Recovery
—the sacred art

The
Twelve
Steps as
Spiritual
Practice

Rami Shapiro

Foreword by Joan Borysenko, PhD

Walking Together, Finding the Way ®

SKYLIGHT PATHS®
PUBLISHING
Woodstock, Vermont

Recovery—The Sacred Art:
The Twelve Steps as Spiritual Practice

2012 Quality Paperback Edition, Fifth Printing

Library of Congress Cataloging-in-Publication Data
Shapiro, Rami M.
Recovery—the sacred art : the Twelve Steps as spiritual practice / Rami Shapiro.
  p. cm.
Includes bibliographical references and index.
ISBN-13: 978-1-59473-259-1 (quality pbk.)
ISBN-10: 1-59473-259-0 (quality pbk.)
1. Twelve-step programs—Religious aspects. I. Title.
BL624.S4825 2009
204'.42—dc22

                                                                2009014735

10 9 8 7 6 5
Manufactured in the United States of America
Cover Design: Jenny Buono

SkyLight Paths Publishing is creating a place where people of different spiritual traditions come together for challenge and inspiration, a place where we can help each other understand the mystery that lies at the heart of our existence.

SkyLight Paths sees both believers and seekers as a community that increasingly transcends traditional boundaries of religion and denomination—people wanting to learn from each other, *walking together, finding the way.*

SkyLight Paths, "Walking Together, Finding the Way," and colophon are trademarks of LongHill Partners, Inc., registered in the U.S. Patent and Trademark Office.

Walking Together, Finding the Way®
Published by SkyLight Paths Publishing
A Division of LongHill Partners, Inc.
Sunset Farm Offices, Route 4, P.O. Box 237
Woodstock, VT 05091
Tel: (802) 457-4000   Fax: (802) 457-4004
www.skylightpaths.com

C O N T E N T S

MEETING THE HOLY RASCAL

I have a penchant for reading a book and declaring to all who will listen, "This is the best book I've ever read!" But here is the truth. This *is* the best book I've ever read. If you're holding it in your hands, you can celebrate two acts of grace. The first—the fiercest grace—is that whatever addiction brought you to rock bottom has opened the door to spiritual awakening. The second is that Rami Shapiro is one of the wisest and most accessible spiritual teachers of our time—humble, funny, authentic, and deeply grounded in the world's great wisdom traditions.

If you are addicted to anything—and all of us are addicted to the delusion that we are in control of our lives—Rami opens the door to freedom through a deep inquiry into the Twelve Steps and a stunning collection of practical exercises that will guide you to your true nature, the soul within you that is beyond habits, beliefs, and opinions. The soul that is, despite your past actions and current afflictions, always pure.

Dubbed a "Holy Rascal" by the Native American Catholic nun Sister Jose Hobday, Rami lives up to that description with unabashed joy. He is a rare bird—an iconoclastic spiritual powerhouse who busts through stale doctrines, dogmas, and assumptions so that we can connect authentically—eyeball to eyeball and moment to moment—with the deeper reality of which we're a part. The words "rare bird" were chosen deliberately, since his Tweets on Twitter (he calls them "Jaded Wisdom") are outrageously outside the box. Sign up for his daily dose of crazy wisdom and you'll see for yourself.

Rami has been a friend and teacher to me since 2003 when we met on a sweltering September day at The Crossings Conference Center in Austin, Texas. I was there giving a seminar on optimizing brain function as part of my ongoing teaching in mind/body/spirit healing. Rami was one of the presenters at an interspiritual conference taking place on the same weekend. Interspirituality is a word coined by the late Brother Wayne Teasdale, referring to a universal spiritual experience that transcends belief systems. It is the common ground of deep interconnectedness where we all meet when we're in the moment, free of the need to be whoever we're not.

As Rami writes, we often don't come to that spiritual ground until we've hit bottom and have tasted the medicine of heartbreak. Only when we truly surrender to our powerlessness over life can we touch something larger than our own egos. Whether you are an atheist or a Christian, a Jew or a Muslim, an indigenous person, a Hindu, a Buddhist, or a member of any faith tradition, authentic spiritual experience is the same for us all. That is where this book will take you, drawing on Rami's lifelong experience of the world's wisdom traditions, which he shares in a practical way devoid of the dogma he so respectfully (and often humorously) leaves behind.

When I told my group at The Crossings that Rabbi Rami, Father Thomas Keating, a Muslim Imam, and a number of other spiritual luminaries were on site, we decided to suspend our compelling Powerpoint Marathon (I'm big on left brain information) to attend one of their experiential sessions.

Our ragtag band of spiritual interlopers was welcomed warmly into a huge, sunlit room where we joined Rami in an ecstatic dance that took us beyond words into the timeless realm of the present moment. And that's exactly where this book will take you. It is more than words. It is a direct transmission of the wisdom you need to recover from the primary addiction that almost every human being suffers from … our addiction to the illusion that we're in control of our lives.

Joan Borysenko, PhD

ADDICTION, SPIRITUALITY, AND THE PROCESS OF UNCOVERY

First of all, we had to quit playing God.
—Bill W.

Here is the heart of Twelve Step recovery—quit playing God.[1]

Most of us tend to equate Twelve Step recovery with specific addictions, such as alcohol, drugs, gambling, food, sex, and shoplifting. If we suffer from one or more of these addictions, we may seek out a book like this; if we don't, we won't. That's a pity. Twelve Step recovery is much more than a way to escape the clutches of addictive behaviors. Twelve Step recovery is about freeing yourself from playing God, and since almost everyone is addicted to this game, Twelve Step recovery is something from which everyone can benefit.

What does it mean to play God? It means living under the delusion that life is controllable. It means constantly struggling to maintain the illusion that you are controlling it. It means lying to yourself all day, every day, insisting that, with enough effort, you can get life to do whatever it is you want it to do. It means having to mask your failure at controlling life by blaming others— your parents, your spouse or partner, your children, your colleagues, your friends—for your failure. It means having to dull the pain of failure with booze, pills, television, overwork, or whatever your method of numbing yourself to the reality of life's uncontrollability may be. It means spiraling into the madness of delusional thoughts and addictive behaviors that make sense only to a mind drunk on the insanity of its own divinity.

Addiction is a disease. Most people in Twelve Step recovery assume that their disease is physical: an alcoholic's disease is the inability to drink moderately, just as a drug addict's disease is the inability to cease taking drugs, or a compulsive overeater's disease is the inability to stop eating when full. I disagree. My assumption is that alcoholism, drug addiction, compulsive overeating, and any other addictive behavior are physical symptoms of a deeper psychospiritual disease, a state of mind that all humans share. The real disease from which almost all of us suffer is the disease of playing God, of thinking we are or should be in control of what happens to us in life. As long as you maintain the illusion of control, you are fine, but eventually and inevitably life slips out of control, and you are faced with a very difficult choice: Quit playing God, and abandon the delusion of life's controllability, or find some way to escape reality and maintain the illusion that you are in control.

Most of us opt for the latter. Rather than admit that we are powerless over life, we redouble our efforts to regain control. This is like a hamster on a wheel who, wishing to get off the wheel, keeps running faster, hoping in that way to come to the end that much sooner.

Like the hamster, our quest for control always ends in exhaustion and failure. How you deal with that failure determines what kind of addict you may be. Failure to control life leads you to take refuge in alcohol, drugs, food, sex, gambling, shoplifting, excessive religiosity, workaholism, or any number of mind-numbing behaviors that allow you to continue the delusion that life is controllable by maintaining the illusion that you are controlling it.

This was what Bill Wilson, creator of the Twelve Step program of recovery, knew, and why he said, "First of all, we had to quit playing God." Wilson isn't implying that addicts imagine themselves to be the Creator and Judge of the universe. What he means is that all addicts—and I would say almost all humans—play God by insisting that we can and should control our lives.

Three premises underlie this book. First, it is the obsessive quest for control rather than the compulsive use of a specific substance or behavior that defines an addict. Second, most of us are addicts seeking to play God by trying to control our lives and the lives of those who touch ours. And third, the Twelve Steps can be of service to all of us since we are all addicted to the delusion of control.

This quest for control may play itself out in harder and softer forms; it may involve overt acts of coercion or more subtle acts of manipulation, but it is always there. Always, that is, until we recognize our addiction and takes steps—in this case, the Twelve Steps—to recover from it.

COMPULSIVE THINKING

Bill Wilson's insistence that we must first quit playing God reveals that the underlying addiction from which most of humanity suffers is the addiction to the delusion and illusion of control. Some 2,500 years ago Siddhartha Gautama, the historical Buddha, said something similar: "All that we are is the result of what we have thought. It is founded in our thoughts. It is made up of our thoughts. If one speaks or acts with an evil thought, pain follows one, as the wheel follows the foot of the ox that draws the wagon" (Dhammapada 1:1).[2]

In other words, if you think you can control life you will act to control life, and doing so will invite consequences that will be excruciatingly painful to you and to those who care about you. And because the root cause of your action is your thinking, the deep cure must focus not only on the body and its behavior, but also on the mind and its thoughts. The genius of Twelve Step recovery isn't only that it provides you with a method to stop compulsive behaviors, but that it frees you from the delusion that you are God, the delusion that led to those behaviors in the first place.

The psychoanalyst Carl Jung glimpsed the spiritual dimension of addiction in the wordplay of *spirits* and *spiritus*. The alcoholic's obsession with *spirits* (alcohol) was, in Jung's mind, a misplaced desire for *spiritus,* soulfulness, or God. Jung quoted the opening verse of Psalm 42 to make his point: "As the deer thirsts after water, so thirsts my soul after You, O God." Just as a thirsty deer races to find water, so the spiritually thirsty human races to find God. But where the deer will not be fooled into drinking something other than water, you and I are easily fooled into consuming substitutes for God, be it alcohol, food, sex, gambling, shopping, and the like. We are trying to fill a God-shaped hole in our very being, and are indiscriminate when doing so.

Where does this hole come from? The mind that imagines it is God, and then fails to live up to its imagining. There is no real hole, only an imaginary one. And because it is imaginary, it cannot be filled. Regardless of which behavior we adopt in hopes of filling that hole, the hole always returns. That is because the mind that seeks to fill the hole is the same delusional mind that is digging it. This is like a person who seeks to fill a hole in the yard with the dirt gathered by digging another hole. No matter how many holes he fills, there is always one more. True recovery is the ending of the delusional digging mind, and it is this to which Twelve Step recovery points. It is this understanding of recovery, and not merely Twelve Step's reference to a Higher Power, that makes Twelve Step a spiritual practice.

WHAT IS SPIRITUAL GROWTH?

What do we mean by *spiritual growth*? Your answer to this question may not be the same as mine, nor do we have to agree for you to benefit from either this book or the Twelve Steps in general. But it will be to both our benefits if I am as clear as I can be regarding the terms I use. This way you will have no doubt as to what I am saying, and can respond to it clearly with thoughts of your own.

What I mean by spiritual growth is this: *an ever-deepening capacity to embrace life with justice, compassion, curiosity, awe, wonder, serenity, and humility.*

Notice that there is no mention of God in my definition. I believe in God, and use the term often. In addition, Step One mentions God and Step Three encourages us to define God as we will, so there will be plenty of time for theological exploration. For now, however, let it suffice that for me God is the Source and Substance of All Reality: God is what is and what was and what is not yet. The more mature our spirituality is, that is, the more we embrace life with justice, compassion, curiosity, awe, wonder, serenity, and humility, the more we become aware of God in, with, and as all things. But a specific belief in or idea of God is not essential either to spiritual growth or to working the Twelve Steps.

Books about spirituality number in the thousands, and talk about spirituality pervades radio, television, magazines, newspapers, the Internet, and, of course, the pulpit. Much of the talk about spirituality assumes that spirituality is a state one can achieve. It isn't. Spirituality isn't something you are, but something you do. *Spirituality,* as I shall use it in this book, is not only a noun but a verb and an adjective as well. *Spirituality* refers to behaviors designed to free you from the delusion that your life can be controlled and the illusion that you are controlling it.

Control is delusional because control isn't real. You are not in control of your life. Merely reading this, or even affirming it without experiencing it, however, is useless. The delusion of control must be involuntarily shattered rather than willfully relinquished, and it is shattered only when your life is shattered b' addictive behaviors you use to maintain the illusion of control. *Hitting rock bottom* is the term recovering addicts use to identify those moments when reality demolishes the illusion that you are in control of your life. Rock bottom happens when the addictive behaviors you use to maintain the illusion of control confront the overwhelming power of reality and simply stop working, leaving you defenseless in the face of the fact of your own powerlessness. It is then, and only then, that you have the opportunity to see through the delusional nature of control and live life differently.

In this book I don't talk about spirituality in the abstract. Rather, I talk about spiritual practice, behaviors engaged in for the sake of preparing oneself for the possibility of grace and the ending of the delusional mind that grace achieves. The Twelve Steps are spiritual practices that have the potential to free you from delusional thinking, at least with regard to the idea of control.

THE IRONY OF ADDICTION

The irony of addiction is that we thirst for what we already have. We are, as the Zen proverb puts it, looking for the ox while riding on the ox. We thirst for God—for that sense of belonging, completeness, and grace that reveals the fundamental unity of all life in life—when in fact we are a manifestation of that unity. We are like the fingers of a hand trying to grasp hold of the hand. It can't be done because the hand isn't other than the fingers, though it is greater than them. You and I imagine that God is other and elsewhere. Further, we imagine that when we find God we will find the magic potion that will give us mastery over ourselves and control over our lives. We confuse God with control and then seek control as a way of proving that God exists and loves us.

God has nothing do with control. God, at least as I understand God and will use the word in the context of this book, is reality itself, and reality cannot be controlled, for there is nothing outside reality to do the controlling. Albert Einstein wrote:

A human being is part of the whole called by us the universe, a part limited in time and space. Humans experience themselves, their thoughts, and feelings as something separated from the rest, a kind of optical delusion of their consciousness. This delusion is a kind of prison for us, restricting us to our personal desires and to affection for a few persons nearest to us. Our task must be to free ourselves from this prison by widening our circle of love and compassion to embrace all living creatures and the whole of nature in its beauty.[3]

Our disease is the optical delusion that we are apart from, rather than a part of, the Whole that is God, coupled with the false idea that we need to control the other in order to be happy. Our longing for wholeness can only be met by the realization that we are already whole, but our imagination is too weak to see this. All we see is separation, and we imagine that the only way to overcome separation is to further blur our vision through the misuse of various substances or deeds: alcohol, food, drugs, sex, shopping, and the like. It's not that binge drinking or compulsive overeating brings us closer to the wholeness that already is, but that it shuts down for a moment our capacity to imagine that it isn't. Pema Chödrön, the noted Tibetan Buddhist teacher, teaches that this shutting down is part of what it is to be hooked, *shempa* in Tibetan.

At its subtlest level, we feel a tightening, a tensing, a sense of closing down. Then we feel a sense of withdrawing, of not wanting to be where we are. That is the hooked quality. That tight feeling has the power to hook us into self-denigration, blame, anger, jealousy, and other emotions that lead to words and action that end up poisoning us.[4]

Getting hooked shuts us down. At first what is shut down is our sense of separation from the whole; for a moment we imagine that the hole is filled, but then we turn around to discover that to find the dirt to fill the hole we ended up digging yet another hole. As we become lost in the cycle of addiction and sobriety, what truly shuts down is our capacity to imagine a way out, a way to true wholeness. This is why the way out is always the way in, the way through, or, as the English poet William Blake puts it, "A fool who persists in his folly becomes wise." The addict who succumbs to addiction and hits rock bottom becomes or at least has the opportunity to become wise.

The real gift of Twelve Step recovery is not simply the cessation of our harmful behavior, but the ending of our harmful thinking. For it is ending harmful thinking that is at the heart of spiritual growth, awakening, and recovery.

MATURATION VERSUS MATURITY

For the purposes of this book, I define *addiction* as a state of mind committed to maintaining the illusion of control. In addition, I define *spirituality* as the practice of spiritual maturation, designed to continually cut through the illusion of control and return you over and over again to reality and your powerlessness over it. And I understand spiritual maturation as living life with the ever-deepening qualities of justice, compassion, curiosity, awe, wonder, serenity, and humility.

Notice the phrase *over and over again,* rather than the idea of "once and for all." Maturation is a process with no end point. We mature continually without ever achieving maturity, as if maturity were a fixed state one arrives at once and for all. Nothing is once and for all. The hunger for control is so strong that few of us can simply let it go, and even fewer can let it go once and for all. Most of us never voluntarily divest ourselves of the illusion of control or the delusion that control is possible. Rather, reality painfully rips both from our grasp, and even when this happens most of us still try to get them back. Living without even the possibility of control is so frightening to most of us that we would rather live in an addiction-induced fantasy than face the tough truth of reality. This is why, as addicts, we most often refer to ourselves as "recovering" rather than "recovered." Recovery is a process we work every day, not a destination at which we arrive.

Because recovery in this sense is a verb, rather than a noun, you will want to work the Twelve Steps over and over again. You will want to read this book over and over again as well. *Recovery—The Sacred Art* contains both insights and practices designed to make those insights real in your life. My hope is that you will read the book through once in order to get an overview of the Twelve Steps and my understanding of them. Then you will take up each Step in turn, rereading the chapter devoted to it, and using the practices from the world's religions associated with it. Don't expect anything like perfection when working the Steps and experimenting with these practices. You will get better at both over time, but they are too rich to be mastered. You grow into rather than out of the Steps and the spiritual practices. The more you do them, the more you learn how to do them more profoundly.

Again, I would not do this alone. Invite friends and family members to read and practice with you. And, if it makes sense to you, seek out and attend more formal Twelve Step meetings themselves.

UNCOVERY VERSUS RECOVERY

If it were up to me, I would rather speak of *uncovery* than *recovery*. Of course, I understand that *recovery* is used in the sense of regaining the sanity we once had but lost to the delusion of playing God; *recovery* can also mean to cover over once again. You can recover a lost treasure by both finding what was lost and by reburying it once it is found.

People addicted to control—which means almost all of us—use drink, drugs, food, work, and other substances and actions to cover over and hide the fact that control is a delusion. Workaholics are driven by the delusion that control is possible, and the illusion that working 24/7 can ensure them that control. Their compulsivity covers over the reality of life's fundamental uncontrollability. This is true of all addicts, regardless of the substance or behavior to which they are addicted. A "recovering" addict is a person who is, given my quirky use of the term, trying to re-cover reality. Thus a "recovered" addict would be one who has successfully returned to the illusion of control. This is truer that many would like to think. I have met dozens and dozens of addicts who imagine that practicing the Twelve Steps of recovery will put them back in control of their lives.

The genius of the Twelve Steps is not that it re-covers reality with the blanket of delusion but that it continually uncovers reality and forces the practitioner to face reality and her inability to control reality time after time. It is only by facing the truth of life's uncontrollable nature, and hence our powerlessness over it, that we can shift our lives from the futile quest for control to the potentially rich quest for learning to live without control.

Playing with the word *recovery* beyond this point would be a needless distraction, and I will use the words *recovery* and *recovering* as most people in Twelve Step programs mean them: *Recovery* is "the reclamation of reality and the ending of the delusion of control," and *recovering* is "the affirmation that we are on the path of reclamation and hence ridding ourselves of those behaviors that maintain the illusion that we are in control." But I hope you will keep the notion of *uncovering* in the back of your mind as you read this book and work the Steps, for that is the point of both: to uncover the truth that life is not controllable but yet still navigable. And we navigate it most wisely when we do so most soberly.

SPIRITUAL BUT NOT RELIGIOUS
The Big Book of Alcoholics Anonymous talks about a "Higher Power," and always couples the word *God* with the phrase *as we come to understand Him* or, as I prefer to avoid the anachronistic

gender bias, *God as we come to understand God.* For some, the use of the word *God* suggests that Twelve Step recovery is a religion. Nothing could be further from the truth. Twelve Step recovery offers no defined theology; relies on no professional clergy; collects no dues; and builds no buildings. It is simply a series of practices that can free us from the addictive behaviors that ruin our lives and the lives of those who love us.

Twelve Step recovery offers no image of God other than God as a force capable of helping you recover your sanity by freeing you from the insanity of your addiction and the delusional thinking that feeds it. And the *Big Book* defines *spiritual experience* and *spiritual awakening* in nontheistic terms, saying only that these phrases refer to a "personality change sufficient to bring about recovery."[5]

The Twelve Step program is not a religion, and the *Big Book* is not a bible. Yet the Twelve Steps are a spiritual discipline, and the *Big Book* is a story of revelation. The revelation comes not from God but from recovering addicts who have quit playing God—at least for today. The revelation is the stories of people who have experienced rock bottom, have had the illusion of control stripped from them, and then have taken the heroic step of daring to live without it. To paraphrase Albert Einstein: We cannot solve problems with the same mind that created them. The Twelve Steps take us to a different level of mind, a mind no longer seeking control, and learning instead how to live with justice, compassion, curiosity, awe, wonder, serenity, and humility in a world beyond our control.

HI, MY NAME IS RAMI

I have been struggling with compulsive overeating for at least fifty years. Eating seemed to be the one thing I could control in my life, though in fact it was controlling me. I eat to celebrate small victories, and to comfort myself for small failures. I eat more when the victories are greater and the failures more devastating.

The difference between my eating and most people's is that most people eat until they are full, while I eat until I am disgusted.

I wrote this book not because I have mastered the art of recovery, but because I have succumbed to the madness of addiction. To say I have mastered recovery is to continue to play God. To admit at long last that I am powerless over food and, more important, over life, is to be surrendered to the fact that I am not God, I am not in control, and I will never be in control.

It is important for me to admit and for you to know that I am not an expert on addiction or recovery. My experience with these matters is from the inside: I am a recovering addict; sometimes a successfully recovering addict, sometimes not. But I always come back to the Steps.

Working the Twelve Steps is personal but not private. That is to say, no one can work them for you, but you do not have to work them alone. Indeed, trying to do this alone often assures you of failure. Leaning on and learning from others suffering as you suffer is an essential aspect of successful recovery from specific additive behaviors. There are meetings devoted to your specific problem, where people like yourself gather to share their stories of addiction and recovery; there are Twelve Step workshops and seminars offered around the country; and there is your sponsor who helps you work the Steps one by one, one-on-one. I have and continue to take advantage of all these tools, but none is a substitute for the hard work of taking each Step.

In addition to attending my own weekly Overeaters Anonymous meeting, in the course of writing this book I have sought out different meetings and have spoken to people suffering from a variety of addictive behaviors in order to deepen my understanding of Twelve Step recovery and broaden the scope of the book.

I take the Twelve Steps very seriously, and I honor the intent and the limitations of Twelve Step meetings. I understand that the purpose of meetings is to help one another escape the clutches of addictive behavior. There is no time, and for most participants, no need to explore the larger spiritual world in which Twelve Step recovery functions. But there is so much more to Twelve Step recovery and to the Twelve Steps themselves.

As I go deeper into each Step I find insights that rarely if ever come up in meetings. As I work each Step, I discern in them echoes of spiritual practices from the world's religions of which most people are unaware. And I see in these spiritual practices ways of enhancing and deepening Twelve Step recovery. None of this comes up in most meetings, which is why I have written this book. I want you to see what I see, and to benefit from the practices that I believe enhance recovery and working the Twelve Steps.

But what if you don't suffer from an addictive behavior for which there is a formal support group? What if you simply realize that you are addicted to playing God? There is no God Players Anonymous group that I know of, so what options do you have? Start one.

I'm not thinking of anything formal. Simply invite a few friends to read this book together. Work each Step privately, and share your struggles publicly. Use the group as your sponsor, and let the collective wisdom of your friends inform your recovery from control.

Twenty years ago when I first began studying (but not yet living) the Twelve Steps I formed just such a group for those willing to explore the Twelve Steps as a spiritual practice. The experiment was short-lived because we never moved past learning about the Steps to actually living them. But it wasn't a failure. It set me on the road to recovery, even if it took me years to find the on ramp.

WITH A LITTLE HELP FROM MY FRIENDS

I am a rabbi, and Judaism informs almost everything I do. It cannot help but shape the way I perceive and write about the Twelve

Steps as well. *Recovery—The Sacred Art,* however, is not a Jewish book, nor does it provide a specifically Jewish perspective on Twelve Step recovery. I didn't write this book because I am a Jew, and don't expect readers to be drawn to it because they are Jews. I wrote this book because, as a professor of world religion, I see Twelve Step recovery as a spiritual discipline. I wrote it because I believe each spiritual discipline can benefit from the insights and practices of other spiritual disciplines, so I have drawn on the teachings and practices of many of the world's religions to explore and deepen our understanding of each of the Twelve Steps.

Yet this book contains more than gleanings from the world's religions. For me, the most moving aspect of attending meetings is listening to the stories of real people wrestling with real addictions. The power of story to reveal the deepest truths of our lives makes going to meetings all the more compelling. As I listen to you tell your story, I find aspects of my own life revealed as well. The more honest our telling, the more human we become. And the more human we become, the less we are hooked on playing God. I am grateful to all those who shared their stories with me, and who agreed to let me share them with you as well.

Being a rabbi, an adjunct university professor of religion, and a reporter of stories, however, doesn't make me an expert on addiction and recovery. And while *Recovery—The Sacred Art* isn't a psychology book, it does contain psychological insights, and for those I sought out the advice of Dr. Valerie Goode, a Miami-based psychologist and friend with decades-long experience working with addicts of all types. At various points throughout this book, I add Dr. Valerie's observations about addiction and recovery to deepen our understanding of both. I want to take this opportunity to thank her for both her wisdom and her friendship.

In addition to Dr. Goode's observations I have also turned for comment and advice to my sponsor, Bert. I met Bert long before I began working the Twelve Steps. He was one of my meditation teachers, and I had no idea that he was in recovery.

He told me this only after I had mentioned to him that I had taken up the Twelve Steps to recover from compulsive overeating. His clarity regarding the process of recovery is another invaluable aspect of this book. And to him, too, I offer my thanks.

Mostly, however, I want to thank you, the reader. While I grew in my understanding of Twelve Step recovery while writing this book, it is because of you that I wrote it. Your reading this book, and more—your practicing the Twelve Steps—is a blessing to me. Thank you.

A NOTE ON ANONYMITY

The only reason to be in a Twelve Step program is to work on your recovery. In the context of this book, *recovery* is used to refer to any of the formal addictions to which many people are enslaved, and, more profoundly, to the foundational addiction from which all humans suffer—that is, the general addiction of selfishness and egocentrism that leads us to the madness of living as if we were God, as if we were in control of life.

The work of recovery using the Twelve Step model requires a level of honesty that involves admitting things to yourself and sharing things about yourself with others that are painful, troubling, and deeply embarrassing. For this level of honesty to prevail, people in Twelve Step groups need to trust the group to protect their anonymity, and to not repeat what is said in the group outside the group. This is what most people imagine the principle of anonymity is all about. It is that and more.

The initial concern with anonymity was to help alcoholics associated with AA, Alcoholics Anonymous, avoid the stigma of being called alcoholics. While today there is something almost heroic and even romantic about being in a Twelve Step program, back in the 1930s when AA began, being an alcoholic—even a recovering alcoholic—carried a stigma that could ruin your life.

Bill Wilson, the cofounder of AA, was also concerned that if anonymity were breached, and known AA members were to fall back into their addiction, the validity of the program would be called into question, and the work of helping alcoholics would suffer. So AA members were discouraged from admitting their membership in AA outside of AA meetings.

An additional early concern, and one that I struggled with in writing this book, was furthering one's career at AA's expense. Bill W. knew that egotism was at the heart of addiction, and that the egos of addicts could push them to draw attention to themselves and the program. The principle of anonymity was put in place to temper the ego's desire to show off both its suffering and its success. This is why many books on Twelve Step recovery are often written anonymously, and I respect that decision even as I decided to do otherwise.

I did so with the hope that by removing the veil of my own anonymity I might better reach out to people who suffer. I am a public figure, though not a famous one, and while I do not claim to live a transparent life, when it comes to my compulsive overeating and the insanity it brings to my life, I believe that by being open about my eating disorder I can better reach others who may suffer from this or other addictions.

This is not meant to be a heroic gesture on my part. I am a writer and admit to being attached enough to the words I write to want to be given credit for writing them. I struggled and, in fact, continue to struggle with this, wanting to make sure it is my desire to serve rather than my desire to be recognized that is behind placing my name on this book. I will not pretend that the latter doesn't figure in my motivation, but I do believe it is the former that more powerfully informs this decision.

Which brings me to the last aspect of anonymity: the identities of those I quote in this book. When talking with people for this book I was careful to let them know that I was writing a book on Twelve Step recovery. No one objected to talking with me, but everyone wanted assurance that they would not be named or described in a way that would allow them to be identified by people they knew. I have been very careful about this, and wish to make it clear to you that the names, places, and descriptions of people whose stories you will read in this book have been changed.

There is only one person responsible *for* the material in this book, and that is me. I have done my best to accurately recollect the conversations I have had with people regarding the Twelve Steps, though I admit to working solely from memory, and thus being prone to memory's limitations. And there is only one person responsible *to* the material in this book, and that is you.

If you are reading this book because you suffer from a specific addiction and are curious as to whether or not a Twelve Step program can be of value to you, I welcome you to these pages and warn you that this is not where you need to be. You need to go to meetings. You need to get a sponsor. You need to work the Steps. If this book helps you move in that direction, it has done its job. If you choose to do nothing more than read about the Twelve Steps, you have not done yours.

If you are reading this book because you are curious about the Twelve Step process, but have no specific addiction to which to apply these Steps, think again. Named addictions are few—alcohol, drugs, food, sex, gambling, and shopping, for example—but they are merely symptoms of a general unnamed addiction from which we all suffer. This greater addiction is the addiction to playing God rather than realizing, as I hope this book will show, that, in fact, God is playing you.

CHAPTER ONE

THE GIFT OF
POWERLESSNESS

We admitted we were powerless over our addiction—
*that our lives had become unmanageable.**

"You want to know what powerless is? Powerless is losing your wife, your kid, and your job to booze, and then, when you sober up just enough to maybe pick up the phone and try to call them, you pick up the bottle instead."

Carl had been in program less than three months, and was the first to speak at an open meeting, a meeting not restricted to people suffering from any one specific addiction. He said he hadn't had a drink in the past six weeks, but couldn't guarantee he wouldn't drink today. "One day at a time, right? One friggin' day."

It is very difficult to admit to powerlessness, and most often when we do so, we are lying. In the back of our minds, just beyond what we choose to hear, we are thinking, "If I say I'm powerless, I will be granted the power to deal with this." That's why Step One is an ongoing step. We must continually return to it and reexamine our powerlessness.

*This book is not written for alcoholics, nor does it have any one addiction in mind, and our wording of the Twelve Steps has been adapted to our more inclusive format. Similarly, the references to God as *Him* do not reflect my personal understanding of God, and have been replaced to make the Steps as theologically inclusive as possible.

UNDERSTANDING POWERLESSNESS

The wording of Step One is a challenge. Who wants to admit to being powerless? Even if I say I'm powerless, I know that I'm not. After all, it is me who is working the Steps, so I'm not really powerless. If I were, I couldn't even do that.

The fact is that if you're truly powerless, you're doomed. And that's the point, really. Not to realize some pseudopowerlessness that still allows you the illusion of control, but to realize that you are truly incapable of doing anything to help yourself. Twelve Step recovery is not self-help. At the root of self-help is the notion that you can help yourself. At the root of Twelve Step is the notion that you can't help yourself, and trying to do so only gets you deeper into your addiction. The key to this program has nothing to do with you and your will, and everything to do with God, as you understand God, and you're being surrendered to God.

Being surrendered to God and surrendering to God are two completely different things. If you surrender to God, you are still in control, but when you truly hit rock bottom—when you can do nothing to change your situation and simply howl in anguish and pain—then the situation itself surrenders you to God. You don't do it. Life does it. But as long as you think you are in control of life, forget it.

THE TRUTH OF POWERLESSNESS

The wording of Step One masks the deeper discovery we make when we actually take the Step. Step One says we are powerless over our addiction. It doesn't say we are powerless over life. Yet as we begin to face the fact of our powerlessness, we discover that, in fact, we are powerless over life. We cannot control what happens to us. All we can do is work with what happens moment to moment.

Marcy, a high school student sent to a Twelve Step program for shoplifting as part of her plea agreement with the court, said, "The reason I steal things, you know, shoplift, is to feel powerful, to be in control. It's like I have no control over anything that matters in my life, so I seek to control stuff that doesn't matter, like the junk I steal from department stores and such. I don't even want the stuff, and I usually give it away to people or even throw it away. I just want to take it to prove that I can do what I want."

The fundamental and paradoxical premise of Twelve Step recovery as I experience it is this: The more clearly you realize your lack of control, the more powerless you discover yourself to be. The more powerless you discover yourself to be, the more natural it is for you to be surrendered to God. The more surrendered to God you become, the less you struggle against the natural flow of life. The less you struggle against the flow of life, the freer you become. Radical powerlessness is radical freedom, liberating you from the need to control the ocean of life and freeing you to learn how best to navigate it.

Few of us want to admit to this level of powerlessness. If we can't control our own lives, what's the point of living? Sure, we can see how others are out of control, how they abuse themselves and their loved ones, but they aren't us. If there are changes to be made, we can make them by deciding to make them. We can remake our lives according to our will. The day we can't do that is the day we might as well stop living.

I suggest that that kind of reasoning is backward. The truth as I have come to understand it is just the opposite: As long as I focus on controlling life, I have no time to live it. I can start living only when I at last stop controlling. Why? Because control is an illusion, and spending all my time and energy pursuing an illusion is a waste of all my time and energy. In the end I run out of time and die exhausted and frustrated. Frustration and exhaustion are the only "benefits" I achieve from my quest for control.

Think about this for a moment: What do you really control?

I once heard a recovering heroin addict in Narcotics Anonymous named Kira say that "Addictive thinking is crazy thinking" and that we need to control our thoughts. "We are only one thought away from happiness," she said. Fair enough, but can we control that thought? We can temporarily introduce this or that notion into our minds, but if we are honest and take the time to become aware of our thinking, we will discover that most of our thoughts—crazy and otherwise—arise of their own accord.

If we could control our thoughts, we would be able to keep out negative thoughts and think only joyous thoughts; we would grab that happy thought and install it permanently. Yet negative and unhealthy thinking goes on whether we wish it to or not. Indeed, the only way we know that a thought is unhealthy is to first think it, and by then it's too late. While we like to ignore this, most of the time our conscious minds don't initiate thoughts but rather register thoughts already arising from somewhere else. The only choice we have is whether to run with that thought or not. And as anyone who has tried to override a compulsive thought knows, choosing to not run after it can be a Herculean task.

The same is true of feelings. Like thoughts, feelings arise of their own accord and are not controllable directly by our will. If they were, we would be a lot happier, banishing painful feelings before they arose. But we can't do that. Feelings come and go, and we really have no control over them whatsoever. Even people who tell me they are able to banish feelings of fear when they arise cannot keep those feelings from arising.

Thoughts and feelings just happen. The only choice we have is what to do with them once we are aware of them. Most of us try to cling to the thoughts and feelings we like, and push away those we don't. This may work for you, but it doesn't for me. The more I cling to thoughts or feelings, the more aware I am of how fleeting thoughts and feelings are. The more I try to banish thoughts and feelings I don't want, the more I realize how resilient they are. My thoughts and feelings never do what I want them to do. They are outside my willed control.

What about physical behavior? This certainly seems controllable. I agree that we have more influence over our behavior than we do over our thoughts and feelings, but even here the control is nowhere near complete.

First, there are such things as coercion and manipulation, and then there is the autonomic nervous system. I can hold my breath for a while, but in the end my body insists that I breathe, regardless of my desire not to. Similarly, I don't consciously beat my heart or make my ears hear or my nose smell. On the contrary, if I had to do these things consciously I couldn't do them at all. The fact is that all the millions upon millions of actions that go into keeping me alive are completely outside my conscious control.

And there are those behaviors I would rather not engage in that I seem to fall into habitually. Surely I can decide to cross the street or not to cross the street at any given moment, but, honestly, if you place a gluten-free chocolate fudge brownie in front of me, I am going to eat it whether it is good for me or not. Substitute cigarettes, alcohol, cocaine, or poker for *gluten-free chocolate fudge brownie* and you'll see what I'm getting at. And don't limit your notion of addiction to things. Dr. Valerie Goode, a therapist friend in Miami, once said to me that people can be addicted to intangibles as well as tangibles. "Some people are so addicted to conflict avoidance, for example, that they will continually sacrifice their own best interests just to keep peace in their lives. They are as addicted to tranquility as any alcoholic is addicted to alcohol."

Then there are the people in our lives. We certainly don't control them, and they continue to do things that surprise, frustrate, and infuriate us. They hardly ever seem to do what we expect, and rarely do precisely what we want. And it is not just other people; day to day, nothing ever turns out exactly as we know it should and wish it would. In short, if we look carefully, we aren't in control of much, if anything. And yet we act as if we were or should be in control of everything.

So I am challenging you to go beyond the wording of Step One. If you are an alcoholic or a drug addict, it is imperative for you to admit that you are powerless over alcohol or drugs. But we are all addicted to control, and it is to this greater addiction that I wish to speak. The deepest truth of Step One requires us to admit that we are powerless over our lives, and that life itself is unmanageable.

LIFE IS UNMANAGEABLE

To manage something is to run it. A manager of a restaurant controls the process of welcoming, seating, and serving customers, and of preparing and cooking the food. If a bottleneck happens in the kitchen, there is an assumption that the manager has the power to untangle things. If a conflict erupts among the staff, she is assumed to have the skill and authority to correct matters and, if necessary, fire problematic employees. If customers are dissatisfied, the manager is empowered to satisfy them by adjusting the process to meet their needs and the long-term interest of the restaurant. If a manager cannot do these things, she is an unfit manager. But what if the process itself cannot be managed? Then being the manager is untenable. You are manager in name only. You operate under an illusion of control, and in the end the process will always defeat you, and you will quit the job in disgust.

The same is true of your life. It is an unmanageable process and yet you have been assigned to manage it. When bottlenecks happen and things aren't flowing properly you are supposed to fix things, but you find that you have no power to order things to be other than they are. When people in your life are in conflict, you cannot mandate peace or fire the guilty party. If people are dissatisfied with you, no matter what you do differently they may never change their minds about you. You have been assigned a task that cannot be done.

Perhaps there are moments and situations where you do seem to have a modicum of control, but if you are honest, chances are you will admit that, overall, your life, like all life, is unmanageable. It happens of its own accord. And while you may be good at putting out fires, you just cannot get people to stop lighting them.

So what do you do?

Some of us just struggle on, insisting that we have control, demanding that life be manageable, and agonizing over why we continually fail at managing well. Some of us abandon the struggle and take refuge in self-medication; we drink, or gamble, or eat to distract ourselves from the suffering brought on by our failed attempts at control. And some of us just quit. Not quitting in the sense of committing suicide, but quitting in the sense of giving up on the illusion of personal power, control, and life's manageability. And when we do quit we discover something wonderful: Nothing changes and we are no longer responsible for anything or anyone but ourselves. Life goes on, and at last we are free to live it rather than doomed to try to control it.

ADMITTING WE ARE POWERLESS

Step One calls on us to admit that we are powerless over our addiction. I am asking you to admit something further: that you are powerless over life.

Admitting that we are powerless over our lives requires us to now that this is true. We can know things and yet refuse to admit them, but we cannot admit to things we do not know. To refuse to admit what we know to be true is called *denial*. Denial requires a tremendous act of will. If we do not have the power to control life, we do have the power to deny that we lack the power.

If I deny that I am an addict when, in fact, I am, I have to deny the very facts of my existence. I have to deny my behavior and the implications of my behavior. I have to deny everything I know in my gut to be true about me and the way I live. This is exhausting. It demands all my strength to maintain this illusion, and leaves me no energy for living reality as it is. Denial is living a lie; admitting is taking the first step toward living the truth. Never underestimate the human capacity for rationalization and denial.

To admit something fully, to admit it the way Step One intends for us to admit it, we have to first realize that it is true. I admit that I am a compulsive overeater. I admit that I eat to deal with emotional trauma. I eat to celebrate little victories, and I eat to compensate for little failures. The bigger the victory, the more I eat. The greater the failure, the more I eat. Eating is the way I reward, punish, abuse, and medicate myself.

I admit this without anger, shame, or pride. I admit it the same way I admit that I take a shower after I work out at the gym. But it took me a long time to get to this point.

The word *admitting* is interesting. We say, "John admitted his guilt'" and "Mary was admitted to the university." Two very different usages for the same word! Is there any connection between them? I think there is. When we admit the facts, we gain admittance to the arena of reality. And until we do so, we cannot engage reality at all.

Admit is synonymous with *acknowledge*. *Acknowledge* means "to act in accord (*ac*) with knowledge." To admit your reality, to acknowledge your addiction, is the first step toward acting responsibly in accordance with it. To admit that your life is not under your control, to acknowledge that reality happens regardless of your desire and will is the first step toward learning how to live with it.

Notice that I said "with it" and not "against it." There is no point in fighting reality. You may play out your quest for control in a variety of ways, but however you choose to pretend that you are powerful, that you are in control of your life, the first step in moving beyond the game of control is to admit that you are playing it.

YOU ARE YOUR ADDICTION, BUT NOT ONLY YOUR ADDICTION

"I've quit smoking before," a woman once said to me after lighting up a cigarette and overhearing some offhand remark I made about nicotine addiction. "In fact, I've quit lots of times. I'm sure I can do it again." She wasn't admitting that she was powerless over nicotine; she was arguing just the opposite. She had quit before and could do it again. It is just a matter of willpower. The fact that her quitting is always temporary, and that her desire for nicotine always trumps her desire to avoid it, didn't seem to faze her. She had yet to admit she was powerless over nicotine.

Once you do admit that you have a problem, the natural response is to fight it. I have fought overeating all my life. I have lost every time. As my friend and teacher Byron Katie says, "When you fight reality you always lose. But only one hundred percent of the time."

Fighting an addiction pits your will to resist a craving against your will to succumb to it. You are the addiction, and fighting the addiction is fighting yourself, and fighting yourself gets you nowhere.

You cannot attack your addiction head-on. You cannot simply will it away or seek to kill it. It is you. This is why at Twelve Step meetings we continually identify as alcoholics, overeaters, or drug addicts. When I qualify at a meeting, saying I am a compulsive overeater and powerless over food, I'm not saying this is all I am. I am simply recognizing, knowing, acknowledging, and admitting that this addiction shapes and defines me to a great degree.

THE WAY OF NONDOING

If attacking addiction head-on isn't effective, what is? The answer can be found in the Chinese Taoist concept of *wei wu wei,* noncoercive action. One who acts with *wei wu wei* cuts with the grain, swims with the current, understands the forces at play in his life, and works with them in a manner that often, but not always, leads to results that are in service to his health and the health of others.

The Chinese word *wu* means "not have" or "without." The word *wei* means "action." *Wei wu wei* means "to act without acting." The paradox is only superficial. We act without acting all the time. Right now, as you read this sentence, your eyes are effortlessly scanning the words, sending messages to your brain, which, in turn, translates the dots of light picked up by the eye into shapes associated with letters, sounds, and meaning. Did you do this? When you read these words, are you doing something, or are you allowing something to be done?

Admitting what *is* produces the field in which *wei wu wei* happens. Even the admitting itself is an expression of *wei wu wei*. Admitting is not inventing a truth, or even shifting from one truth to another. There is only one truth: You are addicted, your life is unmanageable, you are powerless. Denying your addiction is a coercive act. It requires you to work mightily to excuse your actions and turn a blind eye to their results. Admitting the truth requires only that you stop denying, stop pretending that you and the things you do are other than they are. As difficult as this may sound, the admitting itself is effortless; you simply observe and confirm what is so.

In Buddhism the just so–ness of things is called *tathata*. *The Awakening of Faith in the Mahayana,* a fifth-century Chinese Buddhist text, describes *tathata* this way:

> In its very origin suchness is of itself endowed with sub-
> lime attributes. It manifests the highest wisdom which
> shines throughout the world, it has true knowledge and a
> mind resting simply in its own being. It is eternal, blissful,
> its own self-being and the purest simplicity; it is invigorat-
> ing, immutable, free ...[1]

Tathata may well be the Buddhist equivalent of your Higher Power, but unlike dualistic notions that separate you and God, *tathata* does not allow for separation. *Tathata* is you, no less than the addiction is you. Indeed, it is more you, for *tathata* includes and transcends the addiction.

Tathata is the way things are at any given moment. *Tathata* is not static; it is changing, but it changes at its own pace. When we want things to stay the same and when we want them to be other than they are at the moment, we are no longer in touch with what is. Of course, even our being out of touch is part of the suchness of the moment. There is no escaping from what is; there is only working with it or working against it. The core of addiction, my sponsor, Bert, once told me, is working against what is.

"The problem is we want to be other than we are. To be other than we are, we have to get control over who we are so we can change who we are. But this can't be done. After all, who would do it? The *you* that seeks control is the *you* that needs controlling. The effort to control is a madness all its own, and we treat it with our addictions. If we didn't want to be other than we are, we wouldn't have a problem. If we didn't have a problem, we wouldn't be addicts. The more you try to be other than you are, the more just like you you become."

Realizing this—admitting it—is what makes Twelve Step recovery valuable for all of us. Many of us have recognizable addictions, but many more of us are addicted to control and live life in pursuit of power that we might exercise control. We are as addicted to control as any coke addict is addicted to cocaine. And the inane and insane things we do to get the power we need to feed our addiction to control are no less inane and insane than the things any other addicts do to get the fix they need to maintain their addiction.

While "official" Twelve Step recovery focuses on "official" addictions, the real craving and the real madness is not limited to those society calls addicts. We are all control freaks; we are all operating under the illusion that we can and should have power over our lives. And we are all in denial over the fact that we don't and we can't. This is the greater message of the Twelve Steps and the greater promise of Twelve Step recovery: Not only do we find ourselves free from whatever named addiction we may carry, we find ourselves free from the core addiction of control.

FUTILITY OR IMPERMANENCE?

Realizing that we are the problem—and that there is nothing we can do about it—is what makes the Twelve Steps a spiritual path not only for people with identifiable addictions, but for anyone. Life is unmanageable for all of us; that is the nature of life.

This is what the Teacher (*Kohelet* in Hebrew) tells us in the opening lines of Ecclesiastes: "*Hevel havalim,* says the Teacher, *hevel havalim,* all is *hevel!* (Ecclesiastes 1:2). The classic English translation of the Hebrew *hevel* is "futility" or "vanity." People who read *hevel havalim* as "all is futile" or "all is vanity" cannot help but understand Ecclesiastes as a depressing articulation of biblical nihilism. But they are reading the book incorrectly, and missing out on one of the wisest texts in all of human literature. The Teacher isn't telling us that life is futile, but that seeking to control life is futile, and all attempts to do so leave us feeling depressed and distraught.

Hevel (*havalim* is the plural) does mean "futility," but it also means "impermanence." Life seems futile when we try to control it, manage it, make it bend to our will and stay bent. And it seems this way because life cannot be controlled, managed, or bent permanently to our will. By its very nature, life is impermanent and changing. It cannot be controlled, and any attempt to do so is vain, both in the sense of being egocentric and in the sense of being a waste of time—futile. What is futile is not life, but our efforts to control life, to control what is intrinsically beyond our control.

"What do people gain from all their efforts [to control life]?" the Teacher asks. "A generation goes and a generation comes and the earth remains forever [uncontrollable]" (Ecclesiastes 1:3–4).

We are born and we die and we control nothing. We glimpsed this when we were toddlers. We demanded that the world conform to our will and when it didn't we threw temper tantrums. Nothing changed then, and nothing much has changed since then. We still demand that the world conform to our desires, and we still throw tantrums when it doesn't.

The only difference is that most of us have found a more subtle way to throw our tantrums. Few of us stamp our feet and scream at the top of our lungs. We do other things: We drink, we eat or gamble compulsively, we do drugs, we bury ourselves in work or in the lives of people who would be better off if we left them alone. There is no end to the ways we throw our tantrums, and no matter how creative we get, the result is the same: We still don't get what we want. Things still remain just the way they are:

> The Sun rises and the sun goes down,
> and hurries to the place where it rises.
> The wind blows to the south, and goes around to the north;
> round and round goes the wind, and on its circuits the wind
>   returns.
> All streams flow to the sea, and the sea is not full ...
> All words are wearisome, more than one can express;
> the eye is never satisfied with seeing, or the ear filled with
>   hearing.
> What has been is what will be,
> and what has been done is what will be done;
> there is nothing new under the sun.
>
> —*Ecclesiastes 1:5–9*

Is the Teacher describing futility or suchness? I think it is suchness. What would happen if the sun rose and set only once? What would happen if the winds made just one circuit and then ceased to blow? What would happen if the seas filled up or the streams dried up? Life would come to an end! Life depends on repetition. It's an open system, and innovations and even mutations do happen, but it is the repetition that allows life to function. Repetition isn't the same as permanence. The sun rises daily, but the day itself is new. It isn't the repetition of the rising sun that bothers us, but the newness of the day.

If we like what is happening in our lives, we crave permanence and try to shape the new day in the mold of yesterday. If we hate what is happening in our lives, we despise permanence and try to make today totally unlike yesterday. In either case, our response to what is happening is to seek to control it. In the first case, we seek to control it in order to ensure that things stay the way they are. In the second case, we seek to control it in order to ensure that things don't stay the way are and in fact conform to the way we want them to be. But both responses are futile. First, because permanence is an illusion; and second, because we can no more control the life in which we manifest than a wave can control the ocean in which it arises.

Seeking control over life is, as the philosopher and spiritual innovator Alan Watts used to say, like trying to bite your own teeth or hear your own ears. When left to do what they are meant to do, teeth and ears work just fine. But when asked to do what they cannot do, they are useless. Ecclesiastes and Step One aren't telling us that life is futile, but that the way we live it is.

THE PROMISE OF POWERLESSNESS

Step One is similar to the first of the Buddha's Four Noble Truths: Life is *dukkha*. *Dukkha*, like *hevel*, is a word not easily rendered into English. A Pali term usually translated as "suffering," *dukkha* is better understood as disquiet, discomfort, and dissatisfaction. The Chinese refer to *dukkha* using the analogy of a coach with a cracked wheel. Every time the wheel rolls over the crack, the coach jerks and sends a shudder through the passengers. So the Buddha's first insight into reality is that it is intrinsically unsettling.

The Buddha spoke of three kinds of *dukkha*. The first is the *dukkha* caused by pain, illness, old age, death, and mourning. The second is the *dukkha* caused by change. The third is the *dukkha* caused by impermanence. Since nothing is permanent, and everything changes, *dukkha* is pretty much all there is; and the inevitability of pain, illness, old age, death, and mourning only makes that all the more obvious.

A woman once approached the Buddha in tears. She presented him with her dead child and said, "Lord Buddha, I have heard that you can bring the dead back to life. This is my son who died only this morning. I beg you, Lord Buddha, restore him to me."

The Buddha agreed, provided that the woman bring him a single mustard seed from a home in the village that had not experienced death. The woman ran to the village and went door to door to find even one household that had not been touched by death. She failed. When she returned to the Buddha, her grief was no less but her attitude toward it had changed. She knew the inevitability of suffering and the futility of seeking to make things other than they are. She could now mourn her child and move on.

This is a hard truth, so let's go into it slowly.

First, the woman's grief was no less. Realizing that all beings die does not make the death of loved ones any easier. Acquiescing to death does not lessen our suffering over our loss and our mourning over our dead. Acquiescing to death only means that we waste no energy denying reality.

Second, sharing her story with the villagers and hearing their tales of death, loss, and mourning opened the woman's heart. It fed her compassion. *Compassion,* from the Latin, means "shared [*com*] suffering [*passion*]." It is not that she cared for her son less, but that she began to care for others as well. The sharing of our story and listening to the stories of others is central to all Twelve Step meetings. It is what the meetings are for. And, as anyone who goes to such meetings regularly will attest, one always emerges from these meetings with a heart more broken, and a greater capacity for compassion.

Third, accepting the present is not the same as accepting the future. "You don't change what is," Dr. Valerie once said to me: "You change what is next. What *is* is what is given to you in the moment. What you do with what *is* creates the next moment. Freedom, if there is such a thing, lies not in changing what is, but in creating what is next."

CHANGING WHAT'S NEXT: STEP ONE AND KARMA

Changing what is next is the deeper meaning of *karma*. We will look at karma more closely when working Step Eight, but for now it is important for us to realize that we are not doomed to repeat the past, we are doomed to engage the present. *Karma* is a Sanskrit term derived from the root *kr,* "to do." *Karma* itself means "action" but is often used to refer to the notion of cause and effect: You do *x,* and *y* happens.

In Hinduism, *karma* is usually understood to mean that what we experience now is the product of actions we took in the past. This is not the same as fate or predestination, two concepts with which karma is regularly confused. Fate and predestination remove the element of free will from our lives. We are not responsible for the life we experience. It was mapped out for us by forces outside ourselves. Karma teaches just the opposite.

Karma simply says that we reap what we sow. Each action we take sets in motion forces that will eventually coalesce to produce a new set of conditions with which we will have to engage, and to which we will have to respond. How we respond is up to us. It is a matter of free will. But once we respond, we cannot escape the consequences of our response, which will manifest in a future karmic moment.

For example, I have a very strong tendency to find humor in things that are just not funny to most people. One morning a friend called to share some deep concern over his career. Having gone through a major career change myself, he thought I would be a good sounding board. All he wanted was an empathic ear, someone to listen to his story and not critique it. I, on the other hand, chose not to critique it, but to make fun of it. My intent was to add some humor to what was a very serious situation of organizational betrayal. Where I expected a laugh, I received only silence. Even over the phone I could feel an icy wall of hurt fall between us.

I tried to back pedal and say something more appropriate, but the damage was done. My words had set into motion forces that I have yet to face fully. While I cannot know for certain how my unintended callousness will play out in our relationship, I doubt if my friend will confide in me again any time soon, or even ever.

My remarks were freely chosen. The fact that I think the way I do may be a conditioned response to years of using humor to avoid dealing with pain, so I may be dealing with a habitual thought pattern, but I was aware of what I was about to say before I said it, and I could have chosen not to say it. I heard the words in my head; I thought they were clever and funny, and I chose to say them out loud. The result, while predictable to someone else, was a surprise to me. But surprise or not, it was out of my control once the words left my lips. Karma did not require that I say those words, but karma does require that the words and my friend's response to them will shape our relationship in the future.

What is valuable about the Hindu notion of karma is that it places us in position of responsibility regarding our lives. It is humbling in that way: We get what we deserve. Karma, however, is not fixed. True, my next encounter with my friend will be shaped by the impact of this last encounter, but my response to that future moment is not predetermined. I am free to act differently, and by acting differently I set in motion new karmic forces that can put the relationship back on track.

Karma does not lock us into the past, it simply does not allow us to escape having to deal with the consequences of the past. Karma basically says you have no choice but to choose how you will respond to *tathata*, the suchness of this moment. Karma does not make you an addict; karma forces you to confront your addiction.

POWERLESSNESS AND UNMANAGEABILITY

How does karma relate to powerlessness? On the surface it seems to contradict it. If karma only conditions the moment and not how I act in it, I'm still in control. If I'm in control, I'm not powerless. If I'm not powerless, my life is not unmanageable; I am only refusing to manage it. The error here is to assume that life's unmanageability stems from our powerlessness. On the contrary, the unmanageability of our lives is not caused by powerlessness; powerlessness is a symptom of life's unmanageability. Life in and of itself is unmanageable. Whether we have an addiction or not, life is not ours to control. While it may be true (and I think it *is* true) that our present actions influence our future, the future is going to happen in one form or another no matter what we say or do, or don't say and do. Life just happens.

At its deepest, Step One is not saying we are powerless over some things and powerful over others. It is saying we are powerless over life itself. Life is not something we control or manage. Life is something that happens to us, in us, and through us. We respond to what life brings; we do not control what it brings.

Recognizing life's fundamental unmanageability can lead either to despair or freedom. It leads to despair if we continue to cling to the notion that life should be manageable, that we should be in control. With this in mind we set out to grab the power needed to manage life and bend it to our will. There is no amount of power that can do this, and in the end we are exhausted, beaten, and apt to assume that life is futile, and all efforts to make our lives successful, meaningful, or joyous are a waste of time.

Recognizing life's fundamental unmanageability leads to freedom if we realize that our inability to control life is not the same as having no way to meaningfully navigate it. Just because I can't control the sea doesn't mean I can't learn how to swim in it. Just because I can't manage the wind doesn't mean I can't tap into its power. Just because I can't manage my life doesn't mean

I can't live it justly and with compassion. Manageability and control are beyond me, but living wisely and well are not.

CALL ME TRIM TAB

I find the notion of navigating life, of learning how to live wisely and well, very compelling. Decades ago I attended a seminar by author and visionary Buckminster Fuller in Boston. One of the ideas Bucky explored was the notion of trim tab.

Trim tabs, as I understand them, are used in boats and aircraft to stabilize the craft without having to control the craft itself. Bucky was in the Navy and explained the use of trim tabs in boats, where they are tiny mechanisms attached to a ship's rudder. Because of the great pressure of the sea against a ship's rudder, turning the rudder itself is arduous, if not impossible. But the small size of the trim tab allows one to adjust it easily. The adjusted trim tab then shifts the pressure on the rudder, making it easier to turn and steer the boat in the desired direction. Applying the idea of trim tab to life, Bucky puts it this way:

> Something hit me very hard once, thinking about what one little man could do. Think of the *Queen Mary*—the whole ship goes by and then comes the rudder. And there's a tiny thing at the edge of the rudder called a trim tab. It's a miniature rudder. Just moving the little trim tab builds a low pressure that pulls the rudder around. Takes almost no effort at all. So I said that the little individual can be a trim tab. Society thinks it's going right by you, that it's left you altogether. But if you're doing dynamic things mentally, the fact is that you can just put your foot out like that and the whole big ship of state is going to go. So I said, call me Trim Tab.[2]

When the realization of life's unmanageability is freeing, it is so because it awakens in us the wisdom of the trim tab. We cannot control our lives, let alone life in general. But we can move the trim tab; we can do small things that may, over time, have major results. To use AA as our metaphor, we may not be able to control our drinking, but we can choose not to drink today. Not drinking today is adjusting the trim tab. It is not pretending that we are no longer alcoholics or that our addiction to drink is conquered. It only means that we chose not to drink this one time. But that small act has tremendous consequences. It is a trim tab.

We must be careful with this analogy. If we think we control the trim tab, then we are still resisting the fundamental idea of surrender at the heart of the Twelve Step program. Our ego, even if it has been reduced to trim tab status, will still trip us up if we continue thinking in this way.

The message of the trim tab is not that we are in control, but that the changes needed to steer us on the right path are little ones, doable ones. We don't need to have our addictions lifted from us in some miraculous way, we only have to be nudged a bit in the right direction. We don't have to say to God, "Lord, I humbly ask You to remove all cravings from me." We only have to adjust the trim tab and say, "Lord, let me not succumb to this craving this time." That is much more modest. That is the trim tab that will over time move the ship of our lives. Start small, stay small, and huge changes can happen.

Practice: Shifting the Trim Tab, Breathing into the Cracks

Vietnamese Zen Master Thich Nhat Hanh, in his introduction to his commentary on the *Sutra on the Full Awareness of Breathing*, writes:

> Breathing is a means of awakening and maintaining full attention in order to look carefully, long, and deeply, see the nature of all things, and arrive at liberation ... We all have a tendency to run away from

suffering. But the fact is that without suffering, there is no way to cultivate understanding and compassion. I don't want to send my friends and children to a place without suffering because a place without suffering is a place without understanding and compassion. Without understanding and compassion there can be no happiness.[3]

Suffering is a gift, a catalyst for compassion. When I first read this, I thought I had misread it. Isn't suffering what Buddhists are supposed to end? And yet here is Thich Nhat Hanh honoring it. Then I remembered a lyric from Leonard Cohen's "Anthem," in which he reminds us that it is because of the brokenness of things—the cracks as Cohen puts it—that light enters the world. Suffering is the crack that lets in the light.

Suffering humbles us; it allows us to have compassion for the foibles of others. Perfection would be the greater evil. If we were perfect, whole, complete unto ourselves we couldn't relate to one another at all. There can be no love between two perfect beings, for one who is perfect needs nothing and has nothing to offer. What is so wonderful about this is that it allows us to honor our addiction and our mistakes. Not to celebrate them, not to perpetuate them, but to honor them as the cracks that let in the light of healing.

There is a crack in everything. Life is broken, and it is its brokenness that makes it livable. But we are somehow of the mind-set that cracks have to be patched. Patching the cracks is trying to control life, rather than engage it. To engage life we have to find the cracks and enter them, rather than deny or patch them.

One way to enter the cracks is to attend to our breathing. Shifting our focus away from whatever patch-up job is capturing our attention at the moment to our breath allows us to be present to the crack, to the light, to the suffering and the compassion for self and others that arises with it. Being present to, rather than controlled by, the moment allows us to freely face the karmic nature of the moment, rather than to habitually repeat the actions that karmicly shaped this moment in the past.

To be able to shift attention to the breath in times of crisis requires that we practice shifting in times of relative noncrisis. Since we are breathing all day long, we can punctuate our day with moments of breath awareness. I take my practice of breath awareness from the *Anapanasati Sutta* or the *Sutra on the Full Awareness* [sati] *of Breathing* [anapana]. This is my own paraphrase of the Sutra:

> When you want to practice *anapanasati,* take note of where you are, sit for a moment and attend to your breathing. As you breathe in, say to yourself, "I am breathing in." As you breathe out, say to yourself, "I am breathing out." Take note of your breath—is it long and even or short and hurried? Don't change it, just notice it. After a few moments it will find its own rhythm.
>
> When it does, change what you say as you breathe.
>
> As you inhale say, "Breathing in, I am aware of my whole body." As you exhale say, "Breathing out, I am aware of my whole body."
>
> As you inhale say, "Breathing in, I calm my whole body." As you exhale say, "Breathing out, I calm my whole body."
>
> As you inhale say, "Breathing in, I watch my thinking." As you exhale say, "Breathing out, I watch my thinking."

As you inhale say, "Breathing in, I am calm in the face of my thoughts." As you exhale say, "Breathing out, I am calm in the face of my thoughts."

As you inhale say, "Breathing in, I watch my feelings." As you exhale say, "Breathing out, I watch my feelings."

As you inhale say, "Breathing in, I am calm in the face of my feelings." As you exhale say, "Breathing out, I am calm in the face of my feelings."

As you inhale say, "Breathing in, control is surrendered." As you exhale say, "Breathing out, control is surrendered."

As you inhale say, "Breathing in, I am free even in the face of my addiction." As you exhale say, "Breathing out, I am free even in the face of my addiction."

As you inhale say, "Breathing in, I am joyful." As you exhale say, "Breathing out, I am joyful."

The practice is simple. Whether or not you are in crisis, make time throughout the day to stop, breathe, and recite this sutra.[4] Reciting the sutra to the cadence of the breath, that is, breathing in as you read about breathing in, and breathing out as you read about breathing out, helps to ensure that your moment of stopping and breathing is long enough to manifest the calm that reciting the sutra brings.

I find this practice extremely helpful when I am trying to stare down a craving. If it is simply me versus ice cream, ice cream always wins. But if I take a few moments to breathe and recite, I find that even if the craving is still present it no longer has its claws in me, and I can walk away from the struggle without eating the ice cream.

Yet do not think that just because you are doing something, you have now gained control. The sutra doesn't say, "Breathing in, I calm myself," it says, "Breathing in, I am calm." The craving will return. You are an addict. You don't have to change the latter or defeat the former. All you have to do is notice what you are already doing, in this case breathing.

By noticing your breath rather than obsessing over the craving, you are shifting the trim tab. It is the breathing in and breathing out that does the work; all you do is observe what is. Take no credit for anything. Just breathe and pay attention.

Step 2

CHAPTER TWO

THE HOPE OF RESTORATION

*We came to believe that a Power greater
than ourselves could restore us to sanity.*

There are three aspects of Step Two that merit exploration: *We
came to believe, a Power greater than ourselves,* and *restore us to sanity.* In this chapter I will focus on the first and last of these, and
leave a *Power greater than ourselves* to Step Three, where we are
encouraged "to turn our will and our lives over to the care of God
as we understood God."

To begin to understand how we "come to believe" anything,
we had best be clear as to what belief really is. Merriam-
Webster's dictionary defines *belief* as "a state or habit of mind in
which trust or confidence is placed in some person or thing." I
am taken with the notion of "habit of mind." What matters is not
the fact behind the belief—there may not be one—but the habitual nature of thinking that belief. The longer we repeat a belief,
the more apt we are to assume that it is true, but the truth of that
belief itself cannot be verified outside the habit of thought.

I saw the power of belief in Reno, Nevada, when I sat down
next to Stan, a sixty-something man who, with no prompting from
me, simply confessed that he was a compulsive gambler. I didn't
meet him at a meeting, but in a casino. I was drawn to him because
he repeated an elaborate ritual of rubbing his hands, pulling his
ears, and praying before dropping dollar coins into any of the three
slot machines he was playing. I asked him what he was doing and
if it helped him win.

"It's true, you know, the power of belief. I believe. You gotta believe. I believe in Lady Luck, she's my Higher Power, man. And if I treat her right she will come through for me. You see that bucket of coins? She gave me that from the fourth machine down. That's why I'm playing the ones in front of it. I rub my hands on my thighs to show her I'm empty, that I have no money. Then I pull my earlobes to show her I am listening for her guidance. Then I ask her to fill my hands with coins. And then I drop a dollar in the slot and punch that button. I don't always play the slots, sometimes I play blackjack, but I do the same thing. I pull my ears to listen to her tell me if I should take a card or not. Never fails."

Stan didn't seem like a winner. His clothes suggested Lady Luck had abandoned him years ago. When I asked him if he won regularly, Stan said, "What's regular, man? You lose, that's your dues. The Lady is expensive, and it costs me, but then she gives me some back so I can play some more. She's a bitch, but I love her."

Belief need have little to do with reality. Put more simply: There is no evidence outside any system of belief proving the assumptions on which that belief system is based. This is what the philosopher, mathematician, and logician Kurt Gödel revealed in his two incompleteness theorems, published in 1931. Limiting himself to mathematics, Gödel showed that mathematical theorems are derived from mathematical axioms, which are themselves unproven.

Applied more broadly, Gödel is saying that any system of belief is based on unproven assumptions, so that while the system of belief may be internally consistent and logical if we assume that the assumptions are true, there is no evidence that the assumptions are, in fact, true.

Take the central Evangelical Christian belief that faith in Jesus as the only begotten Son of God, sent by God to die as ransom for our sins, is the only path to salvation. We call this a belief, but, in fact, it is a series of unproven and unprovable assumptions: There is a God, God has a Son, God sends his Son to die as ransom for human sin; and there is such a thing as salvation. We only know these things because Christians testify to them. But such testimony, like the Jewish testimony that Jews are God's Chosen People or the Muslim belief that the Qur'an is the word of God spoken to Muhammad, is tainted, for the reasoning is circular. Believing in these axioms is what it is to be a Christian or a Jew or a Muslim, so of course Christians, Jews, and Muslims will attest to their validity. But the circular reasoning underlying these beliefs is in no way convincing or compelling outside the system of belief that supports them.

This is a difficult concept for many people to grasp, let alone accept. We want to believe in our beliefs, but this doesn't make them true. What is really at the heart of belief is will: We choose to believe that something is true without requiring any objective evidence to substantiate our belief. We are back to the subtle play of ego in search of control.

I heard one self-identified Buddhist (he actually identified himself as Buddha X) at an AA meeting put it this way: "I have come to believe that even coming to believe is a trick of the ego and another means of asserting a false sense of control. I don't believe that there is a Power greater than myself who can restore me to sanity, because to do so would require an act of will that I just can't trust. This doesn't mean there is no Power, it only means that my insisting on there being this Power doesn't make it so. I need something deeper than belief, and I think that is faith."

Faith is not the same as belief. Belief is about content: One believes in this or that. Faith is an attitude toward life itself. As the philosopher Alan Watts wrote:

> Faith is a state of openness or trust. To have faith is to trust yourself to the water. When you swim you don't grab hold of the water, because if you do you will sink and drown. Instead you relax, and float. And the attitude of faith is the

very opposite of clinging to belief, of holding on. In other words, a person who is fanatic in matters of religion, and clings to certain ideas about the nature of God and the universe, becomes a person who has no faith at all. Instead they are holding tight. But the attitude of faith is to let go, and become open to truth, whatever it might turn out to be.[1]

Watts's comments are very helpful to gaining a deeper understanding of Step Two. Clinging to the idea that there is a Power greater than ourselves who can restore us to sanity is like grasping hold of the water when we are trying to swim. It is an act of ego that will fail to do what we want it to do: save us from drowning. Clinging to beliefs only weighs us down. But if this is so, what are we to do with Step Two and the notion of *coming to believe*?

The way out of this quandary is to realize that the key term here is *coming* rather than *believe*. As Bert put it to me one day, "Believing is a matter of grit; coming to believe is a matter of grace. When we choose to believe one thing or another, we are acting willfully, but when we come to believe we discover that we are convinced of something because reality allows for nothing else." A fellow from an AA meeting told me this story:

When I first started going to meetings, I would stop and take a drink on my way to the meeting. Sometimes I'd do the same after leaving a meeting. Sometimes I'd do both. It was my way of asserting control. If I didn't have control over my sobriety, I would have control over my drinking. I'd drink in defiance of God. Honestly. Where some heretics would curse God and quit church, I'd just down a Scotch on my way to a meeting and another on my way home from one. And then one day I didn't. I was planning to, but as I drove to the liquor store on my way to my meeting, the absurdity of what I was doing just hit me. I started to laugh until the tears just poured out of me. I had

to park for a while and let this work through me. My
behavior was just so absurd I couldn't do it anymore. I
haven't had a drink since.

This man didn't choose to believe anything. He simply was shown
the madness of his behavior, and the seeing caused a change in his
behavior. You can't do anything to make yourself believe in a
Higher Power who can restore you to sanity, but you can experience that Higher Power and come to believe as a consequence.

Step Two is not about choosing to believe or not to believe.
Step Two is about seeing what is. You admit the truth of your
own experience, and doing so is "coming to believe." This is the
faith at the heart of Twelve Step recovery. Not faith in a belief or
creed, but faith in the authenticity of your own experience. Over
time, your experience will show you that life, when approached
with faith—and by *faith* I mean the willingness to surrender to
reality—won't kill you.

Of course, seeing what is isn't as easy as it sounds. We tend
to filter our seeing through the lens of our assumptions. We place
our experience in a narrative that supports the story of our life,
however we understand it. For example, you might see yourself
as a victim of other people's greed. No matter what evil happens
to you, you are never at fault because you know that you would
have succeeded if not for the machinations of others. As long as
you hold to this belief, you will never grasp the truth of your
experience, only the narrative in which you wrap it.

We all do this to one degree or another, and for those
addicted to wearing narrative blinders there is no way to deliberately or willfully see things without those blinders. We can't take
them off because we cannot imagine seeing without them. In
fact, we are convinced that they correct our vision rather than
distort it. We would stay with the distortion our entire lives if we
could, but something happens to make that untenable. That
something is called hitting rock bottom.

Real faith, the faith that will get you working the Twelve Steps forever, requires the surrender of belief. And what causes the surrender of belief is hitting rock bottom, and hitting it hard.

THE BLESSING OF ROCK BOTTOM

I have been fascinated by the idea of rock bottom from the moment I first heard of it. And one of the things that kept me coming back to meetings was having the opportunity to listen to people tell their stories of hitting rock bottom.

"I'll tell you when I hit rock bottom," said Lauren, an African-American woman in an OA group I visited:

> I hit rock bottom when I suddenly realized I was eating chocolate cake out of a Dumpster behind a restaurant. I am not kidding. I wasn't homeless or poor or looking for food. I was simply walking home from my job and I walked down an alley behind a nice restaurant, something I had done hundreds of times. But this time they had just tossed out a chocolate fudge cake—I know we aren't supposed to mention specific foods, but this is such a strong memory for me that I want to be as clear about it as possible so I apologize to anyone who is now haunted by my cake— and it was just sitting there crushed up against some bags of I don't know what and I just couldn't resist it. No, that gives me too much credit. I didn't have to resist it. The thought of resistance never crossed my mind; I just reached in and took it. Not just a taste or even a slice, but the whole thing. I broke off what looked a bit garbagy, but I took the rest and I ate the whole thing in the alley. Or almost the whole thing, because it was when I was near the end of that cake that I suddenly found myself seeing myself eating this cake. It was like I was someone else looking at this person eating garbage. I was so sick by what I saw that I vomited up that cake all over myself. I

started to cry and I ran home covered in and stinking from this chocolate vomit. I threw that outfit in a garbage bag and took a long shower praying to God to kill me. I was so ashamed. I couldn't face myself. I went to my first meeting the next morning.

Hitting rock bottom is the salvation point of every addict I have met in a Twelve Step program. If not for hitting rock bottom, they would never have begun the long climb toward sobriety. Perhaps the most famous story of hitting rock bottom can be found in the New Testament Book of Acts. According to the New Testament, Saul, whom we have come to know as St. Paul, was a rabbi with a deep enmity toward his fellow Jews who chose to follow Jesus of Nazareth. Seeking to defeat the emerging Jesus movement, Saul traveled to synagogues throughout the region preaching against it. It was on a mission to the synagogues of Damascus that Saul hit rock bottom. This is how the Book of Acts tells the story:

> Now as he journeyed he approached Damascus, and suddenly a light from heaven flashed about him. And he fell to the ground and heard a voice saying to him, "Saul, Saul, why do you persecute me?" And he said, "Who are you, Lord?" And he said, "I am Jesus, whom you are persecuting; but rise and enter the city, and you will be told what you are to do." The men who were traveling with him stood speechless, hearing the voice but seeing no one.
> Saul arose from the ground; and when his eyes were opened, he could see nothing; so they led him by the hand and brought him into Damascus. And for three days he was without sight, and neither ate nor drank.
> —*Acts 9:1–9*

Saul/Paul, like many Pharisees before and after him, was all about control. He wanted the world to be the way he insisted it should be, and, projecting his fear of losing control onto those who seemed to be beyond his control, he set out to put down the nascent Jesus movement. But *something* knew better, and this *something* brought Saul/Paul to his knees.

We will explore what this *something* might be in the next chapter. For now, however, let's continue to focus on the nature of hitting rock bottom. Again the Apostle Paul:

> I was given a painful wound to my pride, which came as Satan's messenger to bruise me. Three times I begged God to rid me of it, but God's answer was: "My grace is all you need; my power finds its full strength in weakness." Therefore I shall prefer to find my joy and my pride in the things that are my weakness; and then the power of Christ will come and rest upon me. For this reason I am content, for the sake of Christ, with weakness, contempt, persecution, hardship, and frustration; for when I am weak, then I am strong.
>
> —*2 Corinthians 12:7–10*

In Paul's day Satan was not yet the enemy of God that later Christians thought him to be. For Paul, a Pharisee steeped in the Hebrew Bible, Satan was God's prosecuting attorney, whose task was to "wander and walk about the earth" (Job 2:2), taking note of human behavior and reporting back to God regarding what he had observed. Satan does nothing without God's approval, and cannot act unless it is at God's behest. So when Paul writes that he was given a painful wound to his pride, a wound he calls "Satan's messenger," he knew that God gave this wound to him. And because God gave it to him, God was not eager to remove it from him, but wanted Paul to use the wound to deepen his understanding, the way an oyster uses a grain of sand to produce a pearl.

Hitting rock bottom is a gift from God, a sign of God's grace rather than God's punishment. Without hitting rock bottom, addicts will never be surrendered to change, but will cling indefinitely to their addictions and the illusion of control that addictive behavior maintains.

Linking hitting rock bottom with grace may seem odd at first, but almost every person in recovery with whom I have spoken sees it this way. As Sabrina, a medical technician, told me, "I didn't deserve the addiction as if I had done something wrong, it was a gift from God that pushed me over the edge to rock bottom, and when I hit and found my way into recovery, I knew for a fact that it was God's grace I was receiving."

Hitting rock bottom is how many people in recovery truly encounter a Power greater than themselves. Regardless of the beliefs to which you may subscribe, hitting rock bottom, as the Apostle Paul discovered, knocks the beliefs right out of you.

"It's like getting punched in the gut hard, really hard," Jorge, a retired autoworker, told me. "All the air goes out of you and you can't think at all. All you do is crumble to the ground and gasp for air." A punch like this leaves you helpless; at the moment of impact whatever ideas you entertained regarding your life and its purpose or meaning are literally knocked right out of you. And it is in this state of complete helplessness that you experience the act of being surrendered.

You can't punch yourself hard enough to do this; someone else has to punch you. In the context of the Twelve Steps, the punch comes from Life or, if you prefer, from God. Your addiction itself is not the thing that hits you; it is the consequences of the addiction, the karmic forces unleashed by your compulsivity, that bring you crashing down. Of course, if you weren't in the grip of your addiction, this couldn't happen, but the fact that it does is not a punishment. Karma is not punishment; it is simply consequence. It is the way the universe works; it is the Power greater than you. And when it leads to hitting rock bottom, it is the source of recovery that leads you to sanity as well.

FROM INSANITY TO SANITY

You hear a lot about sanity and insanity at Twelve Step meetings. At first I found this off-putting. When people talked about the "insanity of this disease," I couldn't take them literally. We were neurotic, maybe, but not insane. And while my compulsive eating often made me do crazy, embarrassing things, and while I heard stories of addicts of all types doing terribly hurtful and harmful things, none of the people I met seemed particularly insane to me.

"I didn't know I was insane until I started coming to meetings," Mike, a fifty-something motorcycle mechanic, said at an AA meeting.

> I thought I was just a guy who drank too much and who just needed some other way to cope. When I started coming to meetings, it was clear to me that you all were insane, but not me. I mean the screwed-up things you people do! But I didn't do those things. I didn't. I kept insisting on that. And then slowly I started seeing myself in you. Staying up late and drinking secretly while my wife slept. Starting to drink earlier and earlier in the day. Then one Saturday night when we were having some of my wife's business associates over for dinner, I hid a bottle of gin in the bathroom and pretended to have diarrhea so I could slip away and drink without anyone knowing. Of course they knew, and my wife was mortified, but I didn't care. Her guests left early and awkwardly, she started crying, and I went into the bathroom to drink. Then it hit me. I was you. I was insane.

According to Dr. Valerie, "Sanity is acting in accord with reality, and reality is what is happening in, with, around, and as you right now. Sanity is living with the present, insanity is living from the past."

The more I listened to addicts, myself included, the more I realized that we live from the past. The more I listened to nonaddicts, the more I realized that they too live from the past. In fact, I found it to be the rare individual who lived in the present.

Most of us, addicts and nonaddicts alike, live lives shaped by habit. Habit is simply past action repeated often enough so as to become automatic, unconscious. At one time, such action may have been appropriate, but when habituated and removed from what is happening at the moment, such behavior is, more often than not, an inappropriate response to the current situation.

The key to living authentically, rather than habitually, is engaging the present. We cannot do that while we are locked in the past. As long as we "paste the past over the present," as Sheila, a member of Narcotics Anonymous, told me, "and live today as if it were yesterday, we have no hope. We can't change the past, and living in it means we can't change at all. My experience of my Higher Power tells me that change isn't just possible but inevitable, but only if I live in the present. God is only in the present. Yesterday I was a drug addict; today I am a recovering drug addict. But that can only be true if today is lived fresh."

When you live without the baggage of the past, when you encounter the present fresh, you discover something amazing: Behind the addicted *you*, behind the insane *you*, there is a greater *you*, a sane *you*, a pure *you* that Hindus call *atman* and Westerners call *soul,* a unique manifestation of God that is your true self.

Practice: Seeing the Pure Soul

Living fresh means living from this purity. One way to practice this is to remind yourself each morning that you are that pure self and not the habit-laden self you imagine yourself to be. Traditionally recited by Jews each morning and perfectly applicable to anyone seeking to deepen the wisdom of Step Two, begin each day by reciting: "My God, the soul you have placed within me is pure."

This is one of the most radical affirmations reminding us that no matter what we have done, no matter how far we have fallen, or how insane our living has become, at heart we are pure.

The Power that can restore me to sanity isn't going to make me other than I am, but rather free me to be who I truly am. That means that there is a *me* that is not addicted to food, a *me* that is not bound to repeat yesterday's habits, a *me* that is free from the compulsive behaviors that have defined me in the past. This *me* is my soul, my True Self, and this self is *pure*.

Pure: *Pure* has two meanings. The first is to be without impurities, without blemish. The second is to be transparent. Our obsessions and addictions cloud our thoughts, feelings, and actions, and perpetuate the illusion that we are separate from God, the greater Reality that is all life. The more separate we feel, the more desperate we become for connection, and the more impossible we find making connections to be. We are trapped in an illusory and isolating cage of our own making, and our addictions only make the illusion stronger. As one woman told me, "When I am in my disease, I am alienated from God."

We then compound this problem by imagining not simply that we are helpless but that we are somehow unworthy of help. Until we hit rock bottom, many of us never really knew God's love. We assumed instead that our failures and our addictions made us unlovable. This affirmation tells us something very different.

My God: Here, as in all Twelve Step programs, God is the God of your understanding. For me God is Reality, the creative process of living that includes birth and death, and whatever lies outside of these.

The soul: You are free to imagine the soul to be a truer Self separate from the ego, a greater Self that includes and transcends the ego, or simply the breath of life that is essential to your being. However you think of soul, in this context, know we are talking about the deepest, most true aspect of yourself.

You have placed within me: The soul comes from God. In my understanding this means that you and I are aspects of God the way a branch is a part of the vine, to borrow Jesus's analogy (John 15:5). The soul, as I understand soul, isn't placed in me the way a battery is placed in a toy robot, but rather the way the life force extends the vine into the branch.

Is pure: The soul, the life force that is our truest self, is pure, untainted, sinless, and karma-free. This is what makes this affirmation so radical. We are used to seeing ourselves as sinful, as broken, but there is a greater purity and wholeness beneath all of that. Yes, we have sinned, and yes, we do feel broken, but despite our errors and delusions, our essence is pure. This means that yesterday's habits of body, heart, and mind belong to yesterday only, unless and until we choose to live them again today.

Each morning as part of my daily prayer practice I recite this affirmation:

> My God, the soul you place within me is pure. And because it is pure I am free to live today differently than yesterday. Because it is free, I am free to live today without the burden of past habits, past fears, past mistakes, and past failures. I am free to look at my past without repeating it; to examine it for

lessons to be learned and amends to be made; and to draw from it what guidance I can to live today differently. My God, may I use today's gift of freedom to further my capacity to serve You by serving Your creation with justice, compassion, and humility.

CHAPTER THREE

DECIDING TO BE FREE

*We made a decision to turn our will and our lives
over to the care of God as we understood God.*

Step Three introduces us to a core concept: *God as we understood
God*. Many people who have a problem with Step Three tend to
focus on its overt reliance on God, taking this to mean a reliance
on religion in one form or another. While one cannot deny that
the practice of the Twelve Steps is at its heart spiritual, it is not
in any way religious if by *religious* we mean that it is connected
to one organized faith or another. Alcoholics Anonymous
founder Bill W. makes this very clear in the *Big Book of Alcoholics
Anonymous*:

> I had always believed in a Power greater than myself. I
> had often pondered these things. I was not an atheist.
> Few people really are, for that means blind faith in the
> strange proposition that this universe originates in a
> cipher and aimlessly rushes nowhere. My intellectual
> heroes, the chemists, the astronomers, even the evolu-
> tionists, suggested vast laws and forces at work. Despite
> contrary indications, I had little doubt that a mighty pur-
> pose and rhythm underlay all. How could there be so
> much of precise and immutable law, and no intelligence?
> I simply had to believe in a Spirit of the Universe, who
> knew neither time nor limitation. But that was as far as
> I had gone.

> With ministers, and the world's religions, I parted right there. When they talked of a God personal to me, who was love, superhuman strength and direction, I became irritated and my mind snapped shut against such a theory.[1]

When I first read, this I felt a deep sense of relief. I, too, didn't believe in religion. I, too, placed no trust in rabbis, pastors, imams, gurus, and the like. I still don't. True, I am a rabbi, and maybe it is because I am that I know that rabbis and other clergy know nothing special. We are trained to explain and promote our respective religious systems, and we may even believe that the system to which we belong is the one true system, but belief is not fact, and sincerity is no guarantee of truth. Step Three, however, isn't concerned with fact or truth; it is concerned with *God as we understand God*. Given this phrasing, God is what you imagine God is; God is what you need God to be so that you can recover from the disease that is ruining your life and the lives of those you love.

What does Twelve Step have to say about God? Absolutely nothing. The success of working the Steps isn't dependent on any theological proposition; rather, it is dependent on you finding something or someone greater than yourself to whom you can be surrendered. For some of us, God is the God found in our respective scriptures: Torah, Gospel, Qur'an, or Bhagavad Gita. For others, God is Nature, Tao, the Great Spirit, the Goddess, or even the principles of Twelve Step themselves. Some of us are theists; others are atheists. Some of us have a clear image of a specific God, while others have a vague sense of Something Greater unattached to any religion. The point is, it doesn't matter. God is whatever you need God to be in order to get beyond the insanity that rules your life.

Listen to Bill W. on this:

> The word God still aroused a certain antipathy. When the thought was expressed that there might be a God personal

to me this feeling was intensified. I didn't like the idea. I could go for such conceptions as Creative Intelligence, Universal Mind or Spirit of Nature but I resisted the thought of a Czar of the Heavens, however loving His sway might be. I have since talked with scores of men who felt the same way.[2]

What allowed Bill W. to use the word *God* was his radical notion that he could conceive of God as he wished. Step Three invites you to become your own theologian, to create an idea of God that allows you to trust in something greater than yourself. It is this fact that makes practicing the Twelve Steps a spiritual discipline, but it is also this fact that makes many people, both religious and nonreligious, nervous: "If we know we are imagining God or envisioning God according to our own understanding, how do we know we are surrendering to the true God?" the Reverend Myra, an Episcopal priest with a history of prescription drug abuse, once said to me. "When it comes to God in Twelve Step recovery," she said, "we are like the proverbial blind men and the elephant. We each have a piece of the truth, but the Whole escapes us."

The story of the blind men and the elephant comes from India, and Sufis, Jains, Hindus, and Buddhists all have versions of it. The nineteenth-century American poet John Godfrey Saxe's version is perhaps the best-known telling of the story in the West. The poem opens,

> It was six men of Hindustan
> to learning much inclined
> who went to see the Elephant
> (Though all of them were blind).

Each man explores one part of the elephant and extrapolates from that a picture of the complete animal. One grasps hold of the tail and insists the elephant is shaped like a rope. Another grabs a leg and argues that the elephant is like a pillar. A third holding the trunk insists it is shaped like a snake. The six men argue endlessly as to the true shape of an elephant, and never once imagine that the elephant could incorporate all their notions and could not be reduced to just one.

The difference between the men in Saxe's poem and people in recovery is that we don't argue about God. Our concern isn't with theological accuracy but pragmatic efficacy. If your understanding of God allows you to recover from your addiction and bring some sanity to your life, then your God is as true as God needs to be.

THE REALITY OF NOT KNOWING

The real challenge of Step Three isn't coming to know God, but coming to know ourselves. If we can imagine God any way we wish, then we are not bound to any theology, but once we admit that we are creating God according to our understanding, we cannot help but shift our concern from "who is God" to "who am I." Who is this *you* who decides to turn your will and your life over to the care of God regardless of how you understand God?

Step Three places us in a very interesting situation. If we get to decide who or what God is in order to then turn our will and our lives over to the care of this God, are we not simply surrendering to ourselves? And if that is true, how can we say we are surrendering at all?

Clay, an engineer at an auto plant and a recovering alcoholic, put the problem this way: "If you're powerless over your disease, how can you be powerful enough to understand God? If the disease makes life insane, how do you know your understanding of God is sane? If addicts are obsessed with our own egos, how do we know we aren't simply praying to our egos dressed up as God?"

We don't.

Twelve Step recovery asks us to do the impossible. We are asked to recognize that we are powerless and at the same time to find the power "to turn our will and our lives over to the care of God." We are asked to surrender to God and at the same time to recognize that this God is only the God of our understanding and hence a partial picture at best. We cannot escape the suspicion that we are fooling ourselves.

This means that, even as we trust the program and work the steps, we can harbor doubt in the efficacy of both. This doubt is in fact a key to recovery. Knowing that we cannot know for certain who or what God is, whether or not Twelve Step will work for us, and just who the *you* is who is doing all of this, leads to an ever-deepening sense of humility, and it is this humility that is vital to our recovery.

The humility generated in recovery is the ability to admit that when it comes to the core questions about who you are and why you are here on this planet the only honest answer is, "I don't know." "Humility," Dr. Valerie once told me, "is living the question without settling on an answer."

In the context of Twelve Step recovery, the core question is always the same: "Will I succumb to my addiction today?" And the answer is always the same, "I don't know." Not knowing is not a sign of weakness, but of honesty. Traditionally, people in Twelve Step programs speak of "one day at a time," and commit to abstinence and sobriety just for today. A more accurate rendering of the situation would be to say "one moment at a time." You are abstinent now in this moment, but you cannot be certain about the next moment or the moment after that. Nor do you have to be. The next moment doesn't exist, only this moment needs attention, and in this moment you abstain from whatever addiction haunts you.

Tom, a banker who, according to his own account, has "gambled away three fortunes," put it this way:

> I was a big-picture guy. I looked at my life in terms of years
> not days. And just thinking about giving up gambling for

good made me sick. I mean a lifetime without casinos? No way. When I came into the program and started to hear this one day at a time thing, even that was too much. Then it hit me: How about one hour at a time or one minute at a time? Hey, I'm not gambling right at this moment, so I can live without it. Let's see how to do that in the next moment and the next.

Living the question is living without knowing the answers; living without knowing the answers requires us to live each moment with attention, humility, and curiosity. As the medieval Ch'an (Zen) poet Niu-t'ou Fa-Jung wrote, "Not knowing is knowing the essential ... The highest principle cannot be explained: It is neither free nor bound; lively and attuned to everything, it is always right before you."[3]

What is right before you is this question: "Will I be abstinent in this moment or not?" The answer is not an abstract yes or no, but the reality of your action in that moment. You are either abstinent or you are not. There is no abstract knowing, there is only observing what is right now.

DECIDING OR DEFRAUDING?

If we can't really know God, and all we have is our understanding of God as a projection of our ego, deciding to turn our lives over to this projection is not going to change things. Indeed, on the surface Step Three appears to be simply a subtle gambit of the ego convincing us that we have achieved something when, in fact, we are still in the grips of our addiction to power and control now masquerading as God rather than ego.

I admit that most people in Twelve Step recovery may not think about the steps as deeply as this. They are interested in only one thing—recovery—and parsing the Steps in itself isn't going to help with that. Indeed, at first it might get in the way by bogging us down in extraneous philosophical rambling. But my sense of things is that once we are working the Steps, delving more deeply into them can further our recovery and deepen the spiritual transformation they promise.

Which brings me back to Step One: We are powerless. The ongoing realization that we cannot change reality and must learn to navigate within it is a humbling experience. It continually forces the ego to let go of its grip on the illusion of power and control and allows us to fall into the arms of what *is* rather than into the addiction that promises to protect us from it.

Step Three says we can decide to turn our will and our lives over to God as we understand God. We have seen that the formula "God as we understand God" reduces God to an abstract idea of our own conjuring. Given this, we have to wonder just what value there is in "deciding" to turn to this idea in the first place. And, even if there is value in it, how can we decide to do this if, in fact, we are powerless?

My own experience with Step Three turns the Step on its head, and I am not alone. As Daniel, an accountant in his late thirties with an oxycodone addiction, put it, "I couldn't decide anything. I mean if I can't decide to be clean, how can I decide to surrender to God? And even if I could, I realized that the God I was surrendering to wasn't real. He was just a projection of my own imagination. So I was blocked in on all sides. I did admit I was powerless over this thing, and I do believe that God can restore my sanity, but so what? I couldn't do what Step Three asks me to do."

No one can. And it is only when we realize that we can't that the true gift of Twelve Step recovery begins. We have already turned our lives and our will over to whatever substance we are abusing. It is no longer ours to turn over. My life belongs to food, yours may belong to drugs or alcohol or sex or gambling or compulsive overwork or whatever madness you worship in hopes of getting some control and power over things.

The genius of Step Three is not that we have the power to decide anything, but that it forces us to realize that we can't even make this simple decision to change; we are forced to realize the extent to which the addiction now runs our lives. Step One's admission of powerlessness is now put to the test in Step Three: If we are really powerless, we cannot decide. And if we cannot decide, there is no hope of recovery. Step Three doesn't offer us hope, it confronts us with horror: a lifetime of unending addiction and insanity. And that is its genius, for the horror of our situation is now so acute that we cannot do anything but howl for help. And in that howl is an act of "deciding" far more profound than anything to which the ego can pretend.

Step Three is a radical disruption of the illusion of control that our ego has spent a lifetime constructing. This is, as contemporary spiritual teacher Ram Dass might call it, the fierce grace of God, *regardless* of our understanding of God, tearing the last bit of ego-centered hope from our hands and letting us fall to our deaths.

FALLING INTO THE ARMS OF GOD

The Sufis call this "dying before you die." You are not dying physically but psychologically. Without anything to hold on to—neither your addiction nor the illusion of deciding—you just fall. It is a terrifying experience, until you realize there is no landing. The real problem with falling isn't the falling itself, but the landing. When we truly accept our powerlessness over life, we discover that there is only falling.

This insight at first seems to contradict the idea of hitting rock bottom and requires closer examination. Hitting rock bottom is an experience of the ego. It is the point where the ego, the addicted self clinging to the illusion of control, can no longer maintain that illusion and is surrendered to the reality of powerlessness. It is only when you hit rock bottom that you have the opportunity to begin to climb out of the hole into which you have fallen. Or at least that is the standard metaphor.

What I've learned, however, is that when we are truly surrendered at rock bottom we don't climb out; we fall through. We discover that the bottom is false, part of the ego-centered drama of the addicted personality. We hit rock bottom because the addicted ego takes a perverse delight in degrading itself. As long as we think we are in control, we blame ourselves for our situation, and the blame either motivates us to wallow in our depravity or make some heroic effort to climb out of it. In either case, it is still the ego at work, and this is not yet true surrender.

True surrender involves not only hitting rock bottom but losing even the capacity to wallow or climb out. We are completely broken. In that brokenness we call out not as a tactic for survival but as a last gasp before we die. It is then that we are surrendered.

With that complete surrender, a surrender that comes not as a last-ditch attempt to save ourselves, but as an involuntary death rattle, the bottom of rock bottom opens up and we enter a kind of free fall. Hitting rock bottom shatters the ego, and without the ego there is no more need of rock bottom. Rock bottom was just another illusion of the addicted mind. When you hit it full force, both it and you are shattered by the experience, and you discover a new kind of falling, a free-falling into God.

God, as I understand God, is Reality itself, and reality is infinite and infinitely creative. Free-falling into God is the experience of creativity not as some alien force but as my own true essence. Free-falling into God is the discovery that you are part of the Divine and filled with a creativity that allows you to live free of the addiction that defined the preshattered ego.

It is the nature of total surrender, rather than talk of reliance on God as you understand God, that makes Twelve Step recovery a deeply spiritual practice. As we have said, God as you understand God is most likely a stand-in for the ego; God as you understand God is too often you masquerading as God. But with hitting rock bottom this *you* is shattered, and with it your understanding of God. There is a moment of sheer panic as this *you* dies, followed by a breathless wonder as the bottom itself shatters and you enter the free fall of Divine Reality. Then the *you* that remains—the *you* that you have never met and could never meet as long as you were boxed into the addiction-fueled fantasy of the old *you*—is suddenly called on to live in this new reality. Yet this new *you* doesn't have a clue as to what to do. So you do the only thing you can do: You cry for help.

SELF-POWER OR OTHER POWER

I'm not one who readily calls for help. I live under the conceit that I'm in control, or at least that I should be. All my life I was taught to lift myself up by my bootstraps, and I never questioned the wisdom of that advice.

I think this is what drew me to Zen Buddhism in my teens. *Jiriki* is the Japanese word for self-power, what my dad called "bootstrapping." *Jiriki* is contrasted with *tariki,* other-power. The contrast of *jiriki* and *tariki* is essential to the contrast between Zen and Pure Land Buddhisms, the latter being the most popular form of Buddhism in Japan.

Zen is all about bootstrapping. If you are to reach enlightenment, you must do so under your own power. The self-powered approach of Zen is paradoxical, given that the Buddha taught *anatta,* the nonexistence of this very egoic self upon which Zen seems to rely. I suspect that the paradox is deliberate, forcing us to rely on the illusion—as an addict relies on her addiction—until both illusion and addiction are shattered in the experience of true rock bottom. In both Zen and Twelve Step, *rock bottom* is the shattering of this illusory self and the insanity of thinking you can bootstrap your way through life.

Pure Land Buddhism takes a different approach. Rather than push you toward freedom through self-shattering, Pure Land tells you from the very beginning that you can't free yourself at all. In Pure Land you have no bootstraps on which to pull, and this leaves you barefoot with no self-powered escape. While Zen is rooted in *jiriki,* self-power, Pure Land Buddhism rests on the idea of *tariki,* other-power. While Zen holds that the individual can attain enlightenment under his own power, Pure Land says that in the end only by calling on the power of Amitabha Buddha, the Buddha of Infinite Light, can enlightenment be attained.

The story of Amitabha Buddha is found in an early first-century Buddhist sutra (sacred text) called the Larger Sutra of Immeasurable Life. In this sutra, the historical Buddha tells Ananda, his chief disciple and personal assistant, that there is a long lineage of Buddhas who preceded him, Buddhas who are still alive and aware of him. The Buddha tells Ananda the story of one of these Buddhas, Amitabha.

Amitabha Buddha began life as Dharmakara, a mythic king who, aeons ago, heard a sermon delivered by Lokesvararaja Buddha, the Buddha living at Dharmakara's time. Dharmakara was so taken with the sermon that he abdicated his throne, and became a monk. It was Dharmakara's intent to earn enough merit to create a Land of Bliss where people would go after death and from which they would then attain enlightenment.

The sutra lists forty-eight vows taken by Dharmakara to ensure his success. At the heart of Pure Land Buddhism is Dharmakara's eighteenth vow, the Vow of the Ten Recitations. Dharmakara promises that anyone who calls upon him ten times in his enlightened state as Amitabha Buddha, the Buddha of Infinite Light, will be reborn in the Land of Bliss, or the Pure Land as the Chinese called it, from which they would eventually attain enlightenment themselves.

As Pure Land Buddhism develops, the practice of reciting the *nembutsu,* which is Japanese for "mindfulness of the Buddha," becomes its central practice. Followers of Japanese Pure Land Buddhism recite the phrase *Namu Amida Butsu,* which means both "I trust in the Buddha of Infinite Light," and "Homage to the Buddha of Infinite Light."

I had been practicing the art of bootstrapping most of my life. Zen was my formal practice, but bootstrapping was my way of doing everything. Yet my addiction always got the better of me. No matter how hard I pulled those straps, I never managed to lift myself up. It was then that I realized how Zen, at least for me, was the way to Pure Land.

Zen exhausts the self and leaves us humbled enough to call for help: *Namu Amida Butsu, Namu Amida Butsu*. Yet even that is a kind of *jiriki*, self-power. So we call and call until we discover that we are no longer calling the *nembutsu;* rather the *nembutsu* calls us. Even one recitation of the *nembutsu* in that state of surrender is enough to awaken you to the Pure Land, which, of course, is only this land without the delusion of a separate and volitional self propped up by the illusion of control and the addictions that maintain it.

While most Buddhist commentaries on the Twelve Steps focus on traditions rooted in *jiriki,* it is, I believe, Pure Land Buddhism and its reliance on *tariki,* other-power, that is the Buddhism better suited for people working the Twelve Steps. This becomes clear in the words of Tz'u-min, an eighth-century Chinese Pure Land master:

> The Buddha, in the causal stage, made the universal vow:
> When beings hear my Name and think on me,
> I will come to welcome each of them,
> Not discriminating at all between the poor and the rich
>   and well-born,
> Not discriminating between the inferior and highly
>   gifted,
> Not choosing the learned and those upholding pure
>   precepts,
> Nor rejecting those who break precepts and whose evil
>   karma is profound.
> Solely making beings turn about and abundantly say
>   the *nembutsu,*
> I can make bits of rubble change into gold.[4]

The "bits of rubble" are those broken individuals whose lives are unmanageable, and who cannot, under their own power, do anything about it. The *nembutsu* is the cry of one who has fallen into the pit, hit rock bottom, fallen through, and cannot save himself. As Taitetsu Unno, a Pure Land Buddhist priest, student of Zen, and my professor of Buddhism in college wrote:

> This transformation expresses the boundless compassion, nonjudgmental and all-inclusive, that is the moving force in the Buddhist tradition. It is not, however, a simple naive optimism, for the starting point of Buddhism is a recognition of the universal face to human suffering born of both personal and collective karma. In fact, it is a realistic appraisal of life as it is, not merely on the surface of things but at its most profound depth. In this depth, abundant with the accumulated pain and sorrow of humanity, is also found the capacity of the human spirit to achieve its fullest potential, no matter the obstacles, through awakening to the working of boundless compassion deep within our life.[5]

It doesn't matter if you cry out in Japanese or Chinese as a Pure Land Buddhist might, or if, as a practitioner of another faith, you use some other formula. The cry isn't magic; the words don't matter. What matters is that you have no other choice but to cry.

Practice: Crying Out Loud

The practice of calling out to a power greater than ourselves is universal.

In the Mathnawi of Rumi, the Sufi poet urges us to call out "Allah" repeatedly. "Mention [of the Name] of Allah is pure; when purity has arrived impurity ties up [its] belongings [and] exits [from you]" (Mathnawi 111:185). Rumi teaches that reciting the Name of Allah is the same as Allah saying to you, "Here I am!" (Mathnawi 111:188).

In Hinduism this practice is called *nama-japa*, the recitation of the Name. There are many names for God in Hinduism, and each has its own mantra, or sacred word or phrase. I will mention only two here. The *maha-mantra* (the great mantra): *Hare Rama Hare Rama, Rama Rama Hare Hare; Hare Krishna Hare Krishna, Krishna Krishna Hare Hare*; and the *Shiva mantuma*: *Om Namah Shivaya.*

Like many who went to college in the sixties and seventies, I have had some experience chanting *Hare Krishna.* The context was always that of an ecstatic encounter with Krishna devotees who used the recitation of the Name, along with drumming and dance, to shift themselves into an altered and more expansive state of consciousness. Even today I regularly attend Krishna worship for the sheer exuberance of it.

But my experience with the recitation of *Om Namah Shivaya* has been the more profound. Shiva, to whom this mantra is addressed, is the Hindu God of destruction, that aspect of Reality that shatters all delusions and removes the last vestiges of the separate self. I learned how to chant this mantra from a swami of the Siddha Yoga tradition, and I can attest that, once learned, internalized, and recited, this mantra is a powerful cry for help for those of us who have at last admitted that we are powerless.

In the Christian tradition, the mantra of choice is *The Jesus Prayer* or *The Prayer of the Heart*: "Lord Jesus Christ, Son of God, have mercy on me, a sinner." Twelve Step practitioners who use this prayer tell me they substitute their particular addiction for the word *sinner.* For example: "Lord Jesus Christ, Son of God, have mercy on me, an alcoholic."

The prayer most likely originated among the Desert Mothers and Fathers of the fifth century. These devotees of Jesus withdrew into the Egyptian wilderness to be alone with God. While the prayer itself is from the fifth century, the Christian practice of reciting short lines of sacred text goes back at least two centuries earlier to St. John Cassian (360–435), who taught the repetition of psalm lines to induce inner tranquility.

In Judaism the practice is called *gerushin*, which means "to separate or divorce." Through the repetition of a divine Name of God, you are separated from the addicted ego and released into the infinite Source and Substance of all reality. Reb Nachman of Breslov (1772–1810), the great-grandson of the Baal Shem Tov, the founder of Hasidic Judaism, taught the repetition of the name *HaRachaman*, the Compassionate One. In my own practice this is the Name that I use most often.

It is up to you to find a Name or short prayer that works for you. But once you have settled on one, the practice itself is simple. All you need do is make time each day to sit comfortably and recite the Name or text you have chosen. As the practice of recitation becomes a regular part of your day, extend the practice from formal sitting times to other free moments throughout the day.

I practice calling out the Name of God in different settings. As a formal practice, I spend forty-five minutes or so repeating Names of God each morning as part of my contemplative walking practice. I set out each morning at dawn and walk through town to Lyttle Creek, and then follow the creek to Stones River. I walk along the riverbank for a while and then return home. The whole walk is about six miles, but only the first half is focused on chanting.

I also practice calling out to God silently throughout the day. I do so whenever I am waiting in line at the grocery story or bank, or stuck in traffic. In this way I no longer imagine that I'm wasting time, but rather using it to deepen my awareness of the presence of God. Most importantly, however, I use this practice when I sense the madness of compulsive eating coming over me.

Sometimes when I am in a supermarket or walking by an ice cream parlor and I find myself caught up in crazy thinking about food, an argument starts in my head: to eat or not to eat? The answer to this question is always the same: Eat! What I have come to learn is that it is not the answer that matters, but the madness of the question. If I give myself over to the question, I will succumb to the answer. So I have to shift my attention away from the question, and I do this by repeating the Name of God.

While at first a matter of *jiriki*, self-power, this practice quickly becomes a matter of *tariki*, other-power. Once I recognize that I am falling into the insanity of addictive thinking, the mantra arises in my mind. I don't choose to recite it; it chooses to be recited.

Is this God taking control of my life? The question at that moment is irrelevant to me. I am free from the madness, and that is all that matters.

CHAPTER FOUR

SEARCHING THE EGO

*We made a searching moral
inventory of ourselves.*

The ego, that part of you that feeds on and maintains the illusion of power and control, has a mantra of its own: "It's not my fault." Whatever happens to you, the ego assures you that it isn't your fault. The fault, and there is always fault, lies with others—your spouse; your partner; your children; your boss; your colleagues; or perhaps some racial, ethnic, or religious community other than your own. Step Four silences that mantra.

It *is* your fault. Perhaps not all your fault, but enough your fault for you to begin to notice the beam in your eye and stop cataloguing the specks in another's eye. Step Four asks us to take a close look at that beam by making a searching moral inventory.

A searching moral inventory is one that honestly and unabashedly examines the vices that haunt our lives. The key is to make the list without judgment. It is too easy, as one woman in OA put it, "to binge on our vices," that is, to wallow in our sins and take perverse pride in imagining ourselves to be the most evil people ever to walk the earth.

As Dr. Valerie put it, "A person who sees himself as beyond the reach of redemption is elevating himself beyond the hope of transformation. No one is so wicked as to be beyond redemption, and pretending to be so is just another act of ego inflation that continues to excuse addictive behavior." A searching moral inventory demands that we identify our vices with the same accuracy and objectivity as we bring to any other inventory.

"When I first started taking moral inventory I was sickened by each defect of character I identified," Matt, a recovering alcoholic, said. "The more I discovered anger to be a vice, the more angry at myself for getting angry I became. And the angrier I became, the easier it was to put aside taking a searching moral inventory. I was making this harder than it is, and it is damn hard, so as to have an excuse not to do it. Then one day I was taking inventory at work, something we do quarterly, and I just made the link from one kind of inventory to another. I didn't get mad because we have so many boxes of a product on the shelves; it was just a fact. I began to approach my moral inventory the same way I approach my stockroom inventory. I imagined my life to be a series of stockroom shelves and I just recorded what I found lying on them."

I found Matt's analogy helpful, yet when I went to record my own inventory I discovered so many nuances of behavior that I couldn't bring any order to it at all.

I brought my dilemma to my sponsor, Bert, whose approach to Step Four was rooted in insights from Christianity, Buddhism, and Judaism. Bert suggested that I look at categories of vices catalogued in these faiths and then find how my different behaviors fit into these categories. "Don't focus on any one specific act, but see how many ways you live out the category. Then ask God to eliminate the category itself and not just the behaviors within it."

There are seven such categories in Christianity, three in Buddhism, and seven in Judaism. I took separate sheets of paper for each category and listed behaviors that fell into each category. In this way I brought some order to my inventory, which made it easier to create and to work within the next two Steps.

CHRISTIANITY AND THE SIN OF PRIDE

The listing of sins in Christianity goes back at least to the fourth-century monk Evagrius Ponticus, who listed eight evil thoughts central to sin: gluttony, lust, avarice, sorrow, anger, spiritual lethargy, vainglory, and pride. A student of Evagrius, John Cassian, held that each sin was caused by the one before it, and Pope Gregory the Great (540–604), adhering to Cassian's cascading sin theory, reordered the sins so that *pride,* which according to Gregory was the cause of all other sin, was in a category all its own. He then added *envy* to Evagrius's list and conflated *spiritual lethargy* with *sorrow* to get his final list of the Seven Deadly Sins. Thomas Aquinas (1225–1274) reaffirmed the centrality of pride, calling it the "head" (*caput* in Latin) of all the sins.

In his masterful study of the Seven Deadly Sins, Solomon Schimmel writes:

> It is not difficult to see how pride leads to the other sins. The arrogant person who thinks so highly of himself believes himself entitled to what his heart desires, whether in the social or in the material sphere. Since he expects deference he is easily angered when he doesn't receive it. Assuming himself superior to others, he is especially prone to envy, which is a response to threats to one's self-esteem. Being self-satisfied, the proud person does not feel compelled to activate himself in the pursuit of spiritual goals, and so commits the sin of sloth. Believing his "eminence" to be an entitlement, he will easily trample over the rights of others, as is so frequently done by the greedy, the gluttonous, and the lustful. It is not that pride inevitably leads to these vices, or that all manifestations of these vices are effects of pride. However, since these are frequently the case, Gregory accords pride a separate status, designating it the mother and Queen of all vices.[1]

Given the notion that pride is the one sin that causes all others, we will focus on pride specifically. St. Paul is very concerned with the sin of pride, and speaks of its many manifestations: boasting (1 Corinthians 3:21), conceit (Philippians 2:3), and refusing to "be subject to one another out of reverence for Christ" (Ephesians 5:21).

Among the many Christian writers who focus on pride, it is to C. S. Lewis that people continually directed me when I mentioned my interest in pride and its relation to Step Four. One woman in Gamblers Anonymous told me, "Lewis said pride is the essential vice, the utmost evil. He called other sins 'fleabites' in comparison to pride. Pride is the way the Devil becomes the Devil. Pride, he says, is 'the complete anti-God state of mind.'"

Lewis devotes an entire chapter to pride in his book *Mere Christianity*. He calls pride the "Great Sin":

> Pride leads to every other vice: it is the complete anti-God state of mind ... [I]f you want to find out how proud you are the easiest way is to ask yourself, "How much do I dislike it when other people snub me, or refuse to take any notice of me, or shove their oar in, or patronize [*sic*] me, or show off?" The point is that each person's pride is in competition with every one else's pride ...[2]

Asking Lewis's question is an excellent way to take moral inventory regarding pride, and realizing the competitive nature of pride helps us focus on the motivation behind pride: the need to be one-up on someone—everyone.

> Pride gets no pleasure out of having something, only out of having more of it than the next man. We say that people are proud of being rich, or clever, or good-looking, but they are not. They are proud of being richer, or cleverer, or better-looking than others. If everyone else

became equally rich, or clever, or good-looking there would be nothing to be proud about. It is the comparison that makes you proud: the pleasure of being above the rest. Once the element of competition has gone, pride has gone.[3]

People who suffer from pride suffer from a deep contraction of the spirit. Their worldview is defined by scarcity, and they live life as a zero-sum game: Winner takes all. "The prideful seem inflated," Dr. Valerie said to me, "and come off as having an overabundance of self-esteem. But, in fact, the exact opposite is true. They are deflated. They live in a tiny world where they are forever in fear of losing what little they have. So they focus not so much on getting more, but on making sure others get less."

Pride can mask a deep self-loathing, and it is this aspect of pride that is sometimes evident at Twelve Step meetings as people tell their stories. We tell our story to demonstrate where we have come from and how far we have gone in recovery, yet if you listen closely enough, you can sometimes detect a tone of pride in a person's story—not pride in her recovery but in the depth of her depravity before beginning recovery. It was Bert who first alerted me to this. He called it "the pride that cometh *from* the fall" paraphrasing and reversing the biblical teaching, "Pride goeth before destruction, and a haughty spirit before a fall" (Proverbs 16:18). The idea is that if we cannot excel at excellence, we will excel at depravity. "What the addict fears most," Bert said, "is being ordinary."

We only take pride in that which we can claim to have accomplished. Pride is about power rather than luck, and Lewis's linking of pride with competition further links it with power. The proud take pride in their ability to control their lives. They see themselves as powerful, bigger than life. This is true even in Twelve Step settings where everything depends on admitting our powerlessness.

"The most difficult aspect of recovery is the admission of powerlessness," Craig, a retired postal worker with sixteen years of sobriety, told me, "and that is because it demands a letting go of pride."

> [T]he proud man, even when he has got more than he can possibly want, will try to get still more just to assert his power. Nearly all those evils in the world which people put down to greed or selfishness are really far more the result of Pride ... Power is what Pride really enjoys.[4]

Lewis argues that pride separates us from God and is the greatest source of antagonism between people. "As long as you are proud," he says, "you cannot know God."[5] But the real link between C. S. Lewis, pride, and Twelve Step recovery is his notion that pride is a "spiritual cancer: it eats up the very possibility of love, or contentment, or even common sense."[6] The madness that so many people discover in their lives prior to working the Steps illustrates the lack of common sense that power, even the illusion of power, creates.

How do we become free from pride? By continually recognizing our powerlessness, for powerlessness cultivates humility and humility is the antidote to pride. As C. S. Lewis writes, "If anyone would like to acquire humility, I can, I think, tell him the first step. The first step is to realise [sic] that one is proud. And a biggish step, too. At least nothing whatever can be done before it."[7]

Lewis gives us no guidance for cultivating humility, but we can find exactly what we need in the Seventh Chapter of the Rule of St. Benedict, the Italian monk Benedict of Nursia (480–545) who was central to the creation of Christian monastic life. My guide in all things pertaining to the Rule of St. Benedict is Sister Joan Chittister, who has written two excellent books on the rule: *The Rule of Benedict,*[8] and *Wisdom Distilled from the Daily: Living the Rule of St. Benedict Today.*[9]

Sister Joan defines humility this way:

Humility is simply a basic awareness of my relationship to the world and my connectedness to all its circumstances. It is the acceptance of relationships with others, not only for who they are but also for who I am … Humility is not a false rejection of God's gifts [but] the acknowledgement that I have been given them for others. Humility is the total continuing surrender to God's power in my life and in the lives of those around me.[10]

Practice: Cultivating Humility

In his writings, St. Benedict outlines twelve steps for cultivating humility. I have reworked and simplified them here to speak more directly to those of us working the sacred path of recovery.

1. Be aware of God's presence always. Remind yourself that if God is everywhere, God is present as everyone. Each encounter is an encounter with God, demanding your utmost respect and attention.
2. Place God's will above your own. What is your will? To control life to your own advantage, or, when you realize this is impossible, to blind yourself to your powerlessness with addictive behaviors. What is God's will? To liberate you from the places in which you are enslaved. Doing God's will is freeing yourself and helping to free others as well.
3. Seek guidance only from those who have your best interests at heart, those who support your liberation from the illusion of power and the addictions it carries with it.
4. Be patient and still in the face of difficulties and contradictions, and even personal injustice; respond not

from a sense of injured pride or frustrated will, but from a place of objective calm and mindful tranquility.

5. Recognize when evil thoughts arise in your heart; see them for what they are: the chains of enslavement; and release them by confessing your dark thoughts and secret sins to a trusted confidant. As the Twelve Step proverb puts it, "We are only as sick as our secrets."

6. Be content with whatever life brings to you, seeing nothing as reward or punishment, and everything as an opportunity to deepen your capacity for humility and the liberation humility brings.

7. Consider yourself lower than others, not in hopes that "the last shall be first" (Matthew 20:16) but in order to help lift the other toward freedom.

8. Do nothing that serves yourself alone; make all your deeds of benefit to the community.

9. Discipline your speech and strengthen your capacity for silence.

10. Avoid silliness, mockery, and playing the fool.

11. Speak gently and forthrightly, and avoid the fog of words that comes with speech that is designed to deceive.

12. Keep your heart humble and your appearance simple, engaging each moment as an opportunity to release fear and the need to control.

BUDDHISM: THE THREE POISONS AND THE FIVE HINDRANCES

According to Buddhist teaching found in the Avatamsaka, or Flower Adornment Sutra, Three Poisons lie at the root of the suffering that defines life: greed (*raga*), hatred (*dvesa*), and delusion (*moha*). Collectively, these are called *akusala-mula*, unwholesome actions, and as long as we live lives polluted by these Three

Poisons we will suffer endlessly. As soon as we try to remove these Three Poisons from our lives, however, we run headlong into Five Hindrances (*nivarana*): sensuousness, hatred, anxiety, sloth, and doubt. The Five Hindrances make removing the Three Poisons very difficult.

In the *Samaññaphala Sutta,* the Buddha's discourse on *The Fruit of Contemplative Living* that sets forth a clear portrait of Buddhist life and training, we are told that "so long as the Five Hindrances are not abandoned, a monk considers himself as indebted [the Buddha's term for *addicted*], as ailing, as imprisoned, as enslaved, as traveling in a wilderness." This is how many of us feel. We are sick and imprisoned in a world defined by our enslavements and addictions. And what keeps us from changing are the Five Hindrances.

The Buddha offers us a way to free ourselves from the Five Hindrances and from the Three Poisons they support. His method is called *vipassana*. The word *vipassana* is composed of two words, *vi,* meaning "through," and *passana,* meaning "perceiving." The freedom the Buddha offers in this meditation practice is the freedom that comes from seeing through the delusions that define us and living free of the addictions these delusions foster.

Vipassana practice leads to mindfulness, a state of bare attention in which you are aware of and yet unattached to whatever sensations, thoughts, or feelings arise in the present moment. Mindfulness is a nonjudgmental encounter with reality; you simply note what is happening without rejecting it, embracing it, or engaging it in any way. By simply observing what is happening within and around you, you are not controlling things, but neither are you controlled by them. Over time *vipassana* practice allows you to be present to your addiction without being enslaved by it.

There are many fine books on *vipassana* practice, and many wonderful teachers from whom to learn it. What follows is my own brief overview of the practice. It is adapted from an essay by Buddhist teacher Sakyong Mipham Rinpoche, published in *Shambhala Sun* magazine.[11]

Practice: *Vipassana* Meditation

Place: Set aside a place that is only used for meditation. Train yourself to associate that place with calm, tranquility, and self-awareness so that as you settle into that place these virtues begin to awaken within you.

Beginning the Practice: While you will ultimately want to meditate for at least twenty minutes once or twice each day, in the beginning set more reasonable goals—five or ten minutes perhaps. Adapt the Twelve Step slogan "one day at a time" to meditating "one moment at a time."

Posture: Body and mind are part of a single system, with each influencing the other. Settle into a posture that is upright, sturdy, and calming. If you choose to sit on a chair, do not lean against the backrest. If you use a meditation cushion, cross your legs comfortably and place your hands, palms down, on your thighs. Whether in a chair or on a cushion, keep your hips and shoulders level. Proper posture should reflect and reinforce a sense of stability and inner strength. Improper posture will cause you to feel tense, distracted, and sleepy.

Gaze: Imagine a spot on the floor about eighteen inches in front of you, and rest your eyes there. Don't sharpen your focus; there is nothing to see or look for on that spot. Soften your gaze, and keep your eyes open to avoid falling asleep. Resting your eyes on one spot will minimize visual stimulation and distraction.

Breath: Your breathing is key to meditation. Don't seek to control your breath, but rather allow it to find its own rhythm. Attend to the rhythm. Notice the breath flowing in when you inhale and out when you exhale. Focusing on the flow of breath in and out relaxes the body and the mind, and is a good way to settle into your meditation period.

Thoughts, Feelings, Sensations: Trying to control the mind and put an end to thoughts, feelings, and physical sensations is as impossible as trying to control any other aspect of your life. Thoughts, feelings, and sensations arise of their own accord and arguing with them, berating yourself for having them, or seeking to repress them is counterproductive. Just notice the activity of your mind, and label it for what it is: When thoughts arise, simply say to yourself, "thinking" and then return your attention to your breathing. When feelings arise, say to yourself, "feeling" and return to your breathing. When physical sensations arise, say to yourself, "sensation" and return to your breathing.

According to Sakyong Mipham Rinpoche, every time we sit in meditation we enter upon a "journey of discovery to understand the basic truth of who we are." At first you may be awed by the wildness of the mind and the speed with which it continually spins thoughts, feelings, and sensations, distracting you from watching your breath. Over time you realize that this habit of mind is just that, a habit, and one that will eventually fade if it is not continually reinforced. By allowing the mind to be itself, and returning your attention over and over again to the breath, you help your mind through the painful process of withdrawal from obsessive thinking and feeling. The addiction of the mind is incessant thinking and feeling, and as you free the mind from its addiction, it frees you from yours. "And because we are working with the mind that experiences life directly, just by sitting and doing nothing, we are doing a tremendous amount."[12]

JUDAISM: AVOIDING HATEFUL SPEECH

To find the Jewish categories of vice we turn to the Book of Proverbs and the seven things God hates:

> Six things God hates,
> Seven things are detestable to him:
> A proud eye, a false tongue,
> Hands that shed innocent blood,
> A heart that forges thoughts of mischief,
> And feet that run swiftly to do evil,
> A false witness telling a pack of lies,
> And one who stirs up quarrels between neighbors.
> —*Proverbs 6:16–19*

If we take God as that force that leads to creative and moral living, the author of this proverb is telling us that there are seven blocks to living freely and creatively: pride, lying, murder, obsession with mischief, eagerness to do wrong, lying under oath, and evil speech. As Judaism evolves over time, all seven remain stumbling blocks, but the seventh one—using words to stir up enmity—takes on special concern among the sages. For example, the Talmud, the anthology of rabbinic teachings compiled between the years 200 BCE and 550 CE, tells us there are three sins whose punishment is loss of one's place in heaven: murder, adultery, and idolatry. To these, the Rabbis say, "And the practice of evil speech is equivalent to all three" (Babylonian Talmud,

Erchin 15b). This is the Rabbis' way of saying that evil speech, *lashon harah* in Hebrew, is the greatest sin of all. Why? Because our words, used wrongly, can destroy relationships between persons, peoples, and nations, and undermine the trust needed to sustain the world in an orderly and just manner.

Within the context of Twelve Step recovery, words also play a crucial role. As Reb David, a congregational rabbi volunteering at a rehab center and himself a recovering drug addict, said to me: "We live in a world of words. What we say about ourselves, to ourselves, about others, and to others creates our reality. What does it mean to be in denial? It means to say we are not addicts, that we are in control, that we can stop drugging or boozing anytime we wish. We say this. Our words create and then confirm the delusion under which we live. Words are everything to us. That is why we use words to admit that we are powerless, and to admit our wrongs to God and then another human being. It is through words that we carry the message of recovery to others in Step Twelve—words!"

Evil speech includes gossip, slander, defamation of character, as well as the obvious lying and falsely testifying under oath. Moses Maimonides (1135–1204), the renowned medieval Jewish philosopher, defined evil speech this way: "Anything which, if it would be publicized, would cause the subject physical or monetary damage, or would cause him anguish or fear is evil speech" (Hilchot Deot 7:5).

"When I first started to get sober I found I had to clean up my speech as well as my body," Maureen, a thirty-something recovering alcoholic, said. "I had all this self-defeating self-talk going on in my head. I was gossiping about myself, telling myself I was weak and lazy and an unfit mother who deserved nothing more than to die from alcohol poisoning. To save myself from this inner gossip, I started slandering others. I made other people out to be worse than me so I could look better to myself. I can't tell you how many relationships I destroyed when I was drinking. In some ways I think it was easier to stop drinking than it was to stop talking this way. What saved me was making speech a focus of Step Four. I worked on giving the negative talk over to God as soon as I noticed I was speaking this way. I'd just stop talking. At first it was awkward to just not talk, either to myself or others. But when I got used to the silence I found that I had time to think before I spoke and when I did speak I spoke more truthfully."

According to the ancient Rabbis, evil speech affects three people—"the one who speaks it, the one who hears it, and the one about whom it is said" (Arakin 15b). Indeed, speech is considered the primary source of good and evil in the world (Leviticus Rabbah 33:1), and a community that harbors slanderers suffers plagues (Avot de Rabbi Nathan 19), drought (Ta'anit 7b), and croup (Shabbat 33a–b).

The Baal Shem Tov, the eighteenth-century founder of Hasidic Judaism, taught that each human being is born with a fixed number of words to speak, and when the final word is spoken, the person dies. Notice that it is the number of words we are granted, not the words themselves. Given that our word count is unknown to us, and our next word could be our final word, the question we must ask before saying anything is, "Is what I am about to say worth dying for?"

I take the Baal Shem seriously, if not literally, and ask myself three questions when deciding whether or not the words I want to say are, in fact, worth saying:

1. *Is what I am about to say true?* If it isn't, don't say it. If it is, ask yourself the next question.
2. *Is what I am about to say kind?* If what you are going to say is true and kind, say it. If it is true and unkind, ask yourself the third question.
3. *Is what I am about to say necessary?* If it isn't necessary, don't say it. Yet sometimes it is necessary to say something that is less than kind. Do your best to find a com-

passionate way to say what needs to be said, and then say it. Just know that there will be consequences.

The rabbi most associated with battling evil speech was Yisrael Meir Kagan (1838–1933), known as the Chofetz Chaim (Seeker of Life) after the title of his most famous book. He offered the following guidelines for avoiding hurtful or evil speech:

1. Make sure what you think happened, really happened.
2. Make sure you have your facts right.
3. Make sure the other person intended to cause harm.
4. Make sure you understand the assumptions under which the other person was operating.
5. Make sure the event was not the result of simple human error, rather than a deliberate desire to cause harm.
6. Make sure that you know what else is going on in the person's life that may have triggered the action about which you are to comment.

Here is my translation of a prayer composed by Chofetz Chaim for avoiding evil speech. I suggest that you have it printed up and post it where you and others can see it and regularly take it to heart:

> God, grant me the capacity to keep my mouth and my ears from gossip and slander. Let me not stereotype anyone or fall into the trap of blanket condemnation. May I avoid falsehood, flattery, strife, anger, arrogance, hurt, shame, mockery, and all other manner of hurtful speech. Give me the courage to speak truth with compassion and humility, using my words to further justice, kindness, and respect. May my thoughts, words, and deeds be for healing.

Practice: Evil Speech–Free Zones

Among the ways I have found to deal with *lashon harah* is to create evil speech–free zones, both physical and temporal. These are places and times when I am especially on guard against hurtful speech. My primary physical free zone is my office. While I spend most of my day alone at the computer, I am on the phone a lot, and I respond to a lot of e-mail, and therefore have plenty of opportunity to engage in hurtful speech. The point of an evil speech–free zone is to mark out a place in which you pledge yourself to be vigilant with regard to communications. Nothing that is said or written in that space is said or written without forethought. I keep a copy of the Chofetz Chaim's prayer on my desk, and take note of it throughout my time in my office. I also slow down my verbal and written responses to people to allow myself time to ask the Three Questions: Is it true? Is it kind? It is necessary?

A temporal evil speech–free zone refers to set times during the day that I focus my attention on avoiding hurtful speech. For me, this is class time at the university.

It is so easy for me to use sarcasm and other forms of intimidating speech to cow my students into either agreeing with me or at least not challenging me. While it may seem absurd that a fifty-eight-year-old adjunct college professor should feel threatened by nineteen- and twenty-year-old college kids with their own ideas, there have been times when I find myself getting angry at what I perceive to be the arrogance, ignorance, or stubbornness of certain students. Given that I have all the power in the classroom, it isn't difficult to shut these students down. But to do so involves using hurtful speech. Not only is the student I am "attacking" hurt, but the rest of the class is damaged by my failure to model the dialogical ideal I say I want in my classroom.

So I take a moment to silently recite the Chofetz Chaim's prayer before class, and then I take care to observe the quality of my speech throughout the ninety minutes of class time. This doesn't mean that I never fall into the trap of evil speech, but that even when I do I can stop immediately, apologize, and correct myself. This, too, is a positive modeling of right speech.

Of course, establishing evil speech–free zones doesn't mean you can engage in hurtful speech in other settings and at other times. It just means that you are especially vigilant about avoiding such speech in those places and at those times.

Step 5

CHAPTER FIVE

CONFESSING OUR WRONGS

We admitted to God, to ourselves, and to another human being the exact nature of our wrongs.

Step Five is about hiding and coming out of hiding. It's about shame and being shamed. It's about being so naked that you have nothing to hide, and, having nothing to hide, you are free from shame. My model for Step Five is Genesis 2:25: *And the man and his wife were both naked, and were not ashamed.*

The nakedness here is not merely physical but psychological. Adam and his wife—she is not yet called Eve—were totally transparent to one another. They had no secrets, either from themselves or from each other. And having no secrets, they had no shame.

Having secrets robs us of sanity. The more secrets we have, the more stories we have to invent to keep our secrets secret. And the more stories we have to invent and then remember and keep straight, the more insane our lives become. Living with secrets, our lives become secretive, and the truth is so deeply buried in the mound of lies that passes for life that we have no real life at all.

The ultimate secret in the context of Twelve Step recovery is this: *I am an addict.* The ultimate lie we tell is this: *I can handle it.* Our lies deny reality, and as long as we are committed to the lie we cannot deal with the reality.

"I was in denial for years," Martha Jeanne, a woman at an AA meeting, said. "I was so deep in denial that I was really unaware that I had a problem."

I don't want to judge Martha Jeanne's recollection of her experience, but I would challenge it. As she continued with her story about how her drinking cost her a career, a husband, and two daughters from whom she is still estranged, she kept tossing in the word *denial*. The sense I got from her was that somehow denial excused her drinking: "I didn't know, so I'm really not to blame."

Blame is irrelevant. There is no point in blaming yourself for your behavior. It adds nothing to the facts and is often used to preempt other people's anger and judgment: "I blame myself for everything, so you have no right to blame me for anything."

Blame is also irrelevant because it is based on a lie—denial itself. When we say we are in denial, we are simply saying, "I lie to myself." When we resent people challenging our lie, our resentment focuses on the fact that our lying isn't working. We know we are lying, but at least we can comfort ourselves with the illusion that others don't know we are lying. But when they know we are lying and we know we are lying, and we continue to lie anyway, we can be pretty sure that we are addicted to lying.

Lying is an addiction like any other, and like the others it gives us the false sense of being in control. Reality, which is by definition out of our control, no longer matters because we aren't living in the real world, but in the false world of our lies. This world of lies, since it is a world of our creation, seems to be a world we can control. The problem is that as the lies grow, they take on a life of their own, a reality of their own, and once again we are powerless, and our world and our lies are out of control.

Step Five is all about ending the lie. It is a difficult thing to do, not because we don't know we are lying, but because we don't know what will happen when we stop lying. "Not-knowing" is at the heart of surrender; "not-knowing" is the key to giving up control; "not-knowing" is also the key to the radical freedom offered when we work the Twelve Steps.

If we don't know what will happen when we stop lying, we do know what happens when we do lie:

> When I kept silent, my bones wasted away through my groaning all day long. For day and night Your hand was heavy upon me; my strength was sapped as in the heat of summer.... Then I acknowledged my sin to You and did not cover up my iniquity. I said: "I will confess my transgressions to God" and You forgave the guilt of my sin.
>
> —*Psalms 32:3–5*

When I kept silent, I suffered all day long. What does it mean to keep silent? It means to deny the reality of our failings and misdeeds; to imagine that we did what we did because we had good reason; it means to excuse ourselves; to lie to ourselves; and to lie to everyone else as well. It is this lie that crushes us.

We cannot really lie to ourselves, of course. Somewhere we know the truth and suffer for our refusal to admit it. Maintaining the lie saps us of our strength. We become so fearful of being found out that we spend all our time covering up. This is exhausting and unproductive.

When we keep silent, we lose the will to live and simply groan under the weight of our own guilt and fear. We imagine that God is crushing us, but it isn't God weighing down on us; it is our lying that is crushing us. God doesn't single us out for retribution. We have simply set ourselves up for suffering.

Imagine a little girl who sticks a finger in an electrical socket and receives a shock. Did the socket intend to hurt her? No, the socket simply transmits energy to whatever is inserted into it. The child wasn't singled out for punishment; she placed herself in harm's way. It's the same with us. God doesn't single us out, our misdeeds don't attract God's wrath as if sins were a magnet and God's wrath were iron filings. Our misdeeds simply put us in a relationship with life that is painful. It is simply a matter of karma, cause and effect. But we want to believe that it is God's hand. That way we can blame our suffering on God. But it isn't so. We suffer from the weight of our own behavior—nothing more, nothing less.

What happens when we acknowledge our mistakes and admit our wrongdoing? We no longer cover up iniquity, and we no longer need to maintain the facade of goodness. We no longer need to lie. We cannot be blackmailed by our own guilt when our misdeeds are no longer secret. The weight is lifted because the lie is exposed: *You forgave the guilt of my sin.*

Look carefully at what the psalmist is saying: God forgives the *guilt* of our sin, not the sin itself. This is an important distinction. We cannot undo what has been done. We cannot erase the pain we have caused. Just because we admit to hurtful behavior doesn't release us from responsibility for that behavior. We are relieved of the guilt of what we have done, but not, as Step Six will make clear, the obligation to set things right.

ADMITTING OUR WRONGS

Step Five challenges us to three levels of confession: to God, to ourselves, and to another human being. Yet didn't we just admit our wrongs to ourselves when we took a "searching and fearless moral inventory" in Step Four? Why repeat it here? And if we are to repeat it, shouldn't admitting our faults to ourselves come before admitting them to God and another human being? After all, I cannot admit to another what I have not first admitted to myself.

The difference between Steps Four and Five is one of degree. As difficult and as painful as making a moral inventory may have been, it was still done in the privacy of our own minds. To take an objective moral inventory, we stepped back from our lives and got some distance from our behavior. We took an inventory of ourselves almost as if we were someone else. This need for distance is part of Step Four, and without it we would lack the objectivity we need to make the inventory true and honest.

There is, however, a potential danger with Step Four that Step Five corrects. The danger is that we use the objective distance between the inventory taker and the inventory itself to minimize the severity of the actions we are listing. That is, we identify what was done, but we no longer self-identify as the person who did it. Step Five takes the inventory of Step Four off the page and puts it into our mouths. We speak the truth of our insanity and in this way identify with it so that we might eventually be free from it.

While this explains why we need to admit the exact nature of wrongs to ourselves, it doesn't explain why we should first confess to God rather than ourselves. As Dr. Valerie understands it, the order of Step Five reflects a deep appreciation for human psychology. Admitting our wrongs to God still allows us some distance from those wrongs. We are still telling a story and maintaining a sense of objectivity that allows us to avoid the full impact of our behavior. We are talking about a self from whom we are trying to get some distance, and this distance allows us to hear the reality of our actions without having to shut down in despair. "As you admit your wrongs to God," Dr. Valerie said, "your ego gets to eavesdrop. In this way you ease into the full impact of confession; feeling the pain you have caused to such a degree that the very idea of causing such pain again is anathema."

Having eavesdropped on the confession to God, the ego is now ready to confess the truth to itself: Yes, it was me who did these things. Not a *me* in the past, or a *me* I have outgrown, but the *me* I am today. I am still capable of such things, but now I know that I can avoid them if I avoid the triggers that propelled me into them—my addiction.

Once we accept who we are, a person with the capacity to do great harm, we loosen the bonds of the secret that has strangled us for so long. And now we are ready to cut those bonds altogether by admitting our wrongs to another human being.

"This was the part of Step Five that stopped me in my tracks," Alan said at a Twelve Step meeting focused on Step Five. "I could tell God anything, and I often confessed my sins to God and felt His forgiveness. And I think I was clear with myself about the terrible and sick things I've done while drugging. But admitting this to another human being was almost impossible for me. I avoided it for months. I think what frightened me was the reaction I might get. God never judged me, but I couldn't be sure that another person, even my sponsor, would do the same thing. Telling another person made my past all the more real because I was telling someone who might reject me, and rejection is one of the things I fear the most."

The order of confession from God to ourselves to another human being can be seen as an order of intensity. Pouring our sins out to God is like pouring a bottle of dark-blue ink into an ocean. It stains for a moment, but soon it is lost in the enormity of the sea. Pouring our sins out to ourselves is like pouring the ink into a large vat. The water spreads the ink out to the point where the stain is light and manageable. But pouring our sins out to another human being is like pouring the ink into a glass of water. These sins are all our sponsor knows about us. They color everything. And that is the point.

We have to reach the point where we can see without the shadow of doubt or denial that our misdeeds color everything. We cannot hide in the infinity of God or in the ego's equivocation that while we may have a done some stupid and painful things in the past we have also done plenty of good and kind things as well. No, we have to see the dark side of ourselves; to really feel how the madness of our lives has darkened the lives of others, perhaps even to the point of permanent stain. We have to be so painfully aware of our own wrongs and failings that the very idea of repeating them makes us sicker than the sickness that drives us to do them.

How do we admit our wrongs to God? Moses Maimonides, the Spanish-born physician and leading Jewish philosopher of the Middle Ages, offers this guideline to confession in his commentary on ancient rabbinic law, the Mishneh Torah:

> How does one confess? [He or she] says: "Please God! I have intentionally sinned, I have sinned out of lust and emotion, and I have sinned unintentionally. I have done [such-and-such] and I regret it, and I am ashamed of my deeds, and I shall never return to such a deed." That is the essence of confession, and all who are frequent in confessing and take great value in this matter, indeed are praiseworthy.
> —*Mishneh Torah, Hilchot, Teshuvah, Chapter 1, Law 2*

With all due respect to Maimonides, it just isn't this simple. Since *God* in the Twelve Steps is the God of our understanding—"God as we understood God"—there is a terrible opportunity here to simply imagine an easygoing, omniscient God who already knows our misdeeds and has no real need to hear us repeat them; especially not in detail. But a quick confession does nothing for us because it allows us to bypass the pain we have caused others, and the mess we have made of our lives.

A more powerful tool is offered by Rabbi Nachman of Breslov, one of the spiritual geniuses of Hasidic Judaism. Nachman invites us to engage in a "raw, unadulterated prayer"[1] that he calls the Silent Scream.

Practice: Admitting Our Wrongs to God— The Silent Scream

According to Reb Nachman, this is best done outside in a field away from the hearing of others: "When a person meditates in the fields, all the grasses join in his prayer and increase its effectiveness and power" (Reb Nachman, Likutey Moharan II, 11). If that isn't possible, then any place where you are truly alone and out of earshot will do.

Begin by settling yourself in the place you have chosen. Assure yourself that you are alone and safe. Then begin to speak to God as you might to your best friend. Explain that you are going to share your darkest secrets, and that what you need is the capacity to listen even as you speak. Don't ask God to forgive you, ask God to sustain you as you delve into the madness of your life and the suffering you have caused yourself and others. There is only one "rule" here: "Whatever expression our straight talk may take, it must be straight—that is, honest, sincere, genuine, and true."[2]

Bring your moral inventory with you, but do not recite it as a litany of sins. Rather, take up each wrong in turn. Tell your story regarding it. And then begin to share how those affected by your behavior may have felt. Tell your story from the point of view of those who were hurt by you.

This act of moral imagination rekindles our sense of compassion for others even as it sharpens our sense of pain over the harm we have caused. As we confess our wrongs and feel the pain we caused, we may reach a point where words no longer convey what we are feeling. It is then that we turn to Nachman's silent scream.

> You can shout loudly in a "small still voice" ...
> Anyone can do this. Just imagine the sound of such
> a scream in your mind. Depict the shout in your
> imagination exactly as it would sound. Keep this up
> until you are literally screaming with this soundless
> "small still voice."

> This is actually a scream and not mere imagination.
> Just as some vessels bring the sound from your
> lungs to your lips, others bring it to the brain. You

can draw the sound through these nerves, literally bringing it into your head. When you do this, you are actually shouting inside your brain.[3]

This practice may sound strange to you, and the only way to understand it is to try it. But don't force it. If you are not on the verge of screaming, don't pretend otherwise. This is for those moments of inner despair where you just cannot do anything else.

The gift of the silent scream is absolute release. All the negative energy that confession has built up, most of it fear-based and fear-filled, explodes out into the void and you are free from of it.

ADMITTING OUR WRONGS TO OURSELVES

Having admitted our failings to God, Step Five tells us to repeat them to ourselves. Didn't we just hear them? Didn't we write them down in excruciating detail in Step Four? Why say them aloud to ourselves?

Saying them out loud helps to make them more concrete. There is something about confessing aloud that brings home the reality of what we have done and what we are capable of doing. Having heard our tendency toward sin, we will better be able to recognize it as it arises in the future and thus more quickly and effectively change course.

The repetition allows us to face the reality of our behavior without distortion. When we confessed our sins to God, we spoke outwardly, not just out loud, but in an outer direction. Now we will do the same in an inner direction. And when we do this, something very odd happens: We begin to discover that the *you* we are talking to isn't *us* at all.

Martin, a follower of the Dalai Lama and a recovering alcoholic, shared his insight into this aspect of Step Five. "I hadn't really linked my Buddhist practice with working the Steps until

I began to explore the deeper meanings of admitting my wrongs to myself. The Buddha taught that the self doesn't exist as a fixed thing, but arises from an aggregate of conditions. Without those the self cannot exist, hence the self is not independent but dependent on conditions over which it has no control. I knew this theoretically but when I began to work Step Five I saw it existentially."

What Martin saw, and what we, too, can discover through Step Five, is that the self has no independent existence. In the Buddhist sutra The Questions of King Milinda,[4] the mid-second century BCE Indian sage Nagasena answers questions posed to him by the Indo-Greek king Menander (Milinda in the Pali of the sutra). When asked about the nature of the self, Nagasena uses the analogy of the chariot: Just as there is no chariot without its constituent parts—wheels, axles, cart, yoke, reins—there is no self without its constituent parts: body, mind, consciousness. Just as the chariot is neither reducible to its parts nor separate from them, so the self is neither reducible to its parts nor separate from them. The self, like the chariot, exists only in the interdependence of its parts.

If the self were fixed and permanent, there would be no hope for change, and admitting our hurtful behaviors would do nothing to end those behaviors. However, if, as both the Buddha and Nagasena taught, the self is neither fixed nor permanent, then change is not only possible but also inevitable.

As the Dalai Lama writes, "Can you remember a time when you did something awful and your mind thought, 'I really made a mess of things'? At that moment you identified with a sense of *I* that has its own concrete entity, that is neither mind nor body but something that appears much more strongly."[5]

In other words, this self with which we identify isn't real. It exists only in the context of our admitting wrongs. This doesn't mean that what was done was an illusion, only that the one who did it isn't the one who is admitting it.

"When I first realized this," Martin said, "I thought I was free from the wrongs. After all, *I* didn't commit them. But in time I realized that it isn't a matter of *I,* it is a matter of the conditions. As long as the addiction continues, the *I* that emerges from it will continue to do terrible things. It isn't the *I* that has to change, but rather the conditions."

This realization brings with it a sense of great relief. After all, you can't change yourself because you are yourself. What you can change are the conditions that give rise to the self. For example, if you are an alcoholic and you stop drinking, the *you* that emerges from sobriety isn't the same *you* who emerges from drunkenness. The key is to observe the true nature of self, and this is just what this part of Step Five promises.

Practice: Seeing through the Self

This exercise is based on a much more detailed process articulated by the Dalai Lama in his book *How to See Yourself as You Really Are.*[6] I am adapting it here to help us work Step Five. I urge you to read the book and to practice the full meditation for yourself.

Sit comfortably as you would for meditation. Take a few moments to mentally scan your body for tension in your shoulders, stomach, jaw, or around your eyes. Relax these places of tension to avoid getting defensive during the exercise. When you feel somewhat relaxed, speak aloud in the first person, taking up each of your wrongs in turn.

After each admission, close your eyes and envision yourself doing the wrong you have just admitted. See yourself in your mind's eye, and recall the thoughts and feelings that arose when the wrong was committed. Focus your attention on the *I* who is committing this wrong, and analyze the nature of this *I*:

1. Is this watched *I* identical with the *I* who is doing the watching?
2. Is this watched *I* independent of the body you are watching?
3. Is this watched *I* independent of the thoughts and feelings you are recalling?
4. Is this watched *I* fixed and static, or is it in flux, changing as the mind and body change?

What you will notice is that the *I* you are watching is dependent on the activity you are confessing, and it changes as those activities change. Repeat this process and realize this insight with each confessed wrong. As you do so, you will begin to notice that the watching *I* also does not exist on its own, but only as an extension of physical and mental activity. You begin to realize that the seer is not other than the seeing; the knower is not separate from the knowing. And with this realization comes a sense of liberation: you—a static, addicted, convicted *you* that needs to be radically altered in order to be free from the addiction that haunts you—does not exist. What does exist is the context and content of activity. Do differently and you will *you* differently.

ADMITTING OUR WRONGS TO ANOTHER

While the first two phases of Step Five are serious, time-consuming, and often painful, they pale in comparison to the third phase: confessing our errors to another human being.

"I was scared to death to admit my shortcomings to my sponsor," Natalie, a compulsive gambler and alcoholic, told me. "I was certain she would find me repulsive and drop me like a hot potato. I know that is not how it's supposed to work. I mean, your sponsor isn't supposed to react to what you're confessing, just provide a safe space for the act of confessing, but I was still horrified by the thought of it. But she was great. She listened, that's all. There was no judgment at all, just 100 percent accept-ance. I felt somehow cleansed by the process."

Confession is a powerful tool for self-cleansing, and when used in connection with introspection, it can remove the limita-tions of introspection. Lithuanian Rabbi Israel Salanter (1810–1883), while arguing for the importance of introspection, a process he defines as "searching each and every human action," nevertheless warns us of its limitations: "Most of the time people view themselves mistakenly. They recognize neither their defi-ciencies nor their unworthy character traits."[7]

Rabbi Salanter was the founder of the Musar movement in Judaism. *Musar* means "instruction" and refers to a spiritual dis-cipline focused on character building. At the heart of Musar is the diminution of egocentricity through acts of humility and the confession of wrongs. Rabbi Salanter suggests that we examine ourselves "not only in solitude but also in conjunction with oth-ers. The hazards of self-deception can be materially reduced when an intimate friend points out our unworthy deeds and character traits."[8] He advises us to acquire a close friend with whom to associate continually. In the context of Twelve Step recovery, this friend is our sponsor.

"I had no problem confessing my defects to God," Frank, a middle-aged insurance salesman, said at an AA meeting. "I fig-ured God knew them already, so it was no big deal. And it was easy to confess them to myself because I knew them as well as God did. But when it came to telling someone else, man, that was tough!"

Frank was in multiple Twelve Step programs for a complex of what he knew to be interrelated addictions. "I act compul-sively. I'm afraid of everything. I'm angry with everyone. So I eat and drink and drug myself to oblivion. See, I can say that to you without any worries, but that isn't Step Five. Step Five is like having someone follow you around videotaping your life 24/7 and then sitting down with you and watching it. Nothing is hidden. It isn't just humbling; it's devastating. But I was lucky, my sponsor was a wise old bastard who had heard it all and done even more. He just listened. No judgment, just 100 percent attention. And when I got through it, I felt fifty pounds lighter."

There is no one way to do this final phase of Step Five, but there is a key element: the trustworthiness of your sponsor, teacher, mentor, or spiritual friend. Whomever you ask to hear your confession, make sure you can trust that the person listening will never use what you tell him against you. You want to be perfectly honest with him, but you cannot take that risk unless you are sure you are safe.

How can you be certain this is the right person with whom to do Step Five? There is no foolproof way to make this determination, but here are some hints:

1. Is the person willing to give you enough time to work through this aspect of Step Five? If there is a sense of being rushed, either the timing is wrong, or the person is wrong.
2. Notice whether in other sponsor settings your sponsor is focused. Does she answer the phone during your conversations, or interrupt your time together to deal with others? In other words, if your sponsor is easily distracted, she may not be the person with whom to take Step Five.
3. If your sponsor seems offended by your behavior, or by something you have said during other sponsor meetings; if he seems judgmental in any way, then again he may not be the best person with whom to take Step Five.

Practice: Confession

Though there is a significant difference between Catholic confession and Step Five, when looking for a model for admitting our wrongs to another human being we can learn a lot from the practice of confession in the Roman Catholic Church.[9] The intent of Catholic confession is to receive the forgiveness of God through the priest. Step Five does not mention forgiveness, nor is it in the power of your sponsor or whomever you ask to listen to your confession to forgive you at all. The listener is simply that, one who listens and does not respond. Given this difference, we can still find in the practice of Catholic confession guidelines for admitting the exact nature of our wrongs to another human being.

Before Your Confession: There is no point in taking Step Five unless you are convinced that the behaviors confessed are, in fact, wrongs you have committed. Review your moral inventory and make sure you did not pad the pages simply to have something to confess. Be clear with yourself that these are wrongs you have no desire to repeat. This doesn't mean that you promise never to make mistakes, but that you are ready to commit to not making these mistakes again.

Examining Your Conscience: Within the context of Catholicism, the examination of conscience focuses on your relationship to God, Christ, and the Church as well as more general acts for which you are contrite, such as coming late to mass, acts of pride, jealousy, sloth, and greed. For our purposes we can translate God, Christ, and Church into God as we understand God, the Twelve Steps, and the meeting. Is our relationship with God ongoing and honest? Do we need to strengthen our "walk with God" through greater attention to prayer and meditation? Are we working the Twelve Steps to the best of our ability? Are we maintaining sobriety and abstinence? Are we going to meetings? Do we arrive on time and stay until the end? Are we full participants in the meeting—listening attentively when others speak and speaking honestly when moved to speak ourselves? It may be that we can improve our behavior in any or all of these areas, and admitting that helps us enter into confession with a contrite and humble heart.

The Posture of Confession: Many Catholics kneel during confession, allowing a humble posture to further the humbling of the heart. Kneeling may be inappropriate in a secular Twelve Step context, but posture is always important. The mind often takes its cues from the body. When we are tense—our eyes narrowed, our fists clenched, our breathing rapid and shallow—we can induce an angry and defensive state of mind. Conversely, when we deliberately do the opposite, we can release anger and find some semblance of tranquility. The posture we want when admitting our wrongs to another person is one that invites fearlessness and eschews pride and defensiveness. Sit comfortably with legs and arms uncrossed. Don't slump in your chair, but sit upright to allow your breathing to find a natural rhythm. Even if you begin to cry, do your best not to bury your face in your hands, but maintain eye contact with the listener. You may well have done some things for which you are terribly ashamed, but you know that the *you* you are now is not the *you* you were then. Do not allow the admission of wrongs to become a drama of self-flagellation. If that happens, there can be no moving on, for you have now defined yourself as the *you* of the past. In so doing you are robbing yourself of the capacity to be other than you were.

Making Your Confession: Begin with the wrongs that are the most painful for you to admit. Don't recite your inventory robotically. Allow emotion to enter your voice. Feel the pain of the past, even as you remember that you are not doomed to repeat the past. Don't imagine yourself standing before a firing squad. Imagine yourself emptying a stack of bricks strapped to your back, one brick at a time. The listener cannot forgive your sins, but admitting them should leave you feeling lighter.

Contrition: Catholics are apt to offer a prayer at the end of confession saying:

O my God, I am heartily sorry for having offended you and I detest all my sins, because I dread the loss of heaven and the pains of hell. But most of all because I have offended you, my God, who are all good and deserving of all my love. I firmly resolve with the help of your grace, to confess my sins, to do penance, and to amend my life. Amen.

From our perspective, I would offer something like this: My sadness over the pain I have caused myself and others is unbounded, yet I do not despair. I am not chained to the past, and I am free to be new at each moment. I will not let my sadness excuse my mistakes or act as substitute for making amends. Rather, I will use my sadness to remind me that there is a better way to live, a way free from addiction and the insanity addiction brings. I vow to live this new way with the help of these Twelve Steps.

Concluding Your Confession: In Catholic confession, your admission of sin is followed by words of absolution and forgiveness granted by the priest in the name of Christ. This certainly is outside the parameters of Twelve Step practice, though you may find working Step Five with a priest to be very helpful. In the context of Twelve Step recovery, the conclusion of confession is not forgiveness, but freedom. You admit your wrongs and in so doing realize that you are not doomed to repeat them. You admit them and put them aside. No doubt there will be other mistakes to make tomorrow, but at the conclusion of Step Five there is a sense that the past is past, and today need not be a reflection of it.

After Your Confession: Catholics leave confession thanking God for forgiveness and committed to completing the penance the priest assigned them. In our context, gratitude to the person who listened to you is appropriate, as is gratitude to the program for providing you with the way, and to God for sustaining you as you pursue it. And penance for us is the Steps themselves. We do not stop with Step Five. We have not even reached the halfway point. And even when we complete Step Twelve we are not done with this walk; we commit to working the Steps over and over again as a discipline for sanity.

Step 6

CHAPTER SIX

DEFECT REMOVAL

*We were entirely ready to have God
remove all these defects of character.*

You might think that Step Six would be among the easiest of the Twelve Steps to take. After all, we've just gone through the painful and perhaps traumatic experience of making a searching moral inventory of our failings, and then we confessed those failings aloud to God, ourselves, and another human being. We are probably so weighed down by these defects of character that we should be more than ready to turn them over to God. And yet so many of us find ourselves facing Step Six with trepidation.

In fact, it is when confronting Step Six that we discover that rather than being "entirely ready" to be without these defects, we still harbor the hope that they can be controlled. Step Six forces us yet again to confront the ever-more-subtle ways the desire for control creeps back into our psyches and our lives, pushing out the realization of powerlessness that motivated our recovery in Step One.

"There is always something we are clinging to, always something we don't want God to remove," said Gerri, a Christian pastor and OA member. "When I first got to Step Six I was willing to have God round off the rough edges of my character, but not remove them. I thought that with God's help I could learn to control my so-called defects of character, and by doing so show them to be what I knew them to be: not defects at all, but endearing quirks that made me unique. Even after all this effort, I was still excusing my behavior and clinging to the illusion of control."

The reason we cling to our defects of character is that our lives are so invested in our addictions and the insanity they create that we cannot imagine who we will be without them. And because we cannot know who will be, we are afraid to let go of who we have been.

Here is what the Twelve and Twelve (the Twelve Steps and Twelve Traditions of AA) has to say about this:

> Practically everybody wishes to be rid of his most glaring and destructive handicaps ... but ... what we must recognize now is that we exult in some of our defects. We really love them. Who, for example, doesn't like to feel just a little superior to the next fellow, or even a lot superior? Isn't it true that we like to let greed masquerade as ambition? ... Self-righteous anger also can be very enjoyable....[1]

But it isn't just a fear of being ordinary that causes us to flinch at the idea of being defect-free, it is the notion that without these character flaws we would have no character at all. Think about this for a moment: Who would you be without your anger? Who would you be without your resentments? Who would you be without your fears? While you can pretend to know who you might be if you were free from these things, you don't really know. You have no data to go on; you have never been free of them. Being entirely ready to have God remove these defects of character means being entirely ready to be someone you have never been before. And who is entirely ready for that?

"I thought Step Six would be a snap," Sandra said at one AA meeting. "I hated the person I'd become. I was ashamed of the way I was living my life—the lying, the secrets, the double life of a successful administrator and a drunk. I thought I'd jump at the chance to have all my defects lifted from me. But the truth is I wasn't ready. I was afraid that if I sobered up I wouldn't exist, or the *me* that would exist would be worse off than the *me* I was. It isn't that I loved who I was, but rather I feared who I might become. Drinking protected me from that person, and I was afraid that I needed to be protected from her. What finally pushed me to take Step Six was once again hitting rock bottom."

Sandra had gone on a business trip and, after months of sobriety, found herself drinking alone in the hotel bar. "It wasn't that something happened that triggered my drinking, I just walked into the bar and drank. It was as if I were someone else. I watched myself do it and couldn't stop myself. I have no real memory of that night, but in the morning I woke up in a stranger's bedroom sick, horrified, and ashamed. I thought back to Step Six. No matter who I would be without this insanity it had to be better than who I was with it. I was entirely ready."

WHO ARE YOU, REALLY?

The self we imagine ourselves to be is a character in a drama we tell about our lives. We build our identities out of half-remembered events from our past, the feelings these memories generate, and the ideas we have about those feelings. We are like playwrights who so identify with the lead character in their play that they begin to mistake the play for real life and the character for themselves. In time we forget that we are constructing the drama and it becomes so real that we feel powerless to change it. Indeed, we are powerless, for the identification with the character is so complete that we no longer have any idea that we are other than this character. We are so attached to certain memories and certain kinds of feelings and ways of thinking that we cannot imagine being ourselves without them. As long as we maintain this illusion, we will balk at taking Step Six.

Being willing to break the illusion—or more accurately, being willing to have the illusion broken—is what Step Six is all about. Being entirely ready to have our character defects removed means being entirely ready to see who we are without them, to see who we are without the addictive scripts we have written for ourselves. Perhaps the greatest modern master of living without scripts was Ramana Maharshi (1879–1950), an Indian sage who at the age of sixteen underwent a spontaneous spiritual transformation and spent the rest of his life teaching a practice of self-realization he called *atma-vicara,* Self Inquiry.

According to Ramana, you and I suffer from a fatal delusion that there is an independent *I* that does whatever we imagine we are doing at the moment. When we say, "I am thinking," Ramana would argue that there are just thoughts. When we say, "I am walking," Ramana would challenge us to see that there is just walking. There is no *I* separate from the activity. The *I* as doer is a fiction. The truth is the *I,* the egoic self we imagine ourselves to be when we imagine ourselves to be anyone at all, is a by-product of doing. There is no self separate from the process that is unfolding at the moment.

This is very difficult to grasp, and even as we wrestle with it, we should be asking, "Who is it that is wrestling? Who is it that is understanding that the *I* is a fiction?" If very act of saying, "I am this" or "I am that" traps us in the illusion of a separate *I,* so too does the act of saying "I know this" or "I know that." Any *I* statement is a trap, and the only way out is to move more deeply in.

David Godman, one of the leading authorities on Ramana Maharshi, puts it this way:

> Sri Ramana taught that since the individual "I"-thought cannot exist without an object, if attention is focused on the subjective feeling of "I" or "I am" with such intensity that the thoughts "I am this" or "I am that" do not arise, then the individual "I" will be unable to connect with objects. If this awareness of "I" is sustained, the individual "I" (the "I"-thought) will disappear and in its place there will be a direct experience of the Self. This constant attention to the inner awareness of "I" or "I am" was called self-enquiry [*sic*] (*atma vicara*) by Sri Ramana Maharshi and he constantly

recommended it as the most efficient and direct way of discovering the unreality of the "I"-thought. He taught that the "I"-thought only finally disappears when the perception of all objects, both physical and mental, ceases and only Self Awareness exists. This is not brought about by being aware of an "I," but only by BEING the "I." This stage of experiencing the subject rather than being aware of an object is the culminating phase of self-enquiry.[2]

In some ways similar to *vipassana* meditation, I find Ramana's self-inquiry to be a powerful tool for freeing ourselves from the tyranny of the ego moment to moment. To see how best to use the practice, let's take as an example the following statement: "I am afraid." The sentence itself assumes there is an *I* who experiences a separate state called "fear." But is this true? Certainly there is a tightening of the body, accompanied by increased heart rate and rapid breathing. There may also be feelings of panic and deep anxiety. And there may be all kinds of thoughts about what is causing this physical and emotional upheaval, and what it means that you are afraid. Memories of past fears may overwhelm your thinking, enhancing the emotional turmoil and fueling even more physical distress. But are these sensations, emotions, and thoughts really you?

The unexamined assumption at the moment of fear is an unequivocal "Yes, of course this is me. I am afraid." But Ramana asks us to look at this assumption more closely. Is the one who notices the body's distress not separate from that distress? Is the one who is aware of feelings, thoughts, and memories not other than those feelings, thoughts, and memories?

If we examine the situation carefully, we discover that it is analogous to watching a horror film in a movie theater. We so identify with the characters on the screen that we forget for a moment that we are sitting safely in a theater. As the music becomes more intense and we anticipate a fatal attack on a hapless character, our body, heart, and mind take on the trauma we imagine the character must be feeling. And when the fatal blow is struck, we scream as if we were there.

For a moment we are there. But the moment passes, and we delight in the experience of being frightened. It was fun. But it was fun because the identification with the character was temporary, and was replaced with the reality of our experiencing other than the horror-filled sensations, feelings, and thoughts that gripped us a moment earlier. Our fright ceases and we feel a sense of humor at our own overidentification with the fiction we are watching.

What is true of watching a film is true of observing our own lives. The observer is not the observed. Ramana asks us to be aware of ourselves as observers, and to see the physical sensations, emotional turmoil, and obsessive thinking of the *I* we imagine ourselves to be as other than we truly are. In other words, we have a body, but we are not the body; we have feelings, but we are not those feelings; we have thoughts, but we are not those thoughts. Whatever we are, we are other than all that.

And what are we when we look at our actions in this way? We are the field in which the action happens. We are the observer. We have no fixed identity. We have no age or gender or size. We have no habits or addictions. We are the pure self we affirmed in Step Two. My own experience with the self-inquiry brings me to the awareness that whoever this Observer is it isn't other than me and you. There isn't a plethora of Observers; there is only one. I know that the *I* who observes *me* is the same *I* who observes *you*. And this *I* is God.

Apply this to Step Six. You have character defects, but you are not those defects. The *you* who is an alcoholic is not the true *you* who knows you to be an alcoholic. The *you* who is angry and full of resentments is not the *you* who knows the angry and resentful you. The real *you* is other than the fictional *you* created by the narrative of addiction. You cannot define this true *you*.

You cannot label it. You cannot be separate from or other than it. That self is you, the real *you*, the *you* free from all limitations and defects from the very beginning. When you realize this, you are then entirely ready to be that *you* because you realize you already are that *you*.

Practice: Self-Inquiry

Ramana's method of self-inquiry rests on the examination of the *I*, the egoic self that seeks to control life and thereby risks becoming trapped in addictive thoughts, feelings, and behaviors when control proves to be an impossible goal.

For example, when you find yourself thinking, "I need a drink" or "I deserve to eat this" or "I don't deserve to be happy and free," stop for a moment and ask, "Who is this *I* who thinks this thought?" When feelings arise and you hear yourself saying, "I'm angry" or "I'm worthless," or "I'm invincible," stop for a moment and ask, "Who is this *I* who feels this feeling?"

Asking alone gives you distance from the *I*, for the one who asks isn't the *I* attached to these thoughts and feelings. From that position of distance, trace the notion of *I* back to its origin. Where did this *I* come from? If you inquire diligently, you will discover that it comes from a vast sense of awareness that is both nameless and unbounded. This awareness is your true self, the self from which even the *I* that inquires arises.

My Indian friend and teacher Prasana, a lifelong student of Ramana Maharshi now living in northern California, offers a classic Hindu analogy to explain Ramana's teaching: "Think of the relationship between ocean and wave. The wave is the ego, the I-thought. The ocean is your true self. It is the nature of the ocean to wave, and it is the nature of the wave to deny its link to the ocean. When the wave asks *Who am I?* and traces its origin back to the point of its arising from the ocean it discovers it is the ocean and nothing but the ocean. This is *moksha*, liberation!"

Since the I-thought is continually arising in our minds, we have endless opportunities to discover our true self. I have been working with this practice since I first learned it in the late 1990s, and while I make no claim to liberation, I can attest that I am continually granted glimpses of the self through this practice of inquiry. Not that I see the self as an object separate from the *I* that inquires, but that there are moments when all *I*'ing ceases and there is only this self. In such moments there is no *me* to know anything, there is just knowing itself. But when that moment of seeing passes and an *I* returns, I understand directly the meaning of the Sanskrit teaching, *Tat tvam assi*, "You are that"; you are this infinite oceanic consciousness waving in endless diversity.

The endless waving of the ocean, the endless arising of *I*, can be discouraging, but Ramana assures us that if we persevere in our inquiry we will eventually achieve liberation: "Plunge deep into yourself, in the innermost depths of your heart, as the pearl diver holding speech and breath plunges deep into the waters and so secure with mind alert the treasure of the self within."[3]

Not that all thoughts of *I* will disappear, for we need such thoughts to function in the everyday world of seemingly separate people, places, and things, but that you will no longer mistake them for your true self. Thoughts and feelings will still arise, and these will still carry an *I* with them, but you will no longer identify with that *I*, and hence will be free from attaching to these thoughts and feelings and the habitual behaviors they often urge upon you.

CHAPTER SEVEN

ASKING FOR FREEDOM

We humbly asked God to
remove our shortcomings.

The devil is in the details; and the details when it comes to Twelve Step recovery are often lodged in the adjectives used by the steps themselves. If *entirely* is the key word in Step Six, *humbly* is the key word in Step Seven.

The English word *humble* comes from the Latin *humili,* low, which itself is related to another Latin word, *humus,* ground or earth. The word *human* is derived from *humus* as well, though the link between these words is lost on most English speakers. To understand the link, it helps to think of *earth* and *earthling.* This is precisely what the Hebrew Book of Genesis does when it tells us that *adam,* humanity, comes from *adamah,* earth. We humans are, in a sense, one way the earth becomes aware of itself. We are the way the universe looks at itself and says, "Wow!" And when we do, we are deeply humbled by the experience.

Remember lying on your back as a kid and looking up into the night sky? It is harder and harder to do in most neighborhoods because of light pollution, but even as adults, when we can find a place safe enough and dark enough to lie back and melt into the night sky, we begin to know what true humility is. It has nothing to do with our failings and flaws, and everything to do with our place in the universe.

The great Christian mystic and theologian Meister Eckhart speaks of this in terms of our relationship to God:

My lowliness raises up God, and the lower I humble myself the higher do I exalt God and the higher I do exalt God the more gently and sweetly he pours into me his divine gift, his divine influx. For the higher the inflowing thing the more easy and smooth is its flow. How God is raised upon my lowliness I argue thus: the more I abase and keep myself down the higher God towers above me. The deeper the trough the higher the crest. In just the same way, the more I abase and humble myself the higher God goes and the better and easier he pours into me his divine influx. So it is true that I exalt God by my lowliness.[1]

Given the Twelve Step notion of "God as we understand God," and being cognizant that I am interpreting Eckhart here, what I understand him to be saying is that the divine influx is our true self, the ocean that pours into the form of the wave, and that the more open I am to knowing the emptiness of the egoic self, the more receptive I become to realizing my true self as a manifestation of the fullness of God.

In a manner similar to Eckhart, Lao-Tzu, the fifth-century BCE Chinese sage who is thought to have composed the Taoist classic, the Tao te Ching, also uses the notion of being low as an analogy for being filled with virtue:

Know the masculine, hold to the feminine
Be the watercourse of the world
Being the watercourse of the world
The eternal virtue does not depart
Return to the state of the infant
Know the white, hold to the black
Be the standard of the world
Being the standard of the world
The eternal virtue does not deviate
Return to the state of the boundless

Know the honor hold to the humility
Be the valley of the world
The eternal virtue shall be sufficient
Return to the state of plain wood
Plain wood splits, then becomes tools
The sages utilize them
And them become leaders
Thus the greater whole is undivided[7]

By making ourselves low or humble, we work with the gravity of the spirit and ourselves to be filled with God's grace or eternal virtue. Notice that we cannot grasp hold of virtue or gain control of it. But if we humble ourselves, we work with the very nature of reality to invite the flow of virtue to come to us. The question now becomes this: Isn't making ourselves humble still an act of control? It is, and hence making anything of ourselves by ourselves, even if what we seek is to make nothing of ourselves is yet another trap of the ego, insisting ever more subtly that it is and should be in charge.

The ecstatic aspect of humility rarely comes up in meetings, where the focus is most often on human foibles. Yet this second aspect of *humble* is also important. If *humus* reminds us that we humans are low as a valley is low, *humili* reminds us that we are a species that can be brought low in ways no other species can experience. While many animals have rich emotional lives, none has the same capacity for shame and guilt as do we humans.

It is common to hear discussions of shame and guilt that seek to free us from these emotions. Feeling shame can be debilitating, and guilty feelings in and of themselves are said to be unproductive and perhaps even narcissistic, with people seeking to use these feelings tactically, saying, "Hey, I feel bad enough as it is, no need for you to continually throw my failings in my face."

In the context of Twelve Step recovery, however, being brought low is redemptive. As a young meth addict named Tyler put it, "God can't lift me up until I at last admit I'm down." Admitting the truth about our lives is what Twelve Step meetings are all about. We tell our stories over and over again until we at last hear the truth of them for ourselves. We listen to others' stories over and over again and we see ourselves in them. It isn't just the stories of our successes, the moments of recovery that add up to days, then months, then years that motivate us; it is the stories of failure and falling as well. Twelve Step meetings aren't pep rallies. They are safe, loving, and supportive spaces for the sharing of our failures as well as our successes, and as important as it is to have people who can celebrate the latter, it is more important to have people who will support us through the former.

Humans are *homo humili,* the animal that can be brought low, and because we can be brought low, we have the potential to be raised up. In Steps Four, Five, and Six we methodically touched the depths to which we had fallen; with the help of sponsors and meetings, we explored what it is to hit rock bottom; we excavated the lowest part of our lives and the hurtful, destructive behaviors that fester there. And in so doing we realized that we wanted something different. We became entirely ready to have God remove our character defects, to lift the terrible burdens of bad judgment and worse behavior that had brought us so low. We hoped that without these burdens we might rise up to take our rightful place in life again. But it is not enough to be ready; it is not enough to hope. We have to ask, and we have to ask humbly.

To ask humbly, we have to be humbled. To be humbled we have to place ourselves in that place of shame and guilt—not through new destructive behaviors but by telling our story of past destruction so mindfully that we again know what it is to hit rock bottom. It is here from the low place that we ask in the low way; our asking is humble because we have been humbled.

In this sense Step Seven is a direct extension of Step One. With Step One we admitted we were powerless over our lives and that we needed help desperately. With Step Seven we finally asked for that help.

FIERCE GRACE

Humility isn't something we achieve (achievement generates pride, not humility). Humility is something to which we awaken when we see the truth of who we are and how distant we are from who we can become. In other words, humility is not ours to control. It is a gift that is given us through the depths of our suffering. It is only when we accept the fact of our suffering, admit to ourselves that our lives are unmanageable, and confess to God, ourselves, and another human being the exact nature of our wrongs that we truly realize the horror of our lives and humbly ask God for help.

It is only when we can no longer hide from the insanity of our lives that we fall at last into the arms of humility. If not for the suffering, there would be no recovery. If not for the madness, there would be no humility. And we control none of this. It is all a matter of grace, a searing grace that burns away the illusion of control, and leaves us humbly asking God for help. This is the state that Ram Dass calls fierce grace.

Ram Dass is one of the iconic spiritual teachers of the twentieth century. Born Richard Alpert in 1931, he was the son of George Alpert, a wealthy Boston lawyer who helped found Brandeis University and who became president of the New York, New Haven & Hartford Railroad. After earning a PhD in psychology from Stanford, Richard taught at Harvard, and probably would have become a noted researcher if not for his collaboration with Timothy Leary in the investigation into LSD in 1961.

As liberating as his experiences with LSD were, they were temporary, and Alpert suspected there was a way of finding a more permanent freedom that didn't depend on the temporary high generated by drugs. In 1967 he went to India in search of this alternative. It was in India that Richard Alpert became *Ram*

Dass (Servant [*Dass*] of God [*Ram*], the name given him by his guru Neem Karoli Baba, whom his followers called Maharaji.

In 1971 Ram Dass published *Be Here Now,* a groundbreaking book of spiritual wisdom drawn from his experiences with Maharaji. The book has never gone out of print. Devoting himself to sharing the insights and practices of his guru, Ram Dass traveled the world teaching, writing, and counseling. In 1997, however, he suffered a severe stroke that left him with expressive aphasia and partial paralysis on his right side.

As he lay on the floor of his bedroom, having collapsed as he was getting out of bed one morning, Ram Dass realized that all his years of spiritual training had abandoned him. He was scared and nothing he knew was going to get him through this. He called his stroke the "fierce grace" of his guru, a reminder from his teacher (who had died years before) that with all his fame and good works, Ram Dass was no one special and had attained nothing of value. It was the fierce grace of hitting rock bottom. It was humbling and liberating at the same time.

We tend to think of grace as somehow soft and tender. It can be at times, I suppose, but the grace that saves, the grace that lifts from us the crushing weight of our addictions to not only one substance or another but our addiction to the illusion of power and control, isn't tender but fierce. Fierce grace rips the illusion of control from our fingers. And without that illusion we fall even farther than we knew imaginable, hitting that terrible rock bottom with such force as to shatter our illusions and allow us to begin the long road of recovery.

I first met Ram Dass when the two of us were lecturing at an Inner Directions Gathering in La Jolla, California. Ram Dass was wheeled onstage for his talk. He made reference to his stroke and told us that he suffered from expressive aphasia, and that there would be moments in his presentation when he would know what he wanted to say but no longer had the words with which to say it. "You'll know what the words are," he said, "but don't call them out to me. We will sit in silence and the words will come to me, or we will sit in silence and they won't come to me, and I will just change the subject." We laughed in awe of a man so at peace with this suffering. Whatever would happen would happen, and he would deal with it with humor and deep humility. This is the gift fierce grace offers us.

ONLY ONE STEP

What I learned from Ram Dass was the fact that there is only one step: hitting rock bottom, and hitting it so hard that there is no opportunity for denial, no room for ego, no option for anything but a radically humble cry for help.

We can't move through the steps, we can only be moved through them. And the agent that moves us, call it God if you like, does so through the fierce grace of our hitting rock bottom. It is our continual realization of powerlessness that allows us to be surrendered to the flow of recovery. As long as we imagine that we have the power to swim to the far shore of sanity on our own, we will inevitably swim against the current. Only when we are too broken to swim do we collapse into the sea itself and discover the current carrying us where we need to go.

Many people imagine that hitting rock bottom is a one-time-only event. But the hard fact is that we continue to hit it over and over again. I'm not referring to lapses in judgment or falling prey to addictive behaviors. This also happens, but it is not what I am talking about. I am talking about a different kind of rock bottom, the rock bottom we hit when we come face-to-face with our own powerlessness. This rock bottom happens over and over again because our grasping at control happens over and over again.

As my sponsor, Bert, put it, "There's a subtle pride that creeps into many of us who work the Twelve Steps. We begin to believe that we are doing the work of recovery rather than continually deepening our awareness that we are being graced with recovery. We don't necessarily speak of it this way and that is why we may even forget we can't do this for ourselves. God is doing this. And as soon as we forget that, our recovery is threatened."

Yet we do forget it. That's why we go to meetings long after our addictive behaviors have ceased. We go to meetings to hear stories of powerlessness and fierce grace, and to remember the truth of powerlessness that we might be surrendered over and over again to grace. We are, as Bert once said, living the myth of Sisyphus.

THE MYTH OF SISYPHUS

Sisyphus was the son of King Aeolus of Thessaly and the king and founder of Corinth. He was also a very unsavory character— killing travelers and guests he invited to his home, seducing his niece, usurping his brother's throne, and revealing and criticizing the secret sexual exploits of Zeus.

It was these unsavory traits that got him into real trouble. Zeus commanded Hades to bind Sisyphus in chains. Hades sent Thanatos, the god of death, to fulfill the High Lord's command, but Sisyphus tricked Thanatos into chaining himself instead, thereby bringing an end to human death. Aries, the god of war, furious that those he defeated in battle could no longer die, freed Thanatos and sent Sisyphus to the Underworld.

Just prior to his death, however, Sisyphus told his wife not to perform the usual rites of the dead on his behalf. When he arrived in the Underworld, he complained to Persephone, queen of the Underworld, that his wife was dishonoring him, and persuaded the queen to let him return to the world of the living to berate her. When he returned to Corinth, he sought to avoid death a second time, but Hermes eventually captured him and returned him to the Underworld.

All this trickery and hubris angered the gods, who created a unique punishment for Sisyphus. He was compelled to continually roll a huge rock up a steep hill. Each time he drew near the summit, the rock would roll back down to the base, and Sisyphus would be required to roll it up the hill again.

Sisyphus is us. The rock is our addiction. Rolling the rock up the mountain is working the Twelve Steps, and just when we imagine that we might get that rock to the top and leave it there once and for all, it gets away from us, rolls back to the bottom, and leaves us with no alternative but to push it up the mountain once more.

For some this sounds defeatist, but it isn't. The rock can never reach the summit; that is simply not an option. The nature of things is for the rock to roll down the mountain before it reaches the summit. That is reality. This would be defeatist only if the rock could make it to the summit, but we were denied the means of getting there. This would be defeatist only if we had no way to roll the rock up the mountain. But we do: the Twelve Steps. When we realize that rolling the rock up the mountain over and over and over again is simply the nature of our situation, and that we can only do what can be done—namely roll the rock—we cannot be defeated.

As Mike said in an open AA meeting, "I don't feel defeated when I have to wash the same dish over and over again. I wash it, it gets used and dirty, I wash it again. Nothing defeatist about that. I would only feel defeated if I couldn't wash it at all. It is the same with my drinking. I am not defeated by my disease as long as I work the Steps. True, I am never cured, but it isn't about cure. It is about living sanely with the insanity of addiction."

THE THREE *P*s

What the myth of Sisyphus tells us, and what the disease of addiction shows us, is that we are powerless by design. We are created powerless over life, just as a wave is powerless over the ocean and a branch is powerless over the tree. Once we realize this, we are free from what the Twelve Steps call the Three *P*s: *Perfectionism, Procrastination,* and *Paralysis.* Thinking we have to be perfect in our lives and in our working of the Twelve Steps allows us to put off actually doing the Steps and living our lives. And as the procrastination drags on, it morphs into paralysis, and we are incapable of doing anything at all. If we can avoid the first *P* the other two will not arise, but once we fall into the trap of perfectionism, we are doomed to fall into the second two traps as well.

When I first heard of the Three *P*s I thought it was just another of the seemingly infinite list of aphorisms that fills Twelve Step books and conversations. But, like most of the other all too cute sayings of Twelve Step programs, this one contains a deep truth: Perfectionism is paralyzing. Perfectionism is just another addiction, another form of *trishna,* desire, and, like all other manifestations of craving, it leaves us powerless over life.

"Procrastination is just a story you tell yourself to mask the fact of paralysis," Dr. Valerie said. "As long as you imagine that you are procrastinating, you can imagine that someday you will stop procrastinating. This fantasy about 'someday' allows you to continue to ignore the real paralysis today."

To end the paralysis, we must end the perfectionism, and the only way to end the perfectionism is to get back to pushing the rock, knowing full well it is going to roll back down the mountain once again.

Practice: Pushing the Rock, Moving the Bead

A *mala* is a strand of 108 beads used by Hindus and Buddhists to keep count while repeating a mantra. One can find equivalent tools in the three Abrahamic religions as well. Sephardi (Eastern) Jews count the knots and windings on the fringes of their prayer shawls, which add up to the numerological equivalent of God's Name. Ashkenazi (or Western Jews) use a different number of knots and windings numerologically equivalent to the phrase "The Lord is One." Orthodox Christians carry thick, black, wool prayer ropes developed by St. Pachomius in the fourth century that are knotted with 100 knots. Catholics use rosary beads. And Sufi Muslims use a strand of 99 beads called a *tasbi* for reciting the ninety-nine names of Allah.

The specific practices of specific religions aside, the universal message of a *mala* is the eternal round. The garland of beads has no beginning or end, and the mantras are recited over and over again into the hundreds and even thousands of times as the thumb moves the beads either clockwise or counterclockwise.

In our context, the point of using a *mala* is to learn to appreciate the endless round of life. Just as Sisyphus never finishes pushing his rock up the mountain, so we never come to end of the *mala*. Yet as our practice with the *mala* deepens, there is a quiet joy that arises in us each time we move a bead. *Mala* usage can be adapted to any meditation practice where repetition of a sacred name is used, but for our purposes I suggest that you use the beads in conjunction with the simple act of breathing.

In my experience with *malas*, I notice first that counting the breath as I move a bead slows down my breathing, relaxes my body, and quiets my mind. Second, I feel a subtle joy just from moving the beads with my fingers. The tactile quality of the beads is simply pleasant in the hand, and I feel a quiet satisfaction just moving the beads around and around. While I cannot explain why this is so, I can attest to the fact that a sense of well-being and calm arises in me whenever I use my *mala*.

When using a traditional *mala* of 108 beads you will notice a 109th bead somewhat larger than the rest. This is called the *sumeru*,[3] *bindu*,[4] *stupa*,[5] or *guru*[6] bead and marks the completion of one round. Counting the beads always starts with the bead next to the guru bead. When you complete the garland of beads and reach the guru bead, you do not count or cross it, but rather turn the *mala* around and count in the opposite direction.

There is no point to working with a *mala*, and no end to it. And that is why I do it. We are learning to appreciate the endless rounds we make in life. It doesn't matter that we never arrive at the mountain's summit or the *mala*'s end. We find joy in simply rolling the stone and moving the bead. It doesn't matter that we never arrive at recovery once and for all. We find joy in simply working the Steps over and over again.

CHAPTER EIGHT

NAMING THE HARMED

We made a list of all persons we had harmed, and became willing to make amends to them all.

Who have you harmed in your life? When I first confronted this question, I said to myself, "I haven't harmed anyone. I haven't robbed anybody, beaten anybody, or killed anybody. What real harm have I done? I'm a pretty decent human being. Working this Step will be a snap." By the time I had "finished" with Step Eight I had a list of names that rivaled the New York City White Pages—all five boroughs! It would have been easier to list the names of persons I hadn't harmed. It all depends on how we define *harm*. I define it this way: To harm someone is to *deliberately mislead another for one's own gain or benefit*. While the wording of this definition is mine, the idea behind it came from a woman named Connie, a tailor at a dry cleaner whom I met at an NA meeting in Los Angeles.

Talking about Step Eight, Connie said:

This was the worst step for me. I thought admitting my defects was tough, but it was nothing compared to making this list. I had to name names, you know? It was one thing to admit that I'm not perfect; it was another thing altogether to realize how many people I hurt through my imperfections. At first I didn't see it; I didn't see how my lying and my drugging hurt anybody. Or if it did, it only hurt a few people. I was hurting myself mostly, right? But then I realized that I had to manipulate a lot of people to live the stoned life I was living; I had to get them to think they were crazy so that I could maintain the lie that I wasn't crazy. Maybe I didn't steal money from them, but I stole something more important; I stole their sanity. I sacrificed their sanity on the altar of my insanity.

We deliberately mislead people when we lie to them, when we withhold information they need to make sound decisions, when we pretend to be someone we're not. Defined this way, we discover that we have harmed and continue to harm people more than we ever imagined. We do this because we are afraid that if we don't do it people will reject us. We are afraid that if we are truly ourselves no one will like us, so we create a false image of ourselves that others will like. We replace our authentic self with an inauthentic self based not on who we are or even who others want us to be, but on who we imagine others want us to be. This process of false-self creation is so steeped in our own projections and fantasies that the image resulting from it is often a cartoon-like character totally out of sync with our true nature. Unfortunately and inevitably, the projected self overshadows the true self to the point where we begin to believe that we are the self we invented and lose touch with the self we are.

Byron, an unemployed and sometimes homeless alcoholic who had been coming to meetings for a few months, but who was, as he put it, "not yet into the recovery aspect of things," told me:

I hate myself when I'm drinking, but I hate myself more when I'm not drinking. But the *me* I hate isn't the real *me* but a fake *me* I invented to pass in the general world of work and such. But I've been that *me* so long that I really can't tell you who the real *me* is. But I can tell you that they are both hateful. I hate the *me* I made and I hate the *me* that made him. And what's more, I hate other people even more for making me have to make the fake *me* in the first place. I think I started drinking to drown out the hate, but now it just feeds it. I oughta get sober and stay that way, but I don't know how.

The irony here is palpable. Our fear of rejection causes us to invent a false self, which in turn leads us to reject our true self, which in turn leads us to reject those who we imagine want us to be other than we are, and whom we blame for setting this cycle of false selves in motion in the first place. It is no wonder that we are confused, conflicted, and dis-eased. How could we be otherwise?

Because we lack integrity and authenticity, we are incapable of healing the anxiety arising from our living falsely. Since we cannot heal the anxiety, we seek to mask it, and we do that by succumbing to the disease of addiction. We turn to self-destructive self-medicating behavior in order to dull the fear and ease the ache of rejection. As Dr. Valerie put it, "No one drinks or does drugs to feel worse, but to feel less worse." The key phrase here is *less worse*. There is no healing in addiction; we cannot drink ourselves to authenticity; we can only numb ourselves to our inauthenticity.

In the context of Step Eight, the deeper we fall into addiction, the more hurtful our actions become, and the worse we feel about ourselves. It now seems that we are the awful person we feared we might be, and the only way to avoid dealing with that is by taking ever stronger doses of "medicine."

For a time, the medicine works. We become inured to both our fears and our behaviors. We make excuses for them both. We stop worrying about being our authentic self because we can no longer remember any self other than the addicted one. We have become our disease.

It is important to remember that the real disease isn't alcoholism, drug addiction, compulsive eating or gambling, or any of the other ways we self-medicate. These are symptoms of a deeper disorder: the delusion that we are in control of our lives. The harm we cause is colored by the addictions we have, but it is fueled by the desire for control. Control is our real addiction.

Of course, we're not in control, and eventually reality catches up with us. When it does, we often take refuge not in God as we understand God, but in our story as we spin our story. This is what denial really is: the insistence that the story we tell about ourselves—about our false selves—is true. We turn our lives into stories, and then like any good novelist we create backstories, invent motivations for our actions, and shape ourselves into highly nuanced and engaging characters when, in fact, we are ordinary people trying to get through the day without getting the crap kicked out of us or kicking it out of someone else.

The challenge of Step Eight is to make our list of people to whom we are ready to make amends without at the same time feeding our story. As we review our lives and make note of the harm we have done and the people to whom we have done harm, we must be careful not to imagine ourselves as either lost saints or demonic sinners. To do so only feeds the story and makes reality all the more difficult to find.

Life, Bert told me, is really about the Three *M*s: *Money, Meeting,* and *Meaning.* We need enough money to take care of ourselves and, if we have one, our families. We need meeting with other people because we humans are social animals and we tend to shrivel up and die without relationships rooted in mutual love, care, and respect. And we need meaning, a deep and eventually unshakable sense that life matters, that our lives matter, and that they matter for something larger than ourselves.

There may be much more to life than Bert's Three *M*s, but without them whatever else there might be is beyond our reach. Meeting is the most important of the Three *M*s because it is through meeting other people that we discover meaning in our lives, and without meaning, authentic living is impossible.

Step Eight helps us to see the unreality of our relationships. We are forced to look at the pain we cause others, even—if not especially—those we claim to love. And when we see this clearly we begin to change; not overnight, but over time. We stop spinning stories and imagining ourselves to be other than we are. We slowly learn to love the person we actually are: the broken person, the ordinary person, the wounded person. We no longer use our wound as a crutch or a club, but rather as a reminder of our ordinariness, which in turn softens our heart and allows us to embrace the equally imperfect people around us.

KARMA IS AS KARMA DOES

The wisdom of ordinariness dawns on us slowly. It is the gift that comes with working Step Eight. As we humbly review our lives and allow ourselves to honestly experience the pain we have caused and the harm we have done, we begin to notice something very profound: The past is rarely past. We discover a recurring pattern to our ways of relating to others. We begin to notice that while the actors change and the sets are different, the drama of our lives is often the same. We are replaying the same insanity over and over again. We find our lives locked into a karmic cycle of almost unchanging cause and effect.

At first this might seem like cause for despair: If this cycle is unchanging, how can we free ourselves from it? If freedom is impossible, then there is no hope of breaking the chains that bind us to our addictions. If we work Step Eight deeply enough, however, we find that there is a vast difference between karma and fate: The latter leaves us without hope, the former is the very harbinger of hope.

The word *karma,* as we mentioned in Step One, derives from the Sanskrit root *kr,* "to do," and simply means "action." As used in Hinduism it has a larger meaning of "cause and effect." Hinduism speaks of three kinds of karma: *sanchita,* or accumulated karma, which is the sum total of all past actions, good and bad; *prarabdha,* or fruit-bearing karma, which is the effects of *sanchita* karma that are present in our current lives; and *kriya-mana,* or current karma, the karma we are creating with our present actions whose effects will ripen over time and become *prarabdha* karma in the future.

We can't escape our past actions. Each act sets in motion a cascade of events that eventually manifests as the present moment. Whatever we encounter now was conditioned by what we did in the past. What isn't conditioned is what we do with this ripened karma in the present.

This is why karma differs greatly from fate. Fate presupposes that our lives are mapped out in advance of our living them. Whatever happens to us and whatever response we make to what happens to us is scripted in advance. We are characters in a play simply acting out our prescribed parts. Karma tells us something else entirely. As my teacher Prasana once told me, "Fate presumes that life is static, that all change is illusory. Karma presumes that fate is illusory, and that life is always changing. Responding to the ever-changing conditions of life is what karma is all about. Respond in ways that lead to freedom and the karma is called good karma. Respond in ways that lead to slavery and the karma is called bad karma. Good or bad, karma is always a matter of response to what is happening now, while fate is a slavish submission to what you imagine will happen later."

No one is fated to become an addict. Rather our responses to circumstances make addiction more or less likely. As Dr. Valerie puts it, "There is a lifetime of experience between being allergic to alcohol and being an alcoholic." Knowing you have a disease, that you cannot take just one drink but are physically driven to take one drink after another, allows you the opportunity to pass on that first drink. This doesn't eradicate the disease; it simply prevents it from shifting from potential problem to actualized addiction. Accepting the reality of our situation, and acting in a way that does not feed the disease, is working wisely with our karma.

Karma doesn't prescribe action; karma only says that the effects of our actions will set up conditions in which future action will be taken. For example, if I overeat and underexercise, I will gain weight. Overeating and underexercising are the causes of my weight gain, and while habitually overeating and underexercising may make it more difficult for me to eat less and exercise more, they do not preclude me from doing so. All they do is set the stage for my doing so or not doing so.

Working with our karma, we take up the Twelve Steps to set new, more healthy, karmic forces in motion. This does not guarantee a specific result, and there is no assurance that we will stay with the program, but it does place responsibility for our actions and the results of our actions squarely in our own laps, and in so doing refines our understanding of powerlessness.

We began with Step One admitting that we were powerless over life, and could not manage the insanity that had come to define our lives. With Step Eight we begin to realize that while we are powerless over the conditions in which we find ourselves at the moment, we are not powerless when it comes to our actions in response to those conditions. In other words, we realized that there is a difference between power and control. We do have some power, just not enough power to effect control. As long as we insist on control, we will see ourselves as totally powerless. Once we relinquish the idea of control we discover we have the capacity—the power—to do little things, and that these little things can change everything. We can turn our lives over to God as we understand God and in so doing respond to the karmic conditions of the moment in ways that will maximize healthy karmic conditions in the future.

Taking a karmic approach to the Twelve Steps brings us into the world of Karma Yoga, or the Way of Union (*yoga*) through Action (*karma*). The union referred to in yoga is the union with

God achieved by acting in accord with one's dharma, or duty. Each situation in which we find ourselves is a manifestation of some past karma, and contains within it a proper way of engaging that moment—a way that honors the past karma without creating new negative karma in the present. That proper way is one's dharma, and doing one's dharma without thought of self or reward is what Karma Yoga is all about.

Karma Yoga is one of the key teachings of the Bhagavad Gita, the Song (*gita*) of God (*Bhagavan*), a central text of Hinduism. Written sometime between the fifth and second centuries BCE, the Gita is a philosophical exploration of the nature of reality, set in the midst of an epic battle between warring cousins and their armies.

The Gita itself is rooted in Karma Yoga, urging us to act without attachment to the fruits of our actions, "for he who does his duty disinterestedly attains the Supreme (God)" (Bhagavad Gita 3:19).[1] Arjuna, the protagonist of the Bhagavad Gita, is about to lead his people into battle against his cousins, a battle Arjuna himself does not wish to fight. His compassion for his relatives is pushing him to leave the field of battle. It is then that his charioteer, who is in fact the Supreme Lord, Krishna, reveals to Arjuna the key to selfless action: "Surrendering all your actions unto Me, your thoughts concentrated on the Absolute, free from selfishness and without anticipation of reward, with mind devoid of excitement—fight!" (Bhagavad Gita 3:30).

Krishna explains to Arjuna that action is simply part of the human condition. Each of us is forced to act, and to act in accord with the conditions our past karma has created for us. This is the Gita's understanding of *powerlessness,* what it calls acting without attachment, or action as sacrifice.

When we act without attachment, we do not act to achieve some end. There is no thought of manipulating people or situations; there is no thought of control. All we do is accept the reality in which we find ourselves, and act in accord with it in a manner that does not generate bad karma. Doing so is the hallmark of the wise: "As the ignorant act because of their fondness for action, so should the wise act without such attachment, fixing their eyes, O Arjuna! only on the welfare of the world" (Bhagavad Gita 3:25).

Your dharma, your duty, is not to yourself but to God and the world. What that duty is depends on the situation in which you find yourself, but in the context of Twelve Step recovery, our dharma is living free from addictive behavior. Living sanely will create karma that will, when it ripens in the future, establish conditions in which sane living becomes more and more natural.

Most of us act from a desire to control, to achieve some desired result; the action is a means to an end, and it is the end on which we are focused. Karma Yoga suggests a different approach: Since we cannot be certain of what ends may arise from our actions, we are better served, and the world is better served, if we focus not on ends, but on means—on the actions themselves. We do not act in order to achieve a certain result, we act because action is unavoidable. We do not act sanely in order to control the world and achieve a certain desirable outcome, we act sanely because we realize that sane action—action that is compassionate and just and supportive of the welfare of both self and other—is the most appropriate action in the situation at hand.

Acting wisely means acting in accord with our duty in the moment—doing what is right, and letting go of the results. We cannot control the results of our actions, only the actions themselves. Acting in this way is called "sacrificing the fruits of our action." It is how the Gita understands powerlessness.

The Gita's insight into powerlessness is very helpful to those of us who struggle with the seeming inconsistency of Twelve Step thinking: If we are powerless, how can we work the Twelve Steps? If we are powerless, how can we even be willing to have our defects of character removed from us? If we are powerless, how can we ask God, however understood, to remove our defects? These are all actions, and if we can take them, then we are not powerless.

The Gita tells us that powerlessness does not mean we are incapable of taking action. On the contrary, doing and not doing are both "actions," in that both create karma. It is not that we cannot act, it is that we cannot control the conditions in which we are called on to act or the results of our activity or inactivity, which arise from our response to that call. In other words, we are powerless over the past and powerless over the future, but not powerless over our behavior in the present.

Our present power is found in our capacity to act with or without attachment to results. If we act with attachment to results, we are acting with ignorance since, in reality, we have no control over results. If we act without attachment to results, we are acting in harmony with reality, for in reality results are outside our control.

KARMIC UNDERSTANDING

Understanding karma requires seeing how our behavior creates the conditions under which and in which future action is necessitated. For example, if we lie to someone now, that lie will create a condition that will color our next encounter with this person: We will have to remember the lie and shape future conversations in light of it. Similarly, the person to whom we are lying will either accept the lie as truth or suspect that we are lying, in either case creating expectations and conditions for a future encounter with us.

The same, of course, can be said for telling the truth. Every action creates karma that will in time become a condition for future experience. The difference is that lying complicates life while truth telling simplifies it. To maintain a lie requires further lying, which, in turn, requires even more lying, and over time our lives become a thick web of tangled lies and half-truths that strangles any move toward authentic living. Truth telling, while often painful, leaves no residue. Yes, telling the truth creates its own karma, and, if the truth we are telling is one that causes pain to ourselves and others, that pain will create a karmic effect with which we will have to deal, but there is no unnecessary complication. We are always dealing with reality—sometimes loving, sometimes not, but never fabricated. This is what Coleman, an elderly African-American sculptor who told me he marched with the civil rights leader Dr. Martin Luther King, Jr., in Selma, called "cutting with a fresh blade."

> When you carve a piece of wood with a dull blade, you have to hack at it. Your cut is ragged, jagged, and messy. It looks like you don't know what you're doing, and you leave the wood sort of wounded. But when the blade is fresh, sharp, and smooth, you cut right and clean, with nothing extra going on. Same is with people. When you act with a blade dulled by drugs or drink, you mess everything and everyone up. When you act sharp, your mind clear and sane, you do what you have to do without any collateral damage. Even when you have to hurt or disappoint someone, you do it without adding insult to injury by lying and manipulating everyone into thinking you aren't doing what it is you are doing.

The first step in using karmic understanding is to take note of the karma your actions create. As you make your list of people you have harmed, do not be satisfied with a surface understanding of the harm. Look more deeply to see the conditions at play when the harmful action was done. Then look back, if you can, to see what conditions existed before the ones that caused or created the conditions existing during the time of the harmful act. In other words, look deeply enough at your behavior to realize beyond a shadow of a doubt that no incident is isolated, that you are conditioned to cause harm by past acts of harming, and that unless and until you cease to do harm, you will perpetuate these conditions throughout your life.

The second step in working with karma is to cease to produce bad karma. You have no control over the past or the future, and you will have to work through the consequences of past karma in the present, but you can *influence* your future by acting in the present in ways that will produce good karma, karma generated by actions that are compassionate and honest. We will speak of this again in Step Nine, where we seek to make amends to those we have hurt, and again in Step Ten, where we strive to cut the bonds of negative karma even as we create them. But for now it is enough to stop the flow of negative karma by recognizing it.

Practice: Working with Karma

One way to work with karma in the context of the Twelve Steps is to make a karmic spreadsheet. I was shown this by an Indian swami. He told me to make a chart for each of the persons I have harmed. Each chart contains four vertical columns. Label the chart with the name of the person you have harmed. Label each of the four columns Action/Condition, using red ink for *action* and blue ink for *condition*. Begin with the column on the far right and write in red ink the harmful action you wish to explore. Then think through the conditions in which the action took place—not the physical setting but the mental setting. What were you feeling at the time? What thoughts were going through your mind? What was the mental and emotional state of the other person? Write these as best you can recall them in blue.

Now move one column to the left. Using red ink, write down a key action (or actions) that set in motion the energies that created the conditions for the action you just explored in column one. Chances are this action too was negative and harmful. Flesh out the conditions for this action and write them down in blue. Do the same with the next two columns. When you look at the entire chart, you will be able to trace four generations of karmic conditioning. This helps you realize that nothing happens in a vacuum, and that your challenges today are the result of behaviors you initiated in the past.

Creating this karmic spreadsheet removes any thought that our harmful acts are isolated, one-time events. We see clearly that our addictive behavior creates conditions that invite further addictive behaviors, and that this cycle is ongoing. Realizing this gives all the more import to breaking the karmic stranglehold addictive behavior has on us. We can now see that acting in ways that will break the addictive karmic cycle and create healthy karmic conditions for the future will have positive consequences not just for the moment but for the rest of our lives.

While it is true that we can only act "one day at a time," karmic understanding reveals that the impact of today reaches far beyond today.

CHAPTER NINE

MAKING AMENDS

*We made direct amends to such people
wherever possible, except when to do so
would injure them or others.*

What does it mean to make amends? Let's begin our investigation with some advice from God given to us through the Prophet Ezekiel:

> To those who say, "Our misdeeds and our mistakes are crushing us, squeezing the life from us; how then can we live?" say this, "As I live, says God, I take no joy in the death of the wicked, rather the wicked should turn from their ways and live … If they turn away from sin and do what is lawful and right—if they restore the pledge, return what they have stolen, and walk in the statutes of life, committing no further evil—they shall live, they shall not die. None of the sins they have committed will be remembered and held against them; if they do what is lawful and right, they shall surely live."
> —*Ezekiel 33:10–16 [translation mine]*

God's advice is directed to those of us who can no longer avoid facing the harm we have caused. Our faults and misdeeds seem enormous; the suffering we have caused seems to overshadow and outweigh any good we may have done. We look at our moral inventory and we are ashamed; we review our list of those we have harmed and we are doubtful of ever making things right and reclaiming a decent life. We are crushed in the present by the weight of our past, and the future seems doomed to be more of the same. How can we live now knowing how we lived then?

What does God say to us? "I take no joy in the death of the wicked." Reality is not out to punish us or condemn us or see us die beneath the weight of our addictions and our pasts. What Reality wants is for us to live in harmony with what is, for when we do so, life lives at its optimum. To live in this manner we have to learn to swim with the current of life rather than against it. While Reality allows us to swim against the current, doing so robs us and life of our highest potential. If this is what God wants, it must be possible to achieve it, for Reality cannot ask the impossible of us. How then are we to live?

First, God says, we should fix what can be fixed. Tyrone, an auto mechanic with twelve years' sobriety, put it this way:

> I'm a fixer. And I'm not talking about cars only. I like to fix things, both mechanical things and people if they need fixing. Most of my life growing up I only saw that others needed fixing, but today I know it is me who is broken. Or at least I know that when it comes to people, the only one I can fix is me. Getting sober was a beginning, but fixing means more than that. Fixing means doing right today regarding what I had done wrong yesterday. I'm not saying I can change the past, but I can sort of fix it in the present.

If we reneged on a promise, we should fulfill the promise. If we stole property, we must return it. If we slandered someone or ruined her reputation, we must publicly set the record straight. Look over the list of people you have harmed. Can you do something to right the wrong you have done? If you can, you must do so. But much of the harm we cause is more subtle than that. Much of the pain we cause results not from external acts with external results, but from external acts with internal results. We did something that damages another internally, psychologically, spiritually.

Carmine, a part-time model whose parents escaped to the United States from Cuba, spoke at the same meeting right after Tyrone:

> I can't fix what I broke. It's one thing if you did something you can sort of undo, like paying for something you stole, but I broke hearts, man, and there is no one but God who can fix broken hearts. My sister had this boyfriend who she thought was going to marry her. But I was drinking and when I drink I get kind of, let's say, wild? And when I got home to my apartment that I used to share with my sister, her boyfriend was there and I just did him. I wasn't trying to hurt my sister or anything, and I can't even say I wanted to do him, I just did it. Sure he was a bastard for letting me, and that is what I told myself for a long time, you know that I did my sister a favor because he would have cheated on her eventually? But once I got in Program I knew I was just hiding from what I did to her by focusing on what he let me do to him. Anyway I can't fix that. Sure I apologized and everything, and my sister even talks to me, but not the same way. I could sort of fix the anger she had, but not the hurt. That she still carries in her heart, and I worry she won't ever trust nobody anymore.

Carmine was right. There is a level of brokenness that we just cannot repair. We can't take away the emotional pain and suffering we have caused. There is nothing we can say or do that will make the past other than what it is, or transform another's pain into something else. The karmic conditions we set in motion have to be harvested by both the persons we have harmed and by ourselves.

"Some people," Dr. Valerie said, "hope to use Step Nine as an escape hatch to avoid feeling the depth of another's suffering, and their own guilt for causing it. They think that by saying they are sorry they can manipulate people into forgiving them. Or they think that by saying they are sorry they deserve to be forgiven and if the other cannot forgive it is no longer their responsibility to make amends. This is cheap grace and counterfeit healing."

Cheap because it costs us very little: All we have to do is say we're sorry. Counterfeit because simply saying we're sorry doesn't change us or offer the people we have harmed any hope of healing. That is why when dealing with *making amends* we have to make a clear distinction between authentic amends making and apologizing, and between apologizing and asking for forgiveness.

AUTHENTIC AMENDS MAKING

Authentic amends making demands a change in our behavior, and not simply a verbal apology. There is a Hasidic proverb that says, "Stir a pot of filth clockwise or counterclockwise and it will still remain a pot of filth. Better to spend your time stringing pearls for the sake of heaven." In other words, nothing can come from trying to make the past something it wasn't. Searching the past to find an out, an excuse for our behavior, is a waste of time. Even if we think we find one, we are fooling ourselves; and using what we imagine we have found to get away with saying "I'm sorry" and nothing more simply perpetuates the life-crushing evil that already threatens to destroy us. Better to string pearls for the sake of heaven; better to spend our time doing differently than spend it pretending that we didn't really do what we really did.

The first thing to do when making amends is to change the way we live. If we are compulsive liars, today we tell the truth. If we are alcoholics, today we are sober. If we are drug addicts, today we are clean. If we are compulsive overeaters, today we are abstinent.

The second thing we do is ask for forgiveness. There is a crucial distinction between apologizing and asking for forgiveness. The Greek *apologia,* from which we derive our word *apology,* means "a speech in one's own defense." In other words, even when we apologize we are, in fact, justifying our actions, or at least seeking to escape the pain we feel over the pain we cause.

"Being in love is never having to say 'I'm sorry,'" Dr. Valerie said, "because saying 'I'm sorry' has nothing to do with love. It doesn't matter how you feel. It doesn't matter that you're sorry. What matters is how the other person feels. Saying 'I'm sorry' shifts the focus to you and your feelings. You're saying, 'Look, I feel bad for what I did. You don't want me to feel bad, do you? Of course not, so stop feeling hurt yourself and accept my apology, and then I can get on with my life without having to feel bad because I hurt your feelings.'"

Saying "I'm sorry" is just a subtle attempt to manipulate another's feelings, the very condition that caused us to act hurtfully in the first place.

Saying "I'm sorry" doesn't change anything. Our focus should be on how the other person feels. Listening, not speaking, is the real work of Step Nine.

TO LISTEN AND TO LOVE

When asked which of the hundreds of biblical commandments he felt to be fundamental, Jesus quotes Deuteronomy 6:5, "You shall love the Lord your God with all your heart, and with all your soul, and with all your might," and Leviticus 19:18, "You shall love your neighbor as yourself" (Matthew 22:37–39). For Jesus, loving God and loving one's neighbor form a seamless whole; indeed, one might argue that loving one's neighbor is the means by which we love God, especially when we understand *neighbor* to refer to all living things.

Yet how can love be commanded? We don't control our thoughts or feelings, and if we are not in control, how can we be commanded to achieve something as subtle and profound as love?

The answer is found in the commandment just prior to the command to love God: "Listen O Israel, the Lord our God, the Lord is One" (Deuteronomy 6:4). Love cannot be commanded, but listening can, and when we listen well, love inevitably follows.

"You know how I learned to make amends?" Danyyelle, a college coed, said at an OA meeting. "I learned to listen. I thought it was supposed to be about me talking about what I had done, but in the end I learned that it was all about me listening to the other person about how she felt about what I had done. The more I talked, the more distant the other person was. The more I listened, the more close we both felt to one another."

Listening is an act of intimacy. When we truly listen, when we open ourselves to the truth of another without trying to change his experience or our own, when we simply stand undefended in the face of another's reality—be it joyous or sorrowful—a bond is established between the listener and the one being listened to. This is what Step Nine asks of us.

Inviting those we have harmed to speak their pain is risky. We cannot be certain what will happen or what they will say. Once again we are brought face-to-face with our lack of control, but this time we welcome it consciously. Listening to others speak about the effects of our actions without *apologia*, without making excuses for our behavior, is more daring still, for their pain will only add to our own as we realize that we were the agents of their suffering.

Practice: Authentic Listening

In the *Sussusa Sutta* the Buddha lists six qualities for authentic listening that, when applied to Step Nine, translate as: hearing, attention, meaning, focus, understanding, and patience.

Hearing: It is not enough that we invite the other to speak; we have to make ourselves receptive to what is being said. Physically this means we have to soften our faces; if we glare at the other or if we look so pained as to make the other too self-conscious to speak, we are not allowing ourselves to hear what might be said. On the other hand, if we make our faces into blank masks, staring into space or looking through the other rather than at her, we are also not hearing. Rest your gaze lightly on the other's face. Be neither stoic nor overly dramatic. This isn't about your reaction but about the other's healing. Take care that your body language invites honesty. Don't tighten up, or cross your arms and legs defensively. Stay as relaxed and as vulnerable as you can. Feeling another's pain, even when you are the cause of that pain, won't kill you, and it may just "save" the other's life by allowing her to heal from the pain you caused and constructively move on with her life.

Attention: The goal of Step Nine is to allow another to reclaim his voice, to tell his story of suffering that he might begin to be free from it. It isn't enough that you invite the story to be spoken or even that you hear what is being said. You must attend to the words; that is, you must feel the other's pain as if it were your own. The key phrase here is *as if*. This isn't your pain, and if you try to take ownership of it, if you become overly dramatic in your listening and act as if you were the one suffering rather than the one who caused the suffering, you are robbing the other of the capacity to heal through this process. Doing this makes Step Nine all about you, and that shift from other to self is just another manifestation of your addiction. Allow yourself to feel what the other is feeling but never pretend that doing so puts the two of you on par.

Meaning: Authentic listening delves more deeply than the story you are hearing to grasp the meaning the story holds for the person telling it. It is one thing to listen to another tell you how devastated she was to discover that you were stealing from her. It is quite another to realize that by stealing her money you were also robbing her of the capacity to trust. Don't listen only to the words, don't lose yourself in the other's pain or your own guilt; listen more deeply to see what the pain means.

Focus: In our context, *focus* means to focus on the intent of Step Nine. It is not enough that we hear what the other has to say or even that we grasp the meaning of his experience for himself; we are listening in order to make amends. Focus on what you can do to change your behavior so that you never cause this kind of suffering again. You cannot change the past, you cannot undo what you have done, and listening does not excuse you in any way from facing the karmic consequences of your actions. But by focusing on what you can do differently now and in the future, you honor the other by changing yourself in response to his experience with you. By actually doing differently, you set in motion healthy karma that will ripen to create conditions that will encourage healthy actions. In turn, these healthy actions will yield even more healthy karma. What was a vicious circle of selfishness becomes a compassionate circle of selfless caring.

Understanding: Thus far you have been listening to the other; now you must also listen to yourself.

Having carefully examined the karmic conditions that gave rise to the actions that caused the pain to which you are now listening, begin to understand how strong karma is, and how vital it is for you to begin to produce different karma. You come to understand that your behavior creates a field that can produce only that which was sown. Understand deeply that you must sow differently, you must do differently, you must be differently. Changing your actions will not take away the other's suffering, but it will honor it. Listening may not cause the other to like you or love you or trust you, but it will allow you to become more likable, more loving, and more trustworthy. And that is a lot.

Patience: You cannot make amends "on the clock." You cannot say to yourself, "OK, I've been listening to this for ten minutes now. I've got what I can from listening, let's wrap things up and be friends again." You may never be friends again. That isn't the point. You aren't fixing a relationship, though that may happen. You are trying to change yourself into a better human being by deeply listening to another's story. It may take a long time and several conversations for the other to feel comfortable enough with you to do more than yell at you or cry. You may never get beyond these, but if you do, if you earn the other's trust just enough to allow her to open up to the pain you caused her, you must be prepared to listen for a long time. I am not saying that you have to be patient with another berating you; that isn't what Step Nine is about. If that is all the other can do, and you have honestly tried to move deeper than that, then it may be wise to move on to someone else. But if the other can get past the desire to hurt you and becomes willing to share her hurt with you, you must be patient enough to let her finish.

You must be patient with yourself as well. As the pain of another sinks into you, the desire to run from that pain either by ending the conversation or trying to apologize for and excuse your behavior becomes strong. This is the Twelve Step equivalent of the fight-or-flight response. Be patient: Neither fight the other's story nor flee from it. Simply continue to listen. In time the two of you will soften, an intimacy will develop from your shared vulnerability one to the other, and the story will end.

ASKING FOR FORGIVENESS

Yet as difficult as authentic listening may be, it is only the first step toward authentic amends making. The second step is asking for forgiveness. It is only after listening, only after making ourselves absolutely vulnerable to another's pain, that we have any idea as to the suffering we caused. And only when we do know that suffering do we have a genuine opportunity to ask for forgiveness.

"You have to be very mindful when engaging in asking for forgiveness," Bert told me. After listening to the pain and suffering you caused another human being, your natural tendency is to say "I'm sorry," but this, he said, is often a dodge. After apologizing, you expect the other to say, "It's OK." In fact, the reason you apologize in the first place may well be to elicit this response, and in this way to skim over the deeper work of Step Nine. But unless and until we are willing to do the deeper work, real amends making cannot happen. And to do that deeper work, you have to be clear about the difference between asking for forgiveness and apologizing.

The difference was made clear to me by a middle-aged meth addict named Phil, who spoke about making amends to his wife.

The details don't matter as far as what I'd done, but what I learned working Step Nine was a real eye-opener for me. I kept telling her I was sorry for this and sorry for that, but she kept on being pissed at me. And that was making me angry as well. Here I am apologizing and she just doesn't seem to care. In fact, the more I said I was sorry the more pissed she got. So I kept asking her what she wanted and she kept saying she wanted me to apologize and I kept apologizing—you know saying I'm sorry—and we got nowhere. And then it just happened: Instead of saying I'm sorry during one of these attempts at amends, I asked her to forgive me. It wasn't that I planned to say something different, it just came out different. She was suddenly like a new woman. She started crying and saying how much she wanted to forgive me and how much she still loved me and that it would take time but she thought that my behavior was better and that she could and would forgive me.

Saying "I'm sorry" gives you power over the other person. You are affirming that you have made your peace with the past, and the other should do so as well. There is nothing more you can add to "I'm sorry," so there is nothing for the other person to do but acquiesce or push for something more. But what more can you offer, other than "I'm sorry"?

When we ask for forgiveness we admit that we are powerless. We cannot forgive ourselves; we need the other to offer forgiveness to us. Asking for anything is a humbling act. We ask for what we do not have and cannot get for ourselves. We ask because we are powerless to achieve our goal without another's help. After we have truly listened to another's story of suffering; after we have grasped beyond a shadow of a doubt our role in producing that suffering; after we have seen the damage we have caused and how we caused it, we are humbled. But not humbled enough. We must dare to lower ourselves even closer to the earth, to metaphorically prostrate ourselves before another and ask for forgiveness.

What if, however, in the process of telling her story, the other has forgiven you? You heard her say so. She is being magnanimous, so shouldn't you be grateful, accept her gift, and move on without actually asking for forgiveness yourself? No.

Some people cannot bear to tell their story if that story causes another pain, even if the person being hurt is the person who caused the original hurt in the first place. Despite the fact that we are the cause of the pain, the other person cannot bear to hurt us, and so forgives us prematurely. This is an act of self-protection on the other's part that will short-circuit the Step Nine process.

If premature forgiveness is offered, do not reject the gift, but do not be satisfied with it, either. Say something like "Thank you for that, but I'm trying to understand what meaning my actions have for you that I might better understand how my behavior causes suffering and change my behavior more thoroughly. If you would, please tell me more." You need not force the issue, but encourage the person to tell you enough of the damage you caused to make it clear to you that saying "I'm sorry" is insufficient, and asking for forgiveness will, in fact, be a humbling and potentially healing act for both of you.

Receiving another's forgiveness isn't the goal of Step Nine; asking for that forgiveness is what matters. When we ask, we help restore the other's self-worth. By requesting something that only he can give, we help him discover that he is valuable, that he has a role to play in our healing, and that playing it will promote his own healing as well.

But what if forgiveness is not forthcoming? The medieval Jewish philosopher Moses Maimonides offers this advice:

> If the injured person refuses to forgive, the person seeking
> forgiveness must bring a group of three of the injured

party's friends with him to plead with their friend to forgive. If forgiveness is still not forthcoming, this must be repeated a second and third time, with different groups of friends. If the injured one still refuses to forgive, the process may cease and the injured party is now the sinner [for] it is forbidden to be cruel and difficult to appease, rather a person must be quick to forgive and difficult to anger and when a sinner asks for forgiveness one should forgive willingly and wholeheartedly.

—Hilchot Teshuvah 2:9–10

When you ask someone for forgiveness, you place yourself in a position of radical vulnerability. You not only admit to having caused the other person harm, but you admit that you cannot move on with your life without the other person's forgiveness. It is another example of admitted powerlessness. But this does not mean that you turn your life over to the other. Asking forgiveness isn't an invitation for retribution and abuse. It is an invitation for healing for both you and the person you have harmed. If the other doesn't want to heal, or cannot heal, you cannot allow yourself to be held hostage to her illness. If you sincerely ask for forgiveness and it is not given, wait and ask again, and then again. But if after three times the other is still unwilling or unable to forgive, move on. While there may come a time when you once again have an opportunity to make amends with this person, you need not, indeed must not, allow the other's state of mind to dictate your recovery.

If some of the people we have harmed choose to hold on to their pain, if they choose to bear a grudge even in the face of our sincere request for forgiveness, then we are free from the burden of the wrong, and the other is left carrying it alone. But when forgiveness is genuinely beseeched and genuinely bestowed, the burden is lifted from everyone. This is why forgiveness is as good for the giver as for the receiver. Both are freed from the crippling weight of the past. Both are free to move on.

This doesn't mean that forgiveness repairs a relationship or allows it to continue, however. It may be that forgiveness at last allows the relationship to end. Where once a couple were bound in love, then bound in hate or resentment, now they are no longer bound at all. Forgiveness is, at heart, all about freedom.

CHAPTER TEN

Step 10

ATTENDING TO THE MOMENT

We continued to take personal inventory and
when we were wrong promptly admitted it.

To work Step Ten well requires great moral courage, allowing us to attend to our actions in the moment, to continually measure them against the ethical standards we hold, and then to immediately admit and correct matters when we fail to live up to those standards.

There is no absolute moral standard we follow in Step Ten. Indeed, everything about the Twelve Steps rejects outside authority. Just as God is the God of our understanding, so our moral standards are the ones we set for ourselves. While some of us may belong to a formal religious tradition that sets moral absolutes that we choose to follow, others may not. And yet whether or not we belong to a religion and follow an external moral code, we all come to realize that acting justly, compassionately, and humbly is key to our recovery.

Why? Because when we do so we plant the seeds of future conditions that feed our healthy selves rather than our unhealthy selves. When we don't lie today, we don't have to lie tomorrow. When we don't exploit people today, we won't have to deal with their anger and frustration tomorrow. This doesn't mean that we don't find ourselves confronting the ordinary sorrows and even horrors of everyday life, but it does mean that we aren't adding to these with totally unnecessary horrors created by our less-than-honorable behavior.

Paddy, an ordained celebrant with whom I once co-officiated at a wedding, proclaimed herself a master at piling needless suffering on top of unavoidable suffering—something she called "tarring the sumac." It's the opposite of gilding the lily, she told me: "You know some people just can't see the natural beauty in the world and bury it in glitz and faux glamour. This isn't my problem. I see the beauty in the world. And I see the ugliness. But when it comes to the ugliness I caused, I tend to paint it blacker than it is. I exaggerate the negative. I may be responsible for causing a tempest, but I then go on to turn it into a tsunami."

When I asked Paddy for an example, she told me about a time long before her present career when she used to work for an accounting firm. She was in the middle of her annual performance review when she let slip something nasty about a fellow employee. Seeing that her boss's interest was piqued, she elaborated on her comment. "I knew what I was doing was wrong the moment I opened my mouth with the original comment, but I couldn't stop. I kept thinking that if I bad-mouth someone else I might get my boss to overlook a couple of pretty serious black marks on my record."

Paddy did such a good job at making her coworker look bad that the man was fired. Unfortunately for Paddy, she was let go soon afterward as well, and, according to her boss, a major factor in letting her go was the sense that she was too eager to get ahead by bad-mouthing others. "If I had just paid attention to what I was saying, and then stopped midsentence, apologized, and gotten back on track, none of that would have happened. I just wish it had been that easy."

Step Ten isn't easy, and it isn't easy for two reasons. First, because most of the time we operate on autopilot; we aren't paying attention to what we do, we just do it. Second, because admitting mistakes as we make them requires not only a very keen sense of observation and awareness but also a deep humility to free us from the need to protect our image of ourselves.

Addictions are humbling, but only when we acknowledge them. Until we do, they give us a sense of exaltation, inflating the ego, and diminishing the soul. "This is why Twelve Step is a spiritual path, a spiritual discipline," Pastor Paul said to me after a Twelve Step open meeting held at an interfaith conference. "And Step Ten is key. It keeps you alert to the pain and suffering you cause and challenges you to make amends midaction. Making amends doesn't mean you can undo what you just did, but by calling yourself on it, you validate the person with whom you are dealing at the moment and take responsibility for the pain you have caused. This allows both of you to move on. Step Ten is a continuous fine-tuning of your character."

CONFUCIUS SAYS

Pastor Paul was talking about cultivating what the Chinese call *jen* (pronounced *ren*). Often translated as "benevolence," or "goodness," *jen* is better understood as "humaneness." *Jen* is a goal toward which each of us must strive and one none of us can fully achieve. We aren't born with *jen;* we cultivate it through the study of ethics and morality, and by applying these ethical principles to every aspect of our lives. No one is ever perfect, and those who hold *jen* as a supreme value are always working toward perfection. *Jen* is not an end state, but, as Pastor Paul put it, a process of continuously fine-tuning our character.

According to the great Chinese philosopher Confucius (551–479 BCE), *jen* is a mix of *chung* and *shu,* "doing one's best" and "reciprocity." *Chung* is doing your best to live in harmony with all things, and *shu* is similar to the golden rule. In the Analects of Confucius, Tzu-kung asked Confucius "Is there one word that serves as a rule of practice for all one's life?" The Master said, "Is not *shu* (reciprocity) such a word? What you do not want done to yourself, do not do to others" (Analects XV.23).[1] Confucius put it more positively when asked by Fan-ch'ih to define *jen.* Confucius said, "It is to love all people" (Analects XV.22).

The Chinese ideogram for *jen* is the sign for human being coupled with the sign for the number two. In other words, *jen* means people in relationship built on *shu*, reciprocity.

Awareness of *shu* is key to working Step Ten. When we realize that we are all in relationship one to another, we discover that what we do to others we do to ourselves as well. Awakening to *shu* awakens the desire to act justly, kindly, and humbly.

Shu is a Confucian version of Step Ten. Karen Armstrong, in her history of the Axial Age, titled *The Great Transformation,* credits Confucius as the first person to articulate the golden rule, which she believes is both at the heart of *shu* and the result of *shu*. *Jen,* which is what results from living the rule, is "not something you got but something you gave ... Living a compassionate, empathic life took you beyond yourself, and introduced you into another dimension."[2] Living this life meant cultivating *shu,* reciprocity. "*Shu* required that all day and every day we looked into our own hearts, discovered what caused us pain, and then refrained, under all circumstances, from inflicting that distress upon other people. It demanded that people no longer put themselves into a special, separate category but constantly related their own experience to that of others."[3]

Practice: Cultivating *Shu*

There are two keys to living the reciprocity Confucius teaches. The first is coming to know your own emotions. The second is recognizing those emotions in others. You cannot relate to the feelings of others if those feelings are alien to you. The problem many of us have is feeling our own feelings. Indeed, one of the prime "benefits" of addiction is medicating yourself against emotions—at first only those we deem negative, but over time all feelings altogether.

Addictive behavior is emotionally numbing, which is why so many people in recovery find it difficult to face the feelings that arise when they no longer self-medicate. The first step in cultivating *shu*, then, is to allow yourself to feel whatever feelings arise in you. The wider your palate of emotions, the greater your capacity to feel empathy with another and to act in accordance with *shu*.

Recognizing another's feelings is the second principle for cultivating *shu*, reciprocity. Recognizing another's feelings requires that you remain calm in the face of those feelings. If you react to the feelings of another, you will shift from the other's feelings to your own. This is the opposite of *shu*.

One of the quickest ways to generate calm is to shift your attention to your breath. Vietnamese Zen master Thich Nhat Hanh teaches a *gatha*, a short poem, just for this purpose. When you find yourself slipping into a reactive mode, responding to another's feelings in an unhealthy manner designed to shut the other down and put an end to your own discomfort, recite this *gatha*:

In, out.
Deep, slow.
Calm, ease.
Smile, release.
Present moment, wonderful moment!

The first line, "in, out," means breathing in; I know that I'm breathing in. Breathing out, I know that I'm breathing out.

The second one is "deep, slow." Breathing in, I see that my in-breath has become deeper. Breathing out, I see that my out-breath has become slower. In the beginning our breath is very short, but if we continue to follow our breathing for a while, naturally our in-breath becomes slower, deeper, and our out-breath also becomes slower, more relaxed.[4]

As your breathing softens, slows, and deepens, you enhance your ability to perceive what the other is feeling without reacting to it. *Shu* is not feeling what another feels, but understanding what it is to feel that way. When a person is hurt and angry, even if she is hurt by and angry with you, getting hurt and angry yourself isn't a wise response. Nor is it helpful to respond with some robotic memorized line, such as "I can see that I have hurt you and that this is making you angry." I guarantee that such canned responses will only inflame the other's hurt and anger.

Practicing *shu* is not easy for me. My initial response to conflict is to shut it down, and that often means tossing out canned responses. Whenever I do, of course, I find that the response is so stale as to be not only ineffective but counterproductive. Rather than throwing water on the fire as I intend, I am throwing gasoline. So when I suggest the practice of *shu* I know how difficult it can be. Nevertheless it is the best response.

A few weeks ago I found myself (or more accurately, I placed myself) in a situation of extreme verbal conflict. A student in one of my classes mistook a comment I had written on her mid-term paper for a personal attack on her beliefs and integrity. The situation exploded so swiftly that I lost my breath, and when it returned it was strained, tight, and defensive. I tried all the old ways of calming the situation. I attempted to explain how she had misinterpreted my comment, and how, even if she hadn't, her response was inappropriate and unwise. Needless to say, that didn't help. I needed a new approach, and began with my breath.

Following Thich Naht Hanh's advice, I slowed my breathing. I didn't turn inward or shut my ears to what was being said, but I invited my body to breathe differently—calmly, deeply. The shift in breathing shifted my mind as well. I could hear more clearly what was being said because it was no longer being drowned out by my own inner panic and need for peace. I didn't feel my student's pain, but I began to put myself in her place and see that for her this was yet another example of how the world was out to put her down. The more I listened without defenses, the more she talked, and the more she revealed. I quickly came to see what she feared, and how what I had written triggered that fear. Now I knew that I needed to honor her fear; not to agree that the world was out to get her, but to work with the fact that she saw things this way.

With complete sincerity I said, "The world can be a harsh place, and people rarely understand us, and often try to force us into boxes that suit them while suffocating us." I meant this. I think it is often true. And my student, convinced that it is always true, suddenly took a deep breath herself. That was the shift she needed.

What had been a rant became a conversation. I explained what my comment was trying to say, apologized for saying it so poorly, and asked her to respond to my intended question. She grasped my point, added her own thoughts, and discovered, as I had originally hoped she would, another avenue of exploration that her paper had opened but she had not thought to walk down. She left feeling heard, and I had managed to make amends in the middle of a mess and thereby salvage a situation for the good.

When practicing *shu*, rather than having a prepared response, allow yourself to empathize with the other from a place of inner tranquility. This will reveal just what needs to be done and allow you to act rather than react, and to do so in a manner that strengthens the relationship rather than strains it.

CHANGE THE WORLD, CHANGE YOURSELF

Addictions are enslavements. They lock us into fixed emotional cages and isolate us from others and from our true selves. Step Ten is about breaking out of that prison by taking responsibility for our behavior, something addicts are loath to do. Whenever a painful situation presents itself, we are sure its cause rests somewhere other than within ourselves. The problem is our boss, our coworkers, our partners, our spouse, our kids, our parents, African-Americans, Hispanics, Asians, Jews, the media, the elites—somebody, anybody but ourselves.

"I had only one problem in my life," Radha, a fashion designer and recovering anorexic, told me, "and it was them." *Them* she told me referred to white people, African-Americans, Jews, Muslims, homosexuals, and "anyone else who I was certain had it in for me and everyone like me." She blamed everything on *them*: the loss of her husband, who she said divorced her for an African-American woman; her difficulty in finding a job; her inability to live the life she knew she was destined to live. "The only thing I could control was my eating. I ate less and less and kept inflating my ego more and more. The less I ate, the more control I thought I had. But it was all madness. I was out of control, and the only real cause of my suffering was me."

Step Ten makes it clear that the problem is us, and for this we should be eternally grateful. If the problem that is ruining our lives rests with others or with institutions such as the media or the government, there is nothing we can do to rectify matters. But when we realize that we are the problem, we also realize that we are the solution. All we have to do is do things differently. That means stopping the insane behavior, apologizing for it, and then doing something else.

As Bert told me once, "Twelve Step programs aren't about fixing the world, they are about fixing yourself." No doubt this is true, yet as we fix ourselves, we also help make the lives of those around us better by ceasing to do the hurtful and harmful behaviors we were inflicting upon them. When we see we are doing something needlessly hurtful and stop doing it, we break that chain of suffering between ourselves and others. And, when we go even further and ask for forgiveness for the action that just caused harm, we offer the other person a way to heal as well. Now both of us can take ownership of what is happening inside each of us and between the two of us. We can own it, name it, and put an end to both the action and the possible negative repercussions of the action. The key to Step Ten is to be able to observe our actions even as we are doing them.

Practice: Self-Observation

George Ivanovich Gurdjieff (1866–1949) a Greek-Armenian spiritual teacher, spoke a lot about the need for self-observation:

> When a man comes to realize the necessity not only for self-study and self-observation but also for work on himself with the object of changing himself, the character of his self-observation must change ... he must begin to see himself, that is to say, to see not separate details, not the work of small wheels and levers, but to see everything taken together as a whole—the whole of himself such as others see him.
>
> For this purpose a man must learn to take, so to speak, "mental photographs" of himself at different moments of his life and in different emotional states: and not photographs of details, but photographs of the whole as he saw it. In other words these photographs must contain simultaneously everything that a man can see in himself at a given moment. Emotions, moods, thoughts, sensations, postures, movements, tones of voice, facial expressions, and so on. If a man

succeeds in seizing interesting moments for these photographs he will very soon collect a whole album of pictures of himself which, taken together, will show him quite clearly what he is.[5]

Adapting Gurdjieff's idea to Step Ten, imagine yourself to be a photographer documenting your own life. Even as you engage in your everyday obligations, allow a part of you to observe, as if through a camera lens. This will give you some distance from yourself. The camera cannot record the rationalizations you may be spinning to justify whatever action you are taking. The camera only records the action. It doesn't matter what your intent is, or how you excuse what you are doing. All that matters is that you are doing it.

When you see yourself engaging in hurtful behavior, "snap the photograph," freeze that action, and look at it. Literally stop for a moment and take in what you are doing. The "photograph" captures the pain, shock, or hurt on the other's face or in her body language, and you can look at it objectively.

The very act of "taking the picture" will cause your behavior to freeze for a moment, and this moment is your opportunity to do something different, beginning with making amends.

You may find it very difficult to "follow yourself around with a camera" all day, so begin with set periods of time. If you know you are going to have a difficult or potentially difficult encounter with someone, "hire" your photographer to film that event. The more familiar you are at seeing parts of your life this way, the easier it becomes to see your whole life this way. The more photos you take, the more opportunities for change you discover.

CONSCIOUS CONTACT
WITH GOD

We sought through prayer and meditation to improve our conscious contact with God, as we understood God, praying only for knowledge of God's will for us and the power to carry that out.

When I read Step Eleven, I am left with more questions than instructions: What is *prayer?* What is *meditation?* What is God? What is *conscious contact with God?* What is *God's will?* And what does it mean to have *the power to carry it out?* Perhaps Bill W. deliberately left us without specifics in this step, urging us to discover God's will in our own way, just as he encouraged us to define God in our own way: God as we understand God. If so, he left us with a great challenge.

The genius of the formulation "God as we understood God," found in Steps Three and Eleven, is that it frees us from any specific religion or theology. The danger is that it leaves open the possibility of substituting ego for God: God as we understand God can become a cosmic projection of our own selves. Similarly, the genius of Step Eleven is that it frees us from any specific spiritual or religious practice. The danger is that this leaves open the possibility of becoming trapped in our thoughts, rather than freed from them, and hence mistake our own will for God's will.

This is precisely what Wanita said she had done. Speaking at a Twelve Step open meeting, Wanita told us that she had belonged to a church that taught that God wanted her to have everything she wanted. God's love, she was told, was like that of a doting father: He wanted her to be happy and would do whatever it took to make her happy. "I should just ask God for whatever it was that caught my fancy and he'd give it to me."

So she did. "My mistake was in thinking that God meant for me to have all the things I wanted by using my credit cards. I just bought stuff—tons of stuff—and I assumed that God would make the payments. Before it finally began to dawn on me that God wasn't going to make sure I could meet my monthly credit card bills, I was over $25,000 in debt."

Wanita went to her pastor for advice. He suggested that her faith was weak, and evidence of this weakness could be found in her small donations to the church. She should pray more, give more to the pastor's ministry, and trust in God. "I did all that, and I started drinking. None of it helped. I hit rock bottom $5,000 later. It was then that I met the real God who was completely different than the God of my understanding."

It is in order to avoid this pitfall, Step Eleven speaks of prayer and meditation, but to understand these well we must first be clear as to the meaning of *God's will*. Of course you are free to understand God's will as you are free to understand God, so there is no sense of my "laying down the law" here or revealing some absolute truth. All I will do—all I can do—is share my understanding of both God and God's will, and invite you to do the same.

For me, God is Reality—all that was, is, and ever will be. Hence my understanding of God's will is simple: Whatever is happening in this moment is God's will. God's will is to manifest reality in all its wonder and wildness. God's will for my life is no different than God's will for your life: We are all designed to become as conscious as we can in the situation we inhabit. The more conscious we become, the more we actualize our capacity for *jen,* humaneness.

God's will for us is to cultivate *jen* in whatever we are experiencing at the moment—good or bad, sane or insane, abstinent or addicted. As we become more conscious of God's will, we discover our true will as well: What we truly desire is to navigate the reality in which we find ourselves in such a way as to maximize *shu,* reciprocity, love.

There is a wise way to engage life and a foolish way. The wise way is expansive, allowing us to grow in compassion, courage, wisdom, truth, and trust. The foolish way is constrictive, shuttering us up behind walls of fear and anger, and robbing us of both trust and trustworthiness. God doesn't will us to live expansively any more than the ocean wills us to swim with the current. God's will is simply what is at the moment. But that moment always contains the possibility of expansive living.

When we do live expansively, God, like the ocean when we swim with the current, supports us in ways that allow us to achieve more love in our lives than living any other way possibly could. Finding God's will is finding the current of godliness that allows us to live with love.

With this in mind, it is not difficult to inquire into the godliness of any action we may entertain. All we need do is ask ourselves this: *Will this action expand love or constrict love?* If the former, then acting in this way is acting in concert with divine will. If the latter, then acting this way is swimming against it. The first is wise, the second foolish.

So much for *knowledge of God's will for us.* But what about *the power to carry that out?* As I read Step One, we are powerless not only over our personal addictions and demons, but over life itself. We are not in control. We lack the power to make things other than they are. So how are we to generate the power to carry out God's will?

I came to understand this best from a thirty-three-year-old aikido instructor named Mark. We were talking after an AA meeting, and when I expressed surprise that an aikido black belt could have a drinking problem, Mark said, "A third-degree black belt aikido instructor doesn't have a drinking problem. I do." Mark went on to say he had stopped drinking years before taking up aikido, and that he saw a lot of parallels between aikido and recovery, especially Step Eleven.

Developed by Morihei Ueshiba in the 1920s, aikido is a Japanese martial art and philosophy that translates as *the Way of unifying with Life energy,* or *the Way of harmonious spirit.* The key to aikido is blending with, rather than resisting, the force of your attacker. Using a minimum of effort, the *aikidoka* (aikido practitioner) merges with the direction of the attacker, turning the direction through a series of subtle techniques and allowing the other to fall helplessly to the mat.

"Aikido never changes what is," Mark told me, "it only seeks to change what might be. I don't insist that my opponent be other than he is, or desire anything less than my defeat. It is just that by working with his desire, I allow him or assist him in overstepping and thus falling to the ground and failing to topple me as he intended. Too bad I didn't learn this before I took to drinking."

Mark told me that it was his perceived inability to engage life that led him to escape from it through alcohol. "At first drinking just dulled the pain of my past failures. Then it caused the pain of future ones. The more I tried to control things, the more frustrated I became at not being able to do so, and the more I took refuge in the bottle. If I had known then what I know now, I would have seen my weakness as a skill to be honed rather than a failure to be denied. That is the genius of aikido and AA: They both see weakness as our greatest strength."

Step Eleven brings us back to the paradox at the heart of Twelve Step recovery: Our success is through weakness not strength, through surrender to God not the imposition of self. The power we need to carry out the will of God is analogous to the power we need to swim with the current of the sea. This power is the power to let go. When we relax into the sea, the sea holds us and carries us. When we learn to navigate the sea, to merge our will with the current, we learn how to work with the sea to go where we wish to go. This is not power as brute strength, but power as wise action. Or, as we mentioned briefly in our discussion of Step One, the Chinese Taoist philosophy of *wei wu wei,* noncoercive action.

Wei wu wei rests on the understanding that there is only one reality, Tao, and all beings are a part of it. There is no separation between you and reality. Hence there is no working of your will on it or its will on you. There is just the way things are in the moment. You cannot change what is (what we earlier called karma) but you can learn to work with it to influence what will be. Nothing is static; everything is changing. You either learn to work with the change or you try to resist it. When we do the former, we find ourselves free, creative, and hopeful; when we do the latter, we find ourselves exhausted, depressed, and seeking to escape reality in the unreality of addiction.

Practice: Working with Change

How do we work with change? There are, no doubt, many ways, but the way I find most helpful is the *I Ching* (pronounced *ee jing*). My teacher in the *I Ching* is Stephen Karcher. Stephen holds a doctorate in comparative literature and psychology and is the author of several books about the *I Ching* as well as what many scholars consider to be the definitive translation of the *I Ching*. Dr. Karcher's approach to the *I Ching* will occupy us here. I encourage you to explore this further, especially by reading his short book, *How to Use the I Ching: A Guide to Working with the Oracle of Change.*[1]

The *I Ching* was composed over three thousand years ago. It consists of sixty-four hexagrams (symbols made of six pairs of solid and broken lines), each accompanied by often obtuse commentary. The book is not meant to be read as much as consulted. You ask questions of the *I Ching*, generate a hexagram in response to the question, and then consult the *I Ching* as to the possible meaning of the hexagram.

The Chinese word *I* (*ee*) is usually translated as "change," and the *I Ching* is often called the Classic of Change, classic in the sense that a 1956 Chevy is classic, or Shakespeare's plays are classics of English literature. The word *I*, however, has two additional meanings that are relevant to us. The first is "trouble" in the sense of sudden disruptions in the present situation. The second is "response to trouble" in the sense of being able to shift gears at a moment's notice to creatively accommodate changing conditions. Everything is changing, and the purpose of the *I Ching* is to reveal the changes in motion and allow us to navigate them wisely. As Dr. Karcher writes:

> Change is the very essence of living. Our lives change, our dreams change, the seasons change, our world changes. Some changes are predictable, some unpredictable. Some are sought after, some avoided. Some bring joy, others bring grief and sorrow. The *I Ching* is an attempt to understand and work with change. But it does not *describe* change; it *participates in change*. It shows the way change occurs because it is *part of the process it models*. By using it, you participate in the change rather than being its unconscious victim.[2]

Seeing what forces are at play allows us to get a sense of the current and its flow. It allows us to more mindfully engage in the reality unfolding around and within us. The

I Ching isn't a road map, but a weather forecast. A road map depicts a fixed reality and shows you how to move from Point A to Point B. A weather forecast works with probabilities and fluid conditions, trying to deduce future conditions from them.

The sixty-four hexagrams of the *I Ching* are variations of the interplay of two primary forces: yin and yang. Together these forces make up reality or, as the Chinese might put it, the Tao. The Tao "permeates, supports, moves and changes everything in our world, seen and unseen ... It is the ongoing process of the real."[3] When we live in sync with the Tao, moving in accord with its flow, we feel joyous, connected, kind, creative, loving, and free. When we work against the flow, we feel strained, alienated, fearful, dull, constricted, and enslaved. The *I Ching* reveals how best to live in harmony with what is. It shows us which ways are open, transformative, and loving, and which ways are closed, static, and dead. And it does so in cryptic language that invites creative musing and personal interpretation. The *I Ching* functions as a doorway into your unconscious, allowing you to glimpse the "unconscious forces shaping a given problem or situation."[4] We can then engage these forces in a manner that maximizes our sense of meaning, purpose, and living in harmony with life.

The details involved in using the *I Ching* require that all sixty-four hexagrams be articulated and explored, a task clearly beyond the scope of this book. Instead, let me simply outline the procedure for using the *I Ching* and encourage you to investigate this on your own.

When working with the *I Ching*, provide yourself with a quiet place to ask and explore the answer to your question. Settle yourself comfortably in a chair or on a cushion. Close your eyes and quiet your breathing. When you feel fairly settled, invite your question to come into your conscious mind. I always ask the same open-ended question: "What are the forces shaping the conditions of this moment?" You may ask something more specific, but I find that the greatest value of the *I Ching* is in this general exploration of current conditions.

There are four ways to generate a hexagram: the original method of tossing fifty yarrow stalks; a later, yet still ancient method of tossing three coins; the modern method of using a computer *I Ching* program; and Dr. Karcher's marble method, which matches the probability theory behind the yarrow stalks without its complexity. I primarily use the last method. Holding your question lightly in your mind, use whatever method you choose to generate your hexagram.

By way of example, I used Dr. Karcher's marble method, asked the question "What are the forces shaping the conditions of this moment?" and generated the hexagram Field that looks like this:

— —

— —

— —

— —

— —

— —

Field reveals that this is a moment for nourishing what has been planted, rather than planting something new. To engage this moment wisely, I should make myself receptive, supple, welcoming, and gentle.

While there is much more to say about Field, even this short snippet makes clear that there is nothing clear when it comes to reading the *I Ching*. After all, the *I Ching* doesn't tell me what has been planted, only that it needs nourishing. Nor does it tell me how to nourish it, only that I should welcome whatever is coming my way at the moment. In other words, there is more than enough room for interpretation and even misinterpretation.

I don't worry about the latter, however. First of all, the Tao is always changing and Field is only temporary, so if I misread the meaning I am not locked into anything permanent. Second, I am using the *I Ching* to further my recovery, to become more conscious of God's will, the Tao of the moment, and even if I am not 100 percent accurate in my understanding, my aim at living in harmony with God's will always leads me to actions that are loving and just. In other words, using the *I Ching* in concert with Step Eleven cannot yield anything but positive results.

The only caveat with the *I Ching* is the potential for projecting the addictive ego onto the Tao and reading not God's will but the ego's will. To avoid this, I link working Step Eleven to the Christian practice of kenosis, self-emptying.

THE WAY OF SELF-EMPTYING

Kenosis comes from the Greek *kenos*, empty. In Philippians 2:7 St. Paul writes that "Jesus emptied himself" (NRSV) or "made himself nothing" (NIV). Jesus emptied himself of himself that he might be filled with God. Paul urges us to do the same: "Let the same mind be in you that was in Christ Jesus" (Philippians 2:5).

Kenosis is a way of seeing reality without the distortion of ego. It is a way to put on the mind of Christ and see the divine in, with, and as all reality. The "how" of self-emptying in the Christian context is called contemplative prayer or, to focus on its most popular form, Centering Prayer. Centering Prayer should no more be limited to Christians than the use of the *I Ching* should be restricted to the Chinese. It is a powerful tool for deepening Step Eleven that anyone can use. As Father Thomas Keating, who along with Father Basil Pennington, reclaimed Centering Prayer for our time, writes:

> Contemplative Prayer is considered to be the pure gift of God. It is opening mind and heart—our whole being—to God, the Ultimate Mystery, beyond thoughts, words, and emotions. Through grace we open our awareness to God who we know by faith is within us, closer than breathing, closer than thinking, closer than choosing—closer than consciousness itself.[5]

Father Basil Pennington says Centering Prayer helps us "to get in touch with what *is*,"[6] and while the practice itself is meant to be done for a fixed amount of time—twenty to forty minutes—once or twice each day, the effect will in time inform the whole of our lives, allowing us to experience "constantly living out of the center, to loving out of the fullness of who we are."[7]

Centering Prayer is deceptively simple. It is not intended as a substitute for other kinds of prayer, but rather, as Father Thomas writes, as a practice of moving "beyond conversation with Christ to communion with him."[8]

I realize that to non-Christians such talk may be troubling, even off-putting. If that is true for you, you may choose not to experiment with Centering Prayer. But as a Jew who has practiced Centering Prayer for many years, I promise you that "Christ" in this context refers to the consciousness of God's presence and not to any fixed Christology. The mind of Christ is the Buddha mind, the awakened mind, the mind that reads the flow of the Tao in the passing moment. To commune with Christ is to rest in the presence of God, however you understand God.

Practice: Centering Prayer

The following guidelines for practice come from Father Thomas Keating, who taught me the art of Centering Prayer. I have modified his explanation of the practice (though not the practice itself) to help make its link to Step Eleven clearer.

1. Choose a sacred word as an expression of your intention to know the will of God. This word can be anything that sets the right intention. You may choose a name of God, such as Jesus, Allah, Krishna, Adonai, or something less "holy," such as "Yes," "Love," "Peace," "Shalom," or "Salaam." What makes a word sacred in the context of Centering Prayer is that it holds your intention to be present.

2. Sit comfortably with your eyes closed. Take a moment to settle down. Allow your breathing to quiet as your body becomes still. Then introduce your sacred word, repeating it over and over, perhaps in sync with your breathing but perhaps not. As you do so, you are consenting over and again to the will of God.

3. If your mind wanders from your sacred word, gently return your attention to it. Distracting thoughts, feelings, physical sensations are natural to Centering Prayer. They are not your enemy. On the contrary, every distraction is an opportunity for kenosis, self-emptying. By returning to your sacred word you are letting go of distractions, and by letting go of distractions you are emptying yourself of the self that feeds on them.

4. When the allotted time for Centering Prayer is over, allow yourself two more minutes to simply sit in the silence with your eyes closed. If you so choose, you

can formally bring your Centering Prayer time to a close with a vocalized prayer or poem or some gesture of thanksgiving.

You are not trying to focus on your sacred word, or erase all thoughts, feelings, and distractions, or even attain any specific insight or sense of enlightenment. You are simply sitting in a state of receptivity, affirming through your sacred word your willingness to empty the self and become filled with the will and presence of God. In this, Centering Prayer is a perfect example of what the Buddhists call *upaya*.

UPAYA: APPROACHING THE GOAL

Upaya is the Sanskrit word meaning "useful means." It is derived from another Sanskrit word meaning to "bring you up to a goal." The goal here is liberation from the suffering caused by our addictions. In Buddhism *upaya* is often linked with *kaushalya*, cleverness, and *upaya-kaushalya* means that each of us can use whatever licit and healthy means we need to put an end to whatever suffering plagues us. *Upaya* has nothing to do with "truth," and everything to do with expedience. If it works it is valuable, even if it is a lie.

The Lotus Sutra, one of the two major texts of Zen Buddhism (the other being the Heart Sutra) tells a story of a father who comes home to find his house engulfed in flames. Inside the house, oblivious to the danger, his children are playing with their toys. He calls to them and urges them to escape from the house while there is still time, but they don't believe the house is burning and refuse to stop playing. He then calls to them, saying that he has brought home some wonderful new toys—golden carts and giant toy oxen—that are too large to bring into the house. The children race outside to play with the new toys and are saved. Clearly, the father is lying, but the lie is necessary to get his children to leave the burning house.

Step Eleven doesn't offer a fixed form of prayer and meditation, or a fixed definition of God and God's will. Any way you imagine the latter, and any way you practice the former, is fine as long as they free you from addictive behaviors and the delusion of control that fuels them. It doesn't matter if your understanding is "true" in some abstract or objective sense. All that matters is that it is true for you, and hence compelling enough to lift you out of the insanity that has become your life.

In a sense, the entirety of Twelve Step recovery is a kind of *upaya*. It doesn't matter if you are really powerless, or if God as you understand God is real or not, or if you are turning your will and your life over to God or over to a more healthy aspect of yourself. All that matters is that whatever you are doing works to liberate you from your addictive behavior and the karma such behavior generates. Bill W. is like the father in our parable: He invites us to imagine a power greater than ourselves who can free us from our addictions, and once we are outside the house, once we are free from the madness of addictive living, we can face the truth even if that means having to accept the fact that there is no gilded ox cart, giant toy oxen, or God.

I am not saying that there is no God or that there is a God. I am saying that in the context of Twelve Step recovery all that matters is that the God of your understanding has the power to surrender you to the greater sanity of living clean and sober.

Micki, a retired postal worker with fifteen years' sobriety, told me, "The longer I remain sober, the less certain I am about my understanding of God. But it doesn't matter. I no longer rely on any idea of God; I rely on my experience of sobriety. I still believe in God but I have less and less understanding of who or what God is. All I know, and all I need to know, is that if I surrender my will to the larger something at the heart of the universe I can live one more day sober. Something in there or out there responds with love when I don't drink. Alcohol was robbing me of that love, and I had to make a choice: love or addiction. I chose love."

There is something of *upaya* in all religions and spiritual practices. At their best they all point to something beyond what they themselves can imagine or articulate. This is why all religions that talk about God take pains to remind us that God is ultimately beyond language. The Hindus have a wonderful Sanskrit saying for this, *neti, neti*—not this, not that. While God may manifest as everything, God can be reduced to no one thing at all.

The God of our understanding is not God, but rather a working model of God. And this becomes more and more clear as our conscious contact with God deepens. Eventually, we come to a place of gentle not-knowing. We no longer worry about God as we understand God, but accept the fact that we cannot understand God. We no longer imagine that we can discern God's will and take comfort in simply aligning ourselves in a godly direction.

To help remind myself of this, I wrote the following poem, which I keep on my desk where I can see it and be reminded that God is not the God of my understanding:

> The Eternal God is not the
> God of Abraham is not the
> God of Isaac is not the God of Jacob is not the
> God of Sarah is not the God of Rebecca is not the
> God of Leah is not the God of Rachel is not the
> God of my childhood is not the
> God of my youth is not the
> God of my adulthood is not the
> God of my old age is not the
> God of my dying is not the God of my imagining.
> The Eternal God is not my creation.
> The Eternal God is not the

God who chooses is not the
God who commands is not the
God who punishes is not the
God who creates is not the
God who destroys is not the
God who makes me win is not the
God who sees that my enemies lose.
The Eternal God is not my creation.
The Eternal God is the
God who alone exists and who exists alone.
When I am free from ancestors, free from traditions,
free from truths, free from words, free from thoughts,
free from even the need to be free
there is God and there I am not.

All we know is what we came to know in Steps One and Two: We are powerless over life, life is essentially unmanageable, and sanity lies not in surrendering to our egoic selves but to a life rooted in a sense of love, justice, humility that is greater than ourselves. In this way Twelve Step recovery is a reflection of the deepest meaning of the faith of Islam.

ISLAM: THE WAY OF SURRENDER

The Arabic word *Islam* refers to the state of being surrendered to *Allah,* the Arabic for God. The root *s–l–m* yields a series of Arabic words that speak directly to Twelve Step recovery: *As-silmu wa as-salamu* means to be obedient, to surrender (Step Three); *sallama* means to be purified of all defects of character (Steps Four, Five, Six, and Seven); and *as-silm* refers to one who lives with and maintains peace and order (Steps Ten and Eleven).

> Islam, in its ideal form, would be a way of life in harmony
> with the Divine Reality, in which human beings align
> themselves with the highest truth and apply it to the

conditions of life. The conditions then established would reflect god's justice, mercy, generosity, and love.[9]

Given this understanding of Islam, we should not be surprised to find many Islamic practices perfectly suited to Twelve Step recovery. With regard to Step Eleven, the one that comes readily to mind is *zikr,* remembrance.

Practice: *Zikr*/Remembrance

In English, when we say we remember something, we usually mean we recollect something we used to know but had, at least for a moment, forgotten. In Arabic the word has a more profound meaning. *Zikr* is not recalling something from the past, but recollecting oneself in the present. Our egoic minds are scattered, distracted, locked into grieving over or pining for the past, and fantasizing about the future. When we practice *zikr,* we release thoughts about past and future and center ourselves in the present. When we do so, we discover that we are also in the Presence of God.

The great Sufi saint Al-Ghazali offers the following instruction in *zikr:*

> Let your heart be in such a state that the existence or nonexistence of anything is the same—that is, let there be no dichotomy of positive and negative. Then sit alone in a quiet place, free of any task or preoccupation, be it the reciting of the Qur'an, thinking about its meaning, concern over the dictates of religion, or what you have read in books— let nothing besides God enter the mind. Once you are seated in this manner, start to pronounce with your tongue [meaning aloud], "Allah, Allah," keeping your thought on it.

Practice this continuously and without interruption; you will reach a point when the motion of the tongue will cease, and it will appear as if the word just flows from it spontaneously. You go on in this way until every trace of the tongue movement disappears while the heart registers the thought or idea of the word.

As you continue with the invocation, there will come a time when the word will leave the heart completely. Only the palpable essence or reality of the name will remain, binding itself ineluctably to the heart.

Up to this point everything will have been dependent on your own conscious will; the divine bliss and enlightenment that may follow have nothing to do with your conscious will or choice. What you have done so far is to open the window, as it were. You have laid yourself exposed to what God may breathe upon you, as He has done upon His prophets and saints.

If you follow what is said above, you can be sure that the light of Truth will dawn upon your heart. At first intermittently, like flashes of lightning, it will come and go. Sometimes when it comes back, it may stay longer than other times. Sometimes it may stay only briefly.[10]

While Al-Ghazali's instructions are for a set time of practice, *zikr* can be done continually. The more we remember that we are in the presence of God, the more we become aware of God's will for us: that we live emptied of addictions and filled with compassion, justice, generosity, and humility.

We cannot help but note the similarity between *zikr* and Centering Prayer. While each comes from and remains true to its tradition of origin, both point to a reality that transcends religion. What my teacher and friend Sheikh Kabir Helminski says of *zikr* is true of both practices: "This path requires no exceptional leap of faith, no abandonment of reason, no complex theology or intellectual attainment. The simple, mindful invocation of God's essential name will take us to the reality of what is being remembered."[11] In other words both are examples of *upaya* that may be of value to anyone and especially anyone working the Twelve Steps.

CHAPTER TWELVE

CARRYING THE MESSAGE

*Having had a spiritual awakening as the
result of these Steps, we tried to carry this
message to alcoholics, and to practice
these principles in all our affairs.*

What is spiritual awakening? It is waking to the flow of the moment and living in harmony with it. This, I believe, is what the Buddha meant when responding to three men who met him after his enlightenment in Bodh Gaya, India, some 2,500 years ago.

One of the men asked, "Are you a god?" No, the Buddha said. Another asked, "Are you an avatar, an incarnation of a god?" No, he said. The third man asked, "Are you a shaman?" No, he said. "Are you just a man, then?" one asked again. No, he said. "Then just what are you?" they demanded. I am awake, the Buddha said.

Buddha means the "Awakened One." The Buddha was awake to the Tao, to the nature of things in this moment, and to the suffering that arises when we live in ignorance of reality, asleep to the truth. Is this, then, what it means to have a spiritual awakening in Step Twelve?

As with all spiritual questions in Twelve Step recovery, there is no easy answer to this question. Just as we define *God* for ourselves, so we must define *spiritual awakening* for ourselves. Yet I suspect, and my own experience supports, that working the Steps does indeed bring us to an awareness of Reality, God, Tao, Allah,

Brahman. And while we should not be surprised that those who use one of these terms rather than another may feel strongly that they should not be used as synonyms, it is my experience that they are just that. As the five-thousand-year-old Rig Veda of the Hindus puts it, "*Ekam Sat Vipra Bahuda Vadanti*—Truth is one. Different people call it by different names."

Discovering both our own powerlessness and the hope that lies in the Higher Power that embraces and transcends us sets us on the road to recovery. Taking moral inventory, listing the names of all those we have harmed, and reaching out to them to make amends destroys the illusion of the sovereign ego and reveals the reciprocity and interconnectedness of self and other. Cultivating compassion and humility allows us to see more and more clearly that all beings suffer, and that seeing opens us to an even greater sense of compassion and connection.

As we work the Steps, pushing the rock up the mountain only to have it slide down once more that we might push it up again, we realize that nothing is once and for all, that everything is over and over again. Nothing in life is permanent. Even our addictive behaviors can change.

Along with awakening to our interdependence and impermanence, we also awake to love. Not love in a romantic sense; not even love for one thing or another, but a general and all-pervasive sense of love, of belonging, of connecting, of caring. Our hearts are broken, along with our egos, as we work the Steps. The deep shame we felt when we first admitted our addiction is replaced by an even deeper compassion. It is our heartbreak that allows this to happen. It is our heartbreak that is key to spiritual awakening.

Marley, a fifty-something waitress at a coffee shop not far from an AA meeting I attended, spoke movingly of the healing power of heartbreak. She had started drinking around the age of twelve or thirteen. At first it was just fun, and she and her friends got a kick out of being rebellious. But it didn't take her long to realize that she couldn't quit. "My friends in high school drank to get blitzed, but I drank to get through the day. They waited until the weekend to get bombed. By the time I was in twelfth grade, I couldn't wait until noon."

Marley didn't know why she started drinking, but she was clear about why she couldn't stop: "I hated myself when I was sober. I despised my life; the way I slept around; the fact that I couldn't hold a job. None of this mattered when I drank. Just the opposite: When I was drunk I thought I was invincible, on top of the world. I was sure that my luck would change and that I didn't have to." What sent her to AA was getting arrested for prostitution.

"I wasn't a hooker. I was just out of money and needed a drink. I hooked up with some guy near a bar and offered to have sex with him for twenty bucks. I had no idea if that was too little or too much, I just knew it was enough to get what I wanted at the liquor store. Problem was, the guy was a cop. My mom had to bail me out and they gave me a walk as long as I agreed to go to meetings. That was rock bottom for me. Saved my life. Grace of God."

To honor the heartbreak and grace of rock bottom, and to continually put ourselves in the place of spiritual awakening and the surrender and compassion that accompany it, I can think of no better practice than prostration.

When we lie prostrate on the ground, we are saying with our entire bodies that we are powerless; we are symbolically returning to the moment of horror and hope that was hitting rock bottom. We are asking God not to fix us but to love us as we are so that we might love ourselves enough to become what we can be.

We can't get any lower than this, and when we learn to relax into the prostration we awake and discover God holding us, surrounding us. Rather than fall into the hell we thought rock bottom to be, we awake over and over again to the fierce grace of God, a searing love that burns away our delusions of control, and allows us to simply be surrendered to the One who is all.

Practice: Prostration

Not every religious tradition has a formal prostration practice, but they all have a variation of it in bowing. Bowing is as close to a universal human religious practice as any practice can be. Traditional Jews, Christians, Muslims, Hindus, and Buddhists all engage in some form of bowing. In Islam, prostration, *sujud* in Arabic, is the central act of the five-times daily prayer (*salaat*), and proper prostration requires that your forehead, palms, knees, and the base of your toes all touch the prayer rug.

While Jews bow continually during prayer, they don't generally prostrate themselves. Yet the Bible tells us that biblical Jews often "fell on their face" when praying to God. Even today it is customary in more observant synagogues for the rabbi and cantor to prostrate themselves during the Yom Kippur *Amidah* prayer in a manner similar to Muslims. On a daily basis observant Jews recite the *Aleinu* prayer containing the line, "We bend our knees, prostrate, and acknowledge our thanks," and bow deeply when doing so.

Though Catholics and Protestants often kneel in prayer, prostration is more common to Eastern Orthodox forms of Christianity. Prostration goes further than that in Islam, with the person lying flat on the floor with her arms stretched out from her sides.

Buddhists bow three times before and after their formal chanting and meditation sessions. The first bow is to the Buddha, honoring one's intent to become a Buddha oneself. The second is dedicated to the dharma, the teachings of the Buddha, and the third is dedicated to the *sangha*, the community of Buddhist practitioners. Buddhists kneel, and then lower their foreheads to the floor, with their forearms and elbows on the floor. Their hands are placed palm up about four to six inches apart, and their head is placed between the palms. When the head touches the floor, the palms are raised.

The kind of bowing I practice, and the kind I am suggesting here, is full-body prostration adapted from Tibetan Buddhism:

1. Stand with your feet together, and bring your hands together with the base of the palms and the finger-tips touching one another.

2. Place your hands on the crown of your head and give thanks for a pure body, then on your throat to remind yourself to purify your speech, then on your heart to remind yourself to let go of resentments.

3. Gently drop to your knees, and stretch out your entire body on the floor, extending your arms forward, your hands still touching in the sign of thanksgiving.

4. Then bring your hands to the top of your head to acknowledge that it is God, not the ego, that is the greater reality.

5. Remain prone. You may choose to focus on your breath, or offer a prayer of thanksgiving or supplication. I tend to simply rejoice in the feeling of surrender. I am completely vulnerable in this posture, completely at the mercy of whatever is happening. And yet through it all I sense God's support.

6. When you are ready, stretch your arms out in front and push yourself up to the kneeling and then standing posture. Return your hands to your head.

7. Repeat the process as often as you wish.

OUR STORIES, OUR SELVES

There are those who imagine that being spiritually awake means being free from addiction and all harmful and hurtful behaviors. The spiritually awake person, we imagine, lives in a state of perfect *satchitananda:* being, consciousness, and bliss. I have no doubt that there are people like this, but I have never met one. Nor am I eager to. Someone who has transcended this world has nothing to teach those of us still seeking to live authentically in it. I don't want to escape this world. I don't imagine that I can end suffering for myself or others. I think suffering is no less a part of authentic living than is joy, anger, love, or any other emotion. I don't want to stop feeling; I want to stop being driven by my feelings.

I am not drawn to Twelve Step meetings to listen to people who are perfect; I am drawn to listen to people who are broken and who have found the wisdom in that brokenness that allows them to live from a place of love. I am drawn to Twelve Step meetings not simply to be reminded of the Steps, but to hear the stories of those who live them.

Telling our story is a powerful way to work Step Twelve. We are the stories we tell. Living the Twelve Steps helps us add new chapters to our story. We don't ignore the trauma of the past, and our story is still rooted in it, but it is no longer controlled by it. We don't end up where we began. We have learned to move on. We don't reinvent our stories; we simply retell them. We don't try to make the stories more healthy, but use their unhealthiness as catalysts for living differently.

By learning to tell our story over and over, we learn to free ourselves from the emotions attached to it. We begin to tell the story in a detached manner. We own the story; the story no longer owns us.

Working the Steps helps us look at our story dispassionately, with detachment, and it does so by having us repeat the story over and over again. And eventually we reframe it. We aren't telling the story of our current life, but of our past life; and we aren't telling it to excuse insane behavior, but to elicit sane behavior in both ourselves and our listeners.

Storytelling is at the heart of every Twelve Step meeting. We don't speak abstractly about the Steps themselves, but concretely about our lives: about how it was before we entered the program and how it is now. Anyone can pick up a copy of *The Big Book of Alcoholics Anonymous* and read about the Steps, but only in meetings do the Steps come alive in the lives of real people.

What moves me in meetings is listening to other people's stories. I see myself in their stories, I see the madness in their stories, and I see the madness in myself. Seeing it allows me some distance from it, and in that place of distance, change happens. It is like trying to open a stuck door with a crowbar. You need to be able to wedge the crowbar between the door and the doorjamb, and then with a little pressure you can pry the door open. The crowbar is the Twelve Steps. The space is the telling of your story. The pressure is working the Steps. And when the door opens, you want to help others do to the same to their doors.

Practice: Telling Your Story

A few years ago I wrote a book called *Hasidic Tales: Annotated and Explained* (SkyLight Paths). It is an anthology of classic Hasidic tales—tales of rabbis and mystics and their students, designed to impart ethical and spiritual teachings—accompanied by my commentary on each story. In the workshop that I developed to explore the power of Hasidic tales, I created the following practice that has, over the years, proven quite successful.

First, get three sheets of thick, plain white drawing paper, some crayons, a pen or pencil, and a notebook with three tabbed divisions. On one sheet of paper draw a self-portrait: the *you* you were when you first began to work the Twelve Steps. Or, if you have yet to do this, the *you* you were when you hit rock bottom (or at least what seemed like rock bottom at the time). On the second sheet draw a self-portrait of the *you* you are today. And on the third, draw a portrait of the *you* you will be when you have moved beyond the egoic need to control life and have been surrendered to the wildness of Reality as a manifestation of God.

Don't worry about your artistic skills, and don't imagine that you have to limit yourself to an actual portrait. Perhaps an abstract drawing of shapes and colors, or signs and symbols more accurately portrays the selves you are seeking to sketch. Don't worry about being critiqued; there is no critique. While I invite people to share their drawings if we are doing this exercise in a group setting, no one is obligated to do so, and neither are you.

Second, when you have completed your three portraits, lay them out side by side. Imagine that you are explaining each one to your sponsor, close friend, or even to yourself. Articulate aloud why you drew what you drew. Why this shape and not some other? Why the smile or the frown? Why the tears or the scars.

Third, look for a thread running through all three portraits: the *you* you were, the *you* you are, and the *you* you are becoming. Look for and articulate aloud any commonalities and differences among the portraits. Get some distance from the drawings, and imagine that you are looking at someone else's artwork. Be as objective and as creative as you can be.

Fourth, take your notebook and label the tabs as follows: "The Me I Was," "The Me I Am," and "The Me I Am Becoming."

Fifth, set up your three portraits so you can see them separately from one another, and begin to write stories about each one. Begin with the "Me I Was." Tell a story about wrestling with life's unmanageability, or wrestling with an addiction, or hitting rock bottom. Think of it as a "Once upon a time" folktale. Keep it simple, and make it compelling. The story should be very short: a page or two at the most.

Don't seek to exhaust your stories about the "Me I Was"; just write a story or two, and then move on to the "Me I Am" and do the same thing. Tell a story about what you are dealing with today. Be specific, and focus on one issue and not some broad or vague philosophical problem or insight. Focus on behavior.

After writing a story or two in this category, flip to the "Me I Am Becoming" section of your notebook. Don't write an imaginative tale about the *you* you hope to be, however. Instead, go back to one of the stories you wrote in the "Me I Was" section of your notebook. Reread what you wrote, and then retell the story from the perspective of the *you* you are becoming. Look for lessons to be learned and write about how you have learned them and how your newfound insight changes the story. This section is more a work of the imagination than the prior two, and that is its genius. As you imagine how you will be in the future, you are setting patterns in place that you will follow as that future unfolds.

PASSIVE EVANGELIZING: CARRYING THE MESSAGE LIGHTLY

Many people, even those who have had a spiritual awakening, find carrying the Twelve Step message to others somewhat intimidating. We aren't evangelists. As happy as we may be to share our story if asked, we don't find ourselves driven to foist it upon someone who didn't ask to hear it. In the end that is all we have—our story. Touting the Twelve Steps in the abstract is useless. What matters is that the Steps have worked for us, and the only way we can demonstrate that is by living our lives rightly and well, and sharing our story about how we used to live and what we did to change.

In *The Big Book of Alcoholics Anonymous,* in the chapter titled "Working with Others," Bill W. suggests that the recovering alcoholic seek out other alcoholics who wish to change. If you don't know any, the *Big Book* even suggests that you contact local clergy and physicians and offer to work with people they recommend. Regardless of your addiction, this approach may work for you. It doesn't for me.

I am not averse to talking about my experience with Twelve Step recovery, and if it comes up naturally in the course of a conversation I am happy to do so. But I don't force the issue, or presume that someone other than myself needs to hear about Twelve Step recovery. I adhere to what some people working Step Twelve call "passive evangelizing." It focuses more on living the Steps in our everyday lives than making a statement about the lives of others.

"You know I really thought I was cured of all my egotistical bullshit," Cory, a balding middle-aged man, said at an NA meeting. "Then I hit Step Twelve. I started preaching the Steps like I was John the Baptist preparing the way for Christ. And if you didn't listen, you were in denial. I was judgmental, rude, and obnoxious. Just like I was when I was using."

Cory realized his problem and talked with his sponsor. "He set me straight—straight back to Step One. It took me a while to realize that it wasn't enough to just stop using, I had to stop abusing as well."

So how can we carry the message without becoming a judgmental messenger? The easiest way is to continue to attend meetings and share your story. Rather than seek out people you imagine need to hear your tale, simply place yourself in a setting where people come to hear it. Attending meetings ensures that a meeting will survive. There is no organizational development arm in Twelve Step that guarantees that meetings take place.

There are only people who gather at set times and places to hold meetings. There is no leader, only a person who offers to facilitate the meeting that day. The meeting doesn't exist outside the people who attend, so attending is one way to be of service because by attending you ensure that there will be a meeting for those who need it. Of course, as you participate in a meeting you are reminded once again that you, too, need to be there, and this is an added blessing.

A more formal way of carrying the message is to take Bill W.'s advice and volunteer at a recovery center or shelter. If you know people who work with addicts, offer to help; be willing to share your story with those recommended to you by a therapist, clergyperson, physician, or social worker. The key to all of this is to live in such a way that you don't push your story on others, but neither do you keep it hidden from them.

Practice: Practicing the Principles in All Our Affairs

What are the principles we are to practice? Perhaps Bill W. simply meant the Steps themselves, but I would suggest that there are principles behind each Step that are lived by working each Step: powerlessness (Step One), faith (Step Two), surrender (Step Three), humility (Steps Four, Five, Six, and Seven), forgiveness (Steps Eight, Nine, and Ten), wisdom (Step Eleven), and hope (Step Twelve). These principles come to inform our lives as we work the Twelve Steps. Here is my brief take on how to practice each one:

> **Powerlessness:** We practice powerlessness whenever we realize that we are not in control. We can't control our desires, our thoughts, our feelings, or even our attitudes. We can control our behavior to some extent, but when it comes to our addictions and the actions toward which those addictions drive us, we have to admit that we are powerless over

these. Twelve Step recovery is not a self-help program, but a selfless help program. We do not change our lives, we allow them to be changed. We do not change ourselves, we allow ourselves to be changed. Allowing this is perhaps all we control, and even here it is more a gift resulting from hitting rock bottom than it is any willful force coming from our ego.

When in the throes of addiction, powerlessness leads us to harmful and hurtful behavior. But when working the Steps and living a life of sobriety or abstinence, powerlessness leads us to compassion. Just as we realize that we have to cry out to God (as we understand God) day after day for the help we need to live the healthy life we desire, we come to realize that everyone is crying out for help as well. Some are crying to God; some to their parents, friends, partners, or spouses; and some may even be crying out to us. The more we cry, the more we can hear and respond, if and when appropriate, to the cries of others. This is living the principle of powerlessness.

Faith: We practice faith every time we work a Step, speak with a sponsor, attend a meeting, or tell our story. Our faith is in the process. We have faith that if we continually work the Steps and attend meetings, if we are courageous enough to face our powerlessness, admit our failings, and make amends whenever necessary, that something happens to us. We are changed. The claws of addiction no longer sink so deep into our psyches, and we can live with clarity and humility. We may have faith in many other things, but it is faith in the process of Twelve Step recovery—reinforced by the stories we hear of other recovering addicts—that brings us to these steps each day, every day, one day at a time. This is living the principle of faith.

Surrender: We practice surrender every time we allow God, as we understand God, rather than our ego-driven desires to rule our lives. There is an anecdote about Albert Einstein, who, when asked by a reporter to articulate the most important question facing humankind, replied that the most fundamental question we can ever ask ourselves is whether the universe we live in is friendly or hostile. When we live from the ego, seeking to impose our will on the world, we cannot help but see the universe as hostile. Everything appears to be in opposition to us and our desires. But when we surrender to the world, not allowing it to batter us but allowing ourselves to learn its currents and how to navigate them, we discover that the universe isn't out to get us, but that it isn't out to protect us either. Rather, the world is what it is, and if we work in harmony with it the world can be a place of deep beauty and meaning. This, of course, doesn't mean we can avoid suffering or prevent others from suffering. It only means that even suffering can have meaning if it leads us to a deeper appreciation of reality. This is living the principle of surrender.

Humility: We practice humility every time we notice our own failings. There is no perfection in Twelve Step recovery, no final goal, no moment when we are done with the Steps and free from even the possibility of insanity. Even if we never return to addictive substances or behaviors again, the deeper truths of the Steps—our powerlessness, our capacity to hurt ourselves and others in the blind pursuit of our desires—never leave us. We remain ever watchful of our thoughts and feelings, and, seeing that so much of what we think and feel is rooted in the quest for control, we are constantly humbled by our own minds and hearts. But now, rather than trying to escape from this humility and pretending to be superior women and men, we embrace it thankfully, knowing that it is our awareness of the ego's madness that keeps us sane. We smile at the insanity of our thoughts and feelings, and take care that our actions are in harmony with compassion rather than compulsion. This is living the principle of humility.

Forgiveness: We practice forgiveness by asking for forgiveness when warranted and granting forgiveness when asked. Working the Steps we focus on our own deeds and our own need to ask forgiveness from those we have harmed. As the Twelve Steps come to inform our lives ever more deeply, we discover that forgiving others is also an act of health and healing. When we ask forgiveness from another, we once again face our powerlessness: No matter what our intention, we do harm and hence have to atone for it. When we ask forgiveness, we are humbled by the behaviors that belie our high estimations of ourselves. We are brought low but not in a manner that demeans us—rather, in a manner that allows us to regain our humanity by humbly asking forgiveness from those we have harmed.

When asked to forgive, we discover something similar. Forgiving another is not like a sovereign pardoning a serf; pardons inflate differences between people, forgiveness erases them. The giver is invited to heal no less than the asker. Both are engaged in realizing the suffering that arises when we do harm and are harmed. We see that amends can take us only so far, and that in the end some greater healing is required, a healing that only forgiveness can offer. We are both freed from the past in the act of forgiveness, and that is what it means to practice the principle of forgiveness.

Wisdom: We practice wisdom when we see the way of the world, both its insanity and its sanity, and realize that such judgments are not intrinsic to nature but to our encounters with it. Nature is just what it is; neither good nor evil, just nor unjust. These are human concepts that make sense only in the arena of human action and reaction. When we see the truth of nature's neutrality we are no longer haunted by the notion that life is somehow against us, or that reality favors one person rather than another for reasons other than happenstance. We stop imagining that we are victims of anything but our own actions, that if we wish the suffering to cease we have to stop inflicting it upon ourselves and others. The wisdom of Twelve Step recovery, like the wisdom of every spiritual path, reveals the interconnectedness of all things and the karmic impact of present action on future conditions. We realize that to cause harm to one is to cause harm to all, and that for good or ill the situation in which we find ourselves at this moment was set in motion by the actions we took in previous moments. We know that if we want a more healthy future we must take more healthy actions here and now. Living *in* the moment rather than *for* the moment is practicing the principle of wisdom.

Hope: We practice hope every time we attend a meeting, every time we tell our story and listen to the often painful wisdom in another's. We practice hope every time we recognize that we have caused another pain and stop to make amends, ask for forgiveness, and change our behavior. We practice hope every time we allow ourselves to be different in ways that make us more loving, trustworthy, and kind.

Twelve Step recovery is rooted in hope, for if there were no hope of change there would be no point to working the Steps. True, we are not in control of the change, but we can promote it, cultivate it, and invite it into our lives. A farmer cannot control her crops, but she can till the soil, plant the best seed, water the soil well, and nurture the crops as best she can. None of this will guarantee a good harvest, but ignoring these will guarantee a poor one. So we plant seeds of sobriety, seeds of compassion, seeds of abstinence, seeds of humility in the soil of our lives. We water these with watchfulness and prayer, and we wait. Not every seed we plant will yield fine results, but some will, and, as we get better at planting and nurturing, this *some* grows. While the weeds of addictive thinking and reactive behavior can never be uprooted once and for all, the good that grows slowly overcomes the bad, and our lives become more rich, more varied, more meaningful, and more and more worth living. This is practicing the principle of hope.

CHAPTER THIRTEEN

FIRST STEP, LAST STEP

"First step, last step," Bert said after reading a rough draft of this book. "That's all you're really saying. The First Step is crucial, central, and repeatable. *We admitted we were powerless over life—that our lives had become unmanageable.* That's the key. We are powerless. And when we pretend otherwise we are lost."

I admit to pretending otherwise now and again. And every time I do, I invite disaster.

"We all do that," Bert said in response to my admission. "It is the disease of the ego, the addiction to the illusion that it is God, that chaos can be controlled, ordered, commanded. God is wild, creation is wild, living is wild. And that's what makes it so damn wonderful."

It is wonderful. I have come to see that more and more clearly as I live the Steps more and more authentically. Yes, there is terrible suffering in the world, and great evil, but there is also unimaginable love, and compassion enough to match and exceed all the horror. We cannot prevent suffering but neither can we avoid reaching out to help those who suffer. It is all of a piece: life and death, love and fear, horror and hope, injustice and justice. We cannot have one without the other, and trying to do so is at the heart of our addictions. We sought to create for ourselves a world of light alone, and when that failed, we sought to shield ourselves from the dark through acts of self-medication. This ultimately numbed us to the fact that life is constantly changing and that we don't have to initiate change and cannot control it, but can simply allow it and learn to navigate it.

In all of history—whether actual history or literary history—there is perhaps no one more paradigmatic of this than Job. Job was a good and decent man who came by his wealth and prosperity honorably. He was generous, just, and kind, yet God allowed Satan to torment Job almost to death.

According to the Bible, God touted Job to Satan as an example of human devotion, but Satan scoffed, saying that Job's love of God was contingent on God's largesse toward Job. God could not let the taunt go untested, and he instructs Satan to test Job's love of God in any way short of killing him. Satan readily complies: Job's wealth is taken from him in a series of raids on his flocks and herds, and freakish "fires from heaven" that destroy his fields and livestock. His children are killed in a tornado that destroys their home in which they were eating together; and his health quickly deteriorates until Job is left a broken man using broken pieces of pottery to scratch the open sores that cover his body.

Job's wife, heartbroken over her husband's torment, urges him to "curse God and die" (Job 2:9), but Job replies, "Should we accept the good at the hand of God, and not receive the bad?" (Job 2:10).

Job understood the light and dark of reality, the fact that one cannot exist without the other and that you and I cannot live without encountering both. Through all of this, Job maintains what his wife calls his "integrity" (Job 2:9). In other words, as saddened as he is over the death of his children and the loss of his wealth and vitality, he is not moved to blame God, fate, himself, or anyone else. Reality is reality, it does what it does; all we can do is move on.

Yet things change for Job when his friends come to comfort him. At least that is why they say they are coming. Their comfort is limited to cajoling Job into self-recrimination. Bad things, they argue, can only happen to bad people. If Job would simply confess his guilt, God would forgive him and restore his fortune.

While there is no reason for us to assume that Job's friends were anything less than sincere, it is also easy to see that Job's troubles were upsetting their own worldview. They believed one could avoid suffering if one acted in accordance with the wishes of God, and here was Job—a man "blameless and upright, one who feared God and turned away from evil" (Job 1:1)—being punished as if he were the most despicable person on earth. They could imagine only two explanations for this: Either God was malevolent or Job wasn't as upright and blameless as he appeared. Refusing to accept the first possibility, they came to Job to coerce him into admitting to the second. Job refused.

Yet the arguments of his friends do have an effect on Job. Whereas previously willing to accept his fate as part of the light and dark of reality, under the ceaseless badgering of his friends Job begins to question his situation more deeply. He demands that God appear to Job and explain why this is happening. He is not ready to curse God as his wife urged, or beg for divine forgiveness as his friends insist, but he is no longer willing to sit passively as events unfold, either. He wants to know why things are as they are. He neither blames God nor himself, but takes a middle path in search of understanding.

We often hear talk of the "patience of Job," but the word *patience* never appears in the Book of Job at all. Job is neither patient nor impatient; he is relentlessly inquiring. In the end, his relentlessness pays off and God appears to Job in a whirlwind.

The image is striking. A whirlwind killed Job's children, so God's appearing in the whirlwind is ominously threatening. A whirlwind is also blinding, disorienting. It picks up and spins everything in its path, and in this case that would include Job. While the Bible does not depict Job caught up in the centrifugal winds of the storm, the reader cannot help but see Job facing the wildness of the storm, his skin burning with the sands whipping his already raw flesh, and yet not retreating. Job holds his place before God and seeks understanding.

Rather than respond logically to Job's inquiry, God peppers Job with questions designed to disorient his mind as the winds disorient his body. They seem to have nothing to do with Job's situation: "Where were you when I laid out the foundation of the earth? Tell me if you have understanding! Who determined its measurements—surely you know!" (Job 38:5). "Have you entered the springs of the sea, or walked in the recesses of the deep? Have the fates of the dead been revealed to you, or have you seen the gates of deep darkness?" (Job 38:16–17).

What kind of questions are these? Job is asking why he suffers, and God is talking about the grand scheme of the cosmos. Is God not listening or is God trying to get Job to realize something greater than his inquiry into justice allows?

I believe it is the latter. Job is focused on the microcosm: his life, human meaning, and purpose. And God is saying to him, "There is no meaning separate from the whole, and the whole is so much greater than the parts humanity sees. Unless and until you relinquish your narrow focus, you can have no idea what this world is about."

After what must have seemed like an eternity of divine interrogation, Job hits rock bottom and seeks to put an end to God's questioning by humbling himself before God: "See, I am of small account; what shall I answer you?" (Job 40:4). However, God is not interested in humbling Job, but in waking him up. Job's reference to being "of small account" is a tactic by which he hopes to elicit God's compassion and make the questioning stop. It doesn't stop. Rather, God commands Job to gear up for another round of relentless inquiry into the nature of the universe. Hitting rock bottom isn't the end; God wants Job to crash right through it.

When Job next speaks he is changed. He has moved through rock bottom into the fierce grace of God's love. Job is neither humble nor haughty, but wise. Job now knows that "God can do all things, and that no purpose of yours can be thwarted" (Job 42:2). Things are the way they are because it is the will of God that they be that way. God's refusal to speak directly to Job's situation, and Job's silence regarding it, suggest that Job realizes that God isn't rewarding and punishing individuals at all, but rather maintaining a system so intricate, so vast, so impersonal that to imagine God seeking to reward or punish anyone is absurd. We cannot control the current of the sea, but we can swim with it. We don't set the grain of wood, but we can cut with it. We can't control the wind but we can tack, using its force to navigate our lives.

Job says to God, "I have heard of you with the hearing of my ears, but now my eyes see you; therefore I despise myself, and repent in dust and ashes." This translation from the NRSV is typical of English translations, but it is terribly misleading. Can the book really end with a submissive Job, a Job who despises his very existence? Can it be after all the grandeur of the universe revealed to Job by God that his only reaction is to cower and recant? I don't think so.

Job is saying something far more profound, and to affirm the truth of what he has discovered, he must affirm the validity of his experience. I used to know God only with my ears, Job says, only secondhand from books and the teachings of others who claim to know. But things are different now. Now I see God for myself, and what I see has changed me. As Stephen Mitchell says in his marvelous translation of Job:

> Job's final words issue from surrender; not from submission, which even at its purest ... is a gesture in a power transaction, between slave and master or defeated and conqueror, and is always a mode of spiritual depression. Surrender, on the contrary, means the wholehearted giving-up of oneself. It is both the ultimate generosity and the

ultimate poverty, because in it the giver becomes the gift. When Job says, "I had heard of you with my ears, but now my eyes have seen you," he is no longer a servant who fears God and avoids evil. He has faced evil, has looked straight into its face and through it, into a vast wonder and love.[1]

Job's surrender to the wild, mad dance of God is paradigmatic of the surrender each of us seeks. We begin our search imagining that what we seek is information: Why do I suffer from this addiction? What must I do to free myself from it? In the end we discover there is no why, there is only the reality of addiction and sobriety, compulsive behavior and abstinence from such behavior. Meaning is not found in an idea we read or hear, but in the reality we perceive when the lenses of perception are cleared of the fog of addiction.

We don't submit, we surrender. We don't recant, we become calm. We don't despise, we wonder. And ultimately we, like Job, become silent and still; honoring the dust and ash of our physical selves, marveling at the fact that one like us can perceive the creative chaos that is God, and know ourselves as expressions of God. This is really God's will for our lives: to be still in the midst of the madness and to know it is all God.

THE TWELVE STEPS OF ALCOHOLICS ANONYMOUS

1. We admitted we were powerless over alcohol—that our lives had become unmanageable.
2. We came to believe that a Power greater than ourselves could restore us to sanity.
3. We made a decision to turn our will and our lives over to the care of God as we understood Him.
4. We made a searching and fearless moral inventory of ourselves.
5. We admitted to God, to ourselves, and to another human being the exact nature of our wrongs.
6. We were entirely ready to have God remove all these defects of character.
7. We humbly asked Him to remove our shortcomings.
8. We made a list of all persons we had harmed, and became willing to make amends to them all.
9. We made direct amends to such people wherever possible, except when to do so would injure them or others.
10. We continued to take personal inventory and when we were wrong promptly admitted it.
11. We sought through prayer and meditation to improve our conscious contact with God, as we understood Him, praying only for knowledge of His will for us and the power to carry that out.
12. Having had a spiritual awakening as the result of these Steps, we tried to carry this message to alcoholics, and to practice these principles in all our affairs.

NOTES

INTRODUCTION

1. *Alcoholics Anonymous: The Big Book,* 4th ed. (New York: Alcoholics Anonymous, Inc., 2006), p. 62.

2. Jack Maguire, *Dhammapada: Annotated and Explained* (Woodstock, Vt.: SkyLight Paths, 2002), p. 3.

3. Albert Einstein, cited in Ruben Habito, "The Inner Pursuit of Happiness," in Stephanie Kaza, ed., *Hooked: Buddhist Writings on Greed, Desire, and the Urge to Consume* (Boston: Shambhala, 2005), p. 45.

4. Pema Chödrön, "How We Get Hooked, How We Get Unhooked," in Kaza, ed., *Hooked,* p. 28.

5. *Alcoholics Anonymous: The Big Book,* p. 567.

CHAPTER 1

1. Thomas Berry, *Religions of India: Hinduism, Yoga, Buddhism* (New York: Columbia University Press, 1992), p. 170.

2. "Call me Trim Tab, Bucky" is inscribed on a stone placed above the headstone marking the grave of Buckminster Fuller and his wife.

3. Thich Nhat Hanh, *Breathe, You Are Alive!* (Berkeley, Calif.: Parallax Press, 2008), pp. 3–4.

4. For a complete and traditional English translation of the sutra plus commentary, see Thich Nhat Hanh, *Breathe.*

CHAPTER 2

1. Alan Watts, *The Essential Alan Watts* (Berkeley, Calif.: Celestial Arts, 1998), p. 2.

CHAPTER 3

1. *Alcoholics Anonymous: The Story of How Many Thousands of Men and Women Have Recovered from Alcoholism,* 4th ed. (New York: Alcoholics Anonymous World Services, 2001), p. 10.

2. Ibid., p. 12.

3. From the "Song of Mind" by Niu-t'ou Fa-Jung, in *The Poetry of Enlightenment,* Master Sheng-yen (New York: Dharma Drum), p. 33.

4. Taitetsu Unno, *Shin Buddhism: Bits of Rubble Turn into Gold* (New York: Doubleday, 2002), p. 12.

5. Ibid., p. 12.

CHAPTER 4

1. Solomon Schimmel, *The Seven Deadly Sins* (New York: The Free Press, 1992), pp. 33–34.

2. C. S. Lewis, *Mere Christianity* (New York: Simon and Schuster, 1980), p. 110.

3. Ibid., p. 110.

4. Ibid., p. 110.

5. Ibid., p. 110.

6. Ibid., p. 112.

7. Ibid., p. 114.

8. Joan Chittister, *The Rule of Benedict: Insights for the Ages* (New York: Crossroads, 1996), pp. 61–74.

9. Joan Chittister, *Wisdom Distilled from the Daily: Living the Rule of St. Benedict Today* (San Francisco: HarperSanFrancisco, 1991), pp. 51–66.

10. Ibid., p. 65.

11. Sakyong Mipham Rinpoche, "How to Do Mindfulness Meditation," in *Shambhala Sun* (January 2000).

12. Ibid.

CHAPTER 5

1. Ozer Bergman, *Where Earth and Heaven Kiss: A Guide to Rebbe Nachman's Path of Meditation* (Jerusalem: Breslov Research Institute, 2006), p. 27.

2. Ibid.

3. Reb Nathan, *Reb Nachman's Wisdom* (Jerusalem: Breslov Research Institute, 1984), p. 16.

4. Edward Conze, trans., "The Questions of King Milinda" in *Buddhist Scriptures* (New York: Penguin Classics, 1959).

5. Dalai Lama, *How to See Yourself as You Really Are* (New York: Atria Books, 2006), p. 132.

6. Ibid.

7. Rabbi Israel Salanter, as quoted in Hillel Goldberg, *Israel Salanter* (New York: KTAV, 1982), p. 37.

8. Ibid.

9. Scott Hahn, *Lord Have Mercy: The Healing Power of Confession* (New York: Doubleday, 2003).

CHAPTER 6

1. *Twelve Steps and Twelve Traditions* (New York: Alcoholics Anonymous, Inc., 2007), p. 66.

2. David Godman, ed., *Be as You Are: The Teachings of Sri Ramana Maharshi* (New York: Penguin, 1989), p. 47.

3. *Ramana Smirti: Sri Ramana Maharshi Birth Centenary Offering* (Tiruvannamalai, India Ramanasramam, 1999), p. 8.

CHAPTER 7

1. Meister Eckhart, cited in Whitall Perry, *The Spiritual Ascent* (Louisville, Ky.: Fons Vitae, 2007), p. 201.

2. Derek Lin, *Tao Te Ching: Annotated and Explained* (Woodstock, Vt.: SkyLight Paths, 2006), p. 201.

3. *Sumeru,* or sometimes spelled *sineru,* is the Pali name for the central world-mountain in Buddhist cosmology.

4. *Bindu* is Sanskrit for "dot." In its feminine form, *bindi,* it refers to the cosmetic dot worn on the forehead of many Hindus.

5. *Stupa* refers to a Buddhist shrine.

6. *Guru* is the blending of two Sanskrit words, *gu,* meaning "dark," and *ru* meaning "light." A guru is one who shifts our consciousness from the darkness of ignorance to the light of wisdom.

CHAPTER 8

1. All translations of the Bhagavad Gita are from Shri Purohit, trans., and Kendra Crossen Burroughs, annotator, *Bhagavad Gita: Annotated and Explained* (Woodstock, Vt.: SkyLight Paths, 2002).

CHAPTER 10

1. Pastor Paul provided me with the sources of his quotations by e-mail as I was preparing the text of this book.

2. Karen Armstrong, *The Great Transformation* (New York: Alfred A. Knopf, 2006), p. 211.

3. Ibid., p. 208.

4. Thich Nhat Hahn, in a transcript of a talk at Phap Van Temple in Ho Chi Minh City, February 22, 2007.

5. Gurdjieff, cited in P. D. Ouspensky, *In Search of the Miraculous* (New York: Harvest, 2001), pp. 146–47.

CHAPTER 11

1. Stephen Karcher, *How to Use the I Ching: A Guide to Working with the Oracle of Change* (London: Element Books, 1997).

2. Ibid., p. 3.

3. Ibid., p. 5.

4. Ibid.

5. Thomas Keating, *Manifesting God* (New York: Lantern Books, 2005), p. 131.

6. Basil Pennington, *Centering Prayer: Renewing an Ancient Christian Prayer Form* (New York: Image, 1982), p. 19.

7. Ibid.

8. Keating, *Manifesting God,* p. 132.

9. Kabir Helminski, *The Book of Language* (Watsonville, Calif.: The Book Foundation, 2006), p. 92.

10. Al-Ghazali, *The Alchemy of Happiness,* quoted in Kabir Helminski, *A Knowing Heart: A Sufi Path of Transformation* (Boston: Shambhala, 2000), pp. 98–99.

11. Helminski, *A Knowing Heart,* p. 99.

CHAPTER 13

1. Stephen Mitchell, *The Book of Job* (New York: Harper Perennial, 1992), p. xxvii.

SUGGESTIONS FOR FURTHER READING

Aaron, Paul, and Musto, David. "Temperance and Prohibition in America: An Historical Overview." In Mark H. Moore, and Dean R. Gerstein, eds., *Alcohol and Public Policy: Beyond the Shadow of Prohibition*. Washington, D.C.: National Academy Press, 1981.

Afterburn, Stephen, and David Stoop. *The Life Recovery Workbook: A Biblical Guide through the Twelve Steps*. Wheaton, Ill.: Tyndale House Publishers, 2007.

Aitken, Robert. *Taking the Path of Zen*. New York: North Point Press, 1982.

Akhilananda, Swami. *Mental Health and Hindu Psychology*. Boston: Branden Press, 1977.

_____. *Hindu Psychology: Its Meaning for the West*. London: Routledge, 1999.

Alexander, William. *Cool Water: Alcoholism, Mindfulness, and Ordinary Recovery*. Boston: Shambhala, 1997.

Anonymous. *World Scripture*. New York: Paragon House 1991.

_____. *The Twelve Steps for Christians*. San Diego: RPI Publishing, 1994.

_____. *Life Recovery Bible*. Wheaton, Ill: Tyndale House Publishers, 1998.

_____. *Twelve Steps and Twelve Traditions of Overeaters Anonymous*. Rio Rancho, N.M.: Overeaters Anonymous, Inc., 2002.

_____. *Alcoholics Anonymous: The Big Book*, 4th Edition. New York: Alcoholics Anonymous, Inc., 2006.

_____. *Twelve Steps and Twelve Traditions*. New York: Alcoholics Anonymous, Inc., 2007.

Armstrong, Karen. *The Great Transformation*. New York: Alfred A. Knopf, 2006.

Ash, Mel. *The Zen of Recovery*. New York: Jeremy P. Tarcher, 1993.

B., Dick. *The Conversion of Bill W*. Kihei, Hawaii: Paradise Research Publications, 2008.

Ballou, Robert. *The Bible of the World*. New York: Viking Press, 1939.

Batchelor, Martine. *Let Go: A Buddhist Guide to Breaking Free of Habits*. Somerville, Mass.: Wisdom Publications, 2007.

Bayda, Ezra. *Zen Heart: Simple Advice for Living with Mindfulness and Compassion*. Boston: Shambhala, 2008.

Benda, Brent, and Thomas McGovern, eds. *Spirituality and Religiousness and Alcohol/Other Drug Problems*. New York: Haworth Press, 2006.

Bergman, Ozer. *Where Earth and Heaven Kiss: A Guide to Rebbe Nachman's Path of Meditation*. Jerusalem: Breslov Research Institute, 2006.

Berry, Thomas. *Religions of India: Hinduism, Yoga, Buddhism*. New York: Columbia University Press, 1992.

Bien, Thomas, and Beverly Bien. *Mindful Recovery: A Spiritual Path to Healing from Addiction*. Hoboken, N.J.: Wiley, 2002.

Blackburn, Simon. *Lust*. New York: Oxford University Press, 2006.

Brady, Mark. *Wisdom of Listening*. New York: Wisdom Publications, 2003.

Buber, Martin. *The Way of Man according to the Teaching of Hasidism*. Secaucus, N.J.: Citadel Press, 1994.

Carlson, Richard, and Benjamin Shield, eds. *Handbook for the Spirit*. Novato, Calif.: New World Library, 1997.

Carnes, Patrick. *A Gentle Path through the Twelve Steps*. Center City, Minn.: Hazelden, 1994.

Cheever, Susan. *My Name Is Bill: Bill Wilson—His Life and the Creation of Alcoholics Anonymous*. New York: Washington Square Press, 2005.

Chesnut, Glenn. *The Higher Power of the Twelve-Step Program for Believers and Non-Believers*. Bloomington, Ind.: Authorhouse, 2001.

Chittister, Joan. *Wisdom Distilled from the Daily: Living the Rule of St. Benedict Today*. San Francisco: HarperOne, 1991.

_____. *The Rule of Benedict*. New York: Crossover Classic, 1992.

Conze, Edward, trans. "The Questions of King Milinda." In *Buddhist Scriptures*. New York: Penguin Classics, 1959.

Dalai Lama. *How to See Yourself as You Really Are*. New York: Atria Books, 2006.

Das, Surya. *Letting Go of the Person You Used to Be.* New York: Broadway Books, 2003.

Donin, Hayim. *To Pray as a Jew: A Guide to the Prayer Book and the Synagogue Service.* New York: Basic Books, 1991.

Driberg, Tom. *The Mystery of Moral Re-armament: A Study of Frank Buchman and His Movement.* New York: Alfred A. Knopf, 1965.

Dyson, Michael Eric. *Pride.* New York: Oxford University Press, 2006.

Epstein, Joseph. *Envy.* New York: Oxford University Press, 2006.

Godman, David, ed. *Be as You Are: The Teachings of Sri Ramana Maharshi.* New York: Penguin, 1989.

Goldberg, Hillel. *Israel Salanter.* New York: KTAV, 1982.

Goldstein, Joseph, and Jack Kornfield. *Seeking the Heart of Wisdom: The Path of Insight Meditation.* Boston: Shambhala, 1987.

Gregson, David, and Jay Efran. *The Tao of Sobriety.* New York: St. Martin's Press, 2002.

Griffin, Kevin. *One Breath at a Time: Buddhism and the Twelve Steps.* New York: Rodale, 2004.

Groff, Christina. *The Thirst for Wholeness: Attachment, Addiction, and the Spiritual Path.* New York: HarperOne, 1994.

Gunaratana, Bhante Henepola. *Mindfulness in Plain English.* Boston: Wisdom Publications, 2002.

Hahn, Scott. *Lord Have Mercy: The Healing Power of Confession.* New York: Doubleday, 2003.

Hanh, Thich Nhat. *Breathe, You Are Alive!* Berkeley, Calif.: Parallax Press, 2008.

Helminski, Kabir. *A Knowing Heart: A Sufi Path of Transformation.* Boston: Shambhala, 2000.

_____. *The Book of Language.* Watsonville, Calif.: The Book Foundation, 2006.

Hemfelt, Robert. *Serenity: A Companion for Twelve Step Recovery.* New York: Thomas Nelson, 2007.

Hirsch, Samson Raphael. *The Pentateuch*, vol. 1. London: Judaica Press, 1999.

Hirschfield, Jerry. *The Twelve Steps for Everyone.* Center City, Minn.: Hazeldon, 1994.

Huber, Cherie. *Making a Change for Good: A Guide to Compassionate Self-Discipline*. Boston: Shambhala, 2007.

Jung, Carl. *The Symbolic Life: Collected Works of C. G. Jung*, vol. 18. Princeton, N.J.: Bollingen, 1980.

Kapleau, Phillip. *The Three Pillars of Zen: Teaching, Practice and Enlightenment*. New York: Anchor Books, 1989.

Karcher, Stephen. *How to Use the* I Ching: *A Guide to Working with the Oracle of Change*. London: Element Books, 1997.

Kasa, Stephanie. *Hooked! Buddhist Writings on Greed, Desire, and the Urge to Consume*. Boston: Shambhala, 2005.

Keating, Thomas. *Manifesting God*. New York: Lantern Books, 2005.

Kornfield, Jack. *A Path with Heart: A Guide through the Perils and Promises of Spiritual Life*. New York: Bantam Books, 1993.

Kurtz, Ernest. *Not-God: A History of Alcoholics Anonymous*. Center City, Minn.: Hazelden, 1991.

Kurtz, Ernest, and Katherine Ketcham. *The Spirituality of Imperfection*. New York: Bantam Books, 1992.

Lesser, Elizabeth. *Seeker's Guide*. New York: Villard, 1999.

Lewis, C. S. *Mere Christianity*, New York: Harper, 2001.

Maguire, Jack. *Dhammapada: Annotated and Explained*. Woodstock, Vt.: SkyLight Paths, 2002.

Maharshi, Ramana. *Talks with Ramana Maharshi*. San Diego: Inner Directions, 2000.

Matto, Michele. *The Twelve Steps in the Bible*. Mahwah, N.J.: Paulist Press, 2000.

May, Gerald. *Addiction and Grace*. New York: HarperCollins Publishers, 1991.

Melctios, Father Webber. *Steps of Transformation: An Orthodox Priest Explores the Twelve Steps*. Ben Lomond, Calif.: Conciliar Press, 2003.

Mitchell, Stephen. *The Book of Job*. New York: Harper Perennial, 1992.

Morinis, Alan. *Everyday Holiness: The Jewish Spiritual Practice of Mussar*. Boston: Trumpeter: 2007.

Nathan, Reb. *Reb Nachman's Wisdom*. Jerusalem: Breslov Research Institute, 1984.

Olitzky, Kerry M. *100 Blessings Every Day*. Woodstock, Vt.: Jewish Lights Publishing, 1993.

Olitzky, Kerry M., and Stuart Copans. *Twelve Jewish Steps to Recovery,* 2nd ed. Woodstock, Vt.: Jewish Lights Publishing, 2009.

Ouspensky, P. D., *In Search of the Miraculous.* New York: Harvest, 2001.

Pennington, Basil. *Centering Prayer: Renewing an Ancient Christian Prayer Form.* New York: Image, 1982.

Perry, Whitall. *The Spiritual Ascent.* Louisville, Ky.: Fons Vitae, 2007.

Pietsch, William. *The Serenity Prayer Book.* New York: HarperCollins, 1992.

Pitman, Bill. *AA: The Way It Began.* Seattle: Glen Abbey Books, 1988.

Prose, Francine. *Gluttony.* New York: Oxford University Press, 2006.

Ramana Smirti: Sri Ramana Maharshi Birth Centenary Offering. Tiruvannamalai, India: Ramanasramam, 1999, p. 8.

Reynolds, David. *Constructive Living.* Honolulu: University of Hawaii Press, 1984.

_____. *A Handbook for Constructive Living.* Honolulu: University of Hawaii Press, 2002.

Russell, Sharman Apt. *Standing in the Light: My Life as a Pantheist.* New York: Basic Books, 2008.

S., Laura. *12 Steps on Buddha's Path: Bill, Buddha, and We.* Boston: Wisdom Publications, 2006.

Salerno, Steve. *Sham: How the Self-Help Movement Made America Helpless.* New York: Random House, 2005.

Schimmel, Solomon. *The Seven Deadly Sins: Jewish, Christian, and Classical Reflections on Human Psychology.* New York: Oxford University Press, 1997.

Selby, Saul. *Twelve Step Christianity: The Christian Roots and Application of the Twelve Steps.* Center City, Minn.: Hazelden, 2000.

Shafir, Rebecca. *The Zen of Listening: Mindful Communication in the Age of Distractions.* New York: Quest Books, 2003.

Shapiro, Rami. *The Sacred Art of Lovingkindness.* Woodstock, Vt.: SkyLight Paths, 2006.

Soho, Takuan. *The Unfettered Mind.* William Scott Wilson, trans. Tokyo: Kodansha International, 1986.

Sparks, Tav. *The Wide Open Door: The Twelve Steps, Spiritual Tradition, and the New Psychology.* Santa Cruz, Calif.: Hanford Mead Publishers, 1993.

Thurman, Robert. *Anger.* New York: Oxford University Press, 2006.

Tickle, Phyllis. *Greed.* New York: Oxford University Press, 2006.

_____. *The Great Emergence: How Christianity Is Changing and Why.* Grand Rapids, Mich.: Baker Books, 2008.

Trijang, Rinpoche, and Michael Richards. *Liberation in the Palm of Your Hand: A Concise Discourse on the Path to Enlightenment.* Boston: Wisdom Publications, 2006.

Unno, Taitetsu. *Shin Buddhism, Bits of Rubble Turn into Gold.* New York: Doubleday, 2002.

Walshe, M. *Meister Eckhart: Sermons and Treatises,* vol. 3. New York: Lilian Barber Press, 1991.

Wasserstein, Wendy. *Sloth.* New York: Oxford University Press, 2006.

Watts, Alan. *The Essential Alan Watts.* Berkeley, Calif.: Celestial Arts, 1998.

Williams, Don. *12 Steps with Jesus.* Ventura, Calif.: Regal Books, 2004.

Wilson, Andrew, ed. *World Scripture: A Comparative Anthology of Sacred Texts.* New York: Paragon House Publishers, 1991.

Young, Andi. *The Sacred Art of Bowing: Preparing to Practice.* Woodstock, Vt.: SkyLight Paths, 2003.

INDEX OF PRACTICES

Spirituality of the Seasons

Autumn: A Spiritual Biography of the Season
Edited by Gary Schmidt and Susan M. Felch; Illus. by Mary Azarian
Rejoice in autumn as a time of preparation and reflection. Includes Wendell Berry, David James Duncan, Robert Frost, A. Bartlett Giamatti, E. B. White, P. D. James, Julian of Norwich, Garret Keizer, Tracy Kidder, Anne Lamott, May Sarton.
6 x 9, 320 pp, b/w illus., Quality PB, 978-1-59473-118-1 **$18.99**

Spring: A Spiritual Biography of the Season
Edited by Gary Schmidt and Susan M. Felch; Illus. by Mary Azarian
Explore the gentle unfurling of spring and reflect on how nature celebrates rebirth and renewal. Includes Jane Kenyon, Lucy Larcom, Harry Thurston, Nathaniel Hawthorne, Noel Perrin, Annie Dillard, Martha Ballard, Barbara Kingsolver, Dorothy Wordsworth, Donald Hall, David Brill, Lionel Basney, Isak Dinesen, Paul Laurence Dunbar. 6 x 9, 352 pp, b/w illus., Quality PB, 978-1-59473-246-1 **$18.99**

Summer: A Spiritual Biography of the Season
Edited by Gary Schmidt and Susan M. Felch; Illus. by Barry Moser
"A sumptuous banquet.... These selections lift up an exquisite wholeness found within an everyday sophistication." — ★ *Publishers Weekly* starred review
Includes Anne Lamott, Luci Shaw, Ray Bradbury, Richard Selzer, Thomas Lynch, Walt Whitman, Carl Sandburg, Sherman Alexie, Madeleine L'Engle, Jamaica Kincaid.
6 x 9, 304 pp, b/w illus., Quality PB, 978-1-59473-183-9 **$18.99**
HC, 978-1-59473-003-2 **$21.99**

Winter: A Spiritual Biography of the Season
Edited by Gary Schmidt and Susan M. Felch; Illus. by Barry Moser
"This outstanding anthology features top-flight nature and spirituality writers on the fierce, inexorable season of winter.... Remarkably lively and warm, despite the icy subject." — ★ *Publishers Weekly* starred review
Includes Will Campbell, Rachel Carson, Annie Dillard, Donald Hall, Ron Hansen, Jane Kenyon, Jamaica Kincaid, Barry Lopez, Kathleen Norris, John Updike, E. B. White.
6 x 9, 288 pp, b/w illus., Deluxe PB w/ flaps, 978-1-893361-92-8 **$18.95**
HC, 978-1-893361-53-9 **$21.95**

Spirituality / Animal Companions

Blessing the Animals: Prayers and Ceremonies to Celebrate God's Creatures, Wild and Tame *Edited and with Introductions by Lynn L. Caruso*
5¼ x 7¼, 256 pp, Quality PB, 978-1-59473-253-9 **$15.99**; HC, 978-1-59473-145-7 **$19.99**

Remembering My Pet: A Kid's Own Spiritual Workbook for When a Pet Dies
by Nechama Liss-Levinson, PhD, and Rev. Molly Phinney Baskette, MDiv; Foreword by Lynn L. Caruso
8 x 10, 48 pp, 2-color text, HC, 978-1-59473-221-8 **$16.99**

What Animals Can Teach Us about Spirituality: Inspiring Lessons from Wild and Tame Creatures *by Diana L. Guerrero* 6 x 9, 176 pp, Quality PB, 978-1-893361-84-3 **$16.95**

Or phone, fax, mail or e-mail to: SKYLIGHT PATHS Publishing
Sunset Farm Offices, Route 4 • P.O. Box 237 • Woodstock, Vermont 05091
Tel: (802) 457-4000 • Fax: (802) 457-4004 • www.skylightpaths.com
Credit card orders: (800) 962-4544 (8.30AM–5:30PM ET Monday–Friday)
Generous discounts on quantity orders. SATISFACTION GUARANTEED. Prices subject to change.

Bible Stories / Folktales

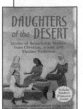

Abraham's Bind & Other Bible Tales of Trickery, Folly, Mercy and Love by Michael J. Caduto
New retellings of episodes in the lives of familiar biblical characters explore relevant life lessons. 6 x 9, 224 pp, HC, 978-1-59473-186-0 **$19.99**

Daughters of the Desert: Stories of Remarkable Women from Christian, Jewish and Muslim Traditions by Claire Rudolf Murphy,
Meghan Nuttall Sayres, Mary Cronk Farrell, Sarah Conover and Betsy Wharton
Breathes new life into the old tales of our female ancestors in faith. Uses traditional scriptural passages as starting points, then with vivid detail fills in historical context and place. Chapters reveal the voices of Sarah, Hagar, Huldah, Esther, Salome, Mary Magdalene, Lydia, Khadija, Fatima and many more. Historical fiction ideal for readers of all ages.
5½ x 8½, 192 pp, Quality PB, 978-1-59473-106-8 **$14.99** Inc. reader's discussion guide
HC, 978-1-893361-72-0 **$19.95**

The Triumph of Eve & Other Subversive Bible Tales
by Matt Biers-Ariel
These engaging retellings of familiar Bible stories are witty, often hilarious and always profound. They invite you to grapple with questions and issues that are often hidden in the original texts.
5½ x 8½, 192 pp, Quality PB, 978-1-59473-176-1 **$14.99**
Also available: The Triumph of Eve Teacher's Guide
8½ x 11, 44 pp, PB, 978-1-59473-152-5 **$8.99**

Wisdom in the Telling
Finding Inspiration and Grace in Traditional Folktales and Myths Retold
by Lorraine Hartin-Gelardi
6 x 9, 192 pp, HC, 978-1-59473-185-3 **$19.99**

Religious Etiquette / Reference

How to Be a Perfect Stranger, 5th Edition: The Essential Religious Etiquette Handbook Edited by Stuart M. Matlins and Arthur J. Magida
The indispensable guidebook to help the well-meaning guest when visiting other people's religious ceremonies. A straightforward guide to the rituals and celebrations of the major religions and denominations in the United States and Canada from the perspective of an interested guest of any other faith, based on information obtained from authorities of each religion. Belongs in every living room, library and office. Covers:
African American Methodist Churches • Assemblies of God • Bahá'í Faith • Baptist • Buddhist • Christian Church (Disciples of Christ) • Christian Science (Church of Christ, Scientist) • Churches of Christ • Episcopalian and Anglican • Hindu • Islam • Jehovah's Witnesses • Jewish • Lutheran • Mennonite/Amish • Methodist • Mormon (Church of Jesus Christ of Latter-day Saints) • Native American/First Nations • Orthodox Churches • Pentecostal Church of God • Presbyterian • Quaker (Religious Society of Friends) • Reformed Church in America/Canada • Roman Catholic • Seventh-day Adventist • Sikh • Unitarian Universalist • United Church of Canada • United Church of Christ

"The things Miss Manners forgot to tell us about religion."

—*Los Angeles Times*

"Finally, for those inclined to undertake their own spiritual journeys ... tells visitors what to expect." —*New York Times*

6 x 9, 432 pp, Quality PB, 978-1-59473-294-2 **$19.99**

The Perfect Stranger's Guide to Funerals and Grieving Practices: A Guide to Etiquette in Other People's Religious Ceremonies Edited by Stuart M. Matlins
6 x 9, 240 pp, Quality PB, 978-1-893361-20-1 **$16.95**

The Perfect Stranger's Guide to Wedding Ceremonies: A Guide to Etiquette in Other People's Religious Ceremonies Edited by Stuart M. Matlins
6 x 9, 208 pp, Quality PB, 978-1-893361-19-5 **$16.95**

Sacred Texts—SkyLight Illuminations Series

Offers today's spiritual seeker an enjoyable entry into the great classic texts of the world's spiritual traditions. Each classic is presented in an accessible translation, with facing pages of guided commentary from experts, giving you the keys you need to understand the history, context and meaning of the text.

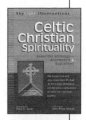

CHRISTIANITY

Celtic Christian Spirituality: Essential Writings—Annotated & Explained
Annotation by Mary C. Earle; Foreword by John Philip Newell
Explores how the writings of this lively tradition embody the gospel.
5½ x 8½, 176 pp (est), Quality PB, 978-1-59473-302-4 **$16.99**

The End of Days: Essential Selections from Apocalyptic Texts—
Annotated & Explained *Annotation by Robert G. Clouse, PhD*
Helps you understand the complex Christian visions of the end of the world.
5½ x 8½, 224 pp, Quality PB, 978-1-59473-170-9 **$16.99**

The Hidden Gospel of Matthew: Annotated & Explained
Translation & Annotation by Ron Miller Discover the words and events that have the strongest connection to the historical Jesus.
5½ x 8½, 272 pp, Quality PB, 978-1-59473-038-2 **$16.99**

The Infancy Gospels of Jesus: Apocryphal Tales from the Childhoods of Mary and Jesus—Annotated & Explained
Translation & Annotation by Stevan Davies; Foreword by A. Edward Siecienski, PhD
A startling presentation of the early lives of Mary, Jesus and other biblical figures that will amuse and surprise you. 5½ x 8½, 176 pp, Quality PB, 978-1-59473-258-4 **$16.99**

The Lost Sayings of Jesus: Teachings from Ancient Christian, Jewish, Gnostic and Islamic Sources—Annotated & Explained
Translation & Annotation by Andrew Phillip Smith; Foreword by Stephan A. Hoeller
This collection of more than three hundred sayings depicts Jesus as a Wisdom teacher who speaks to people of all faiths as a mystic and spiritual master.
5½ x 8½, 240 pp, Quality PB, 978-1-59473-172-3 **$16.99**

Philokalia: The Eastern Christian Spiritual Texts—Selections Annotated & Explained *Annotation by Allyne Smith; Translation by G. E. H. Palmer, Phillip Sherrard and Bishop Kallistos Ware*
The first approachable introduction to the wisdom of the Philokalia, the classic text of Eastern Christian spirituality. 5½ x 8½, 240 pp, Quality PB, 978-1-59473-103-7 **$16.99**

The Sacred Writings of Paul: Selections Annotated & Explained
Translation & Annotation by Ron Miller Leads you into the exciting immediacy of Paul's teachings. 5½ x 8½, 224 pp, Quality PB, 978-1-59473-213-3 **$16.99**

Saint Augustine of Hippo: Selections from *Confessions* and Other Essential Writings—Annotated & Explained
Annotation by Joseph T. Kelley, PhD; Translation by the Augustinian Heritage Institute
Provides insight into the mind and heart of this foundational Christian figure.
5½ x 8½, 272 pp, Quality PB, 978-1-59473-282-9 **$16.99**

St. Ignatius Loyola—The Spiritual Writings: Selections Annotated & Explained *Annotation by Mark Mossa, SJ*
Draws from contemporary translations of original texts focusing on the practical mysticism of Ignatius of Loyola. 5½ x 8½, 224 pp (est), Quality PB, 978-1-59473-301-7 **$16.99**

Sex Texts from the Bible: Selections Annotated & Explained
Translation & Annotation by Teresa J. Hornsby; Foreword by Amy-Jill Levine
Demystifies the Bible's ideas on gender roles, marriage, sexual orientation, virginity, lust and sexual pleasure. 5½ x 8½, 208 pp, Quality PB, 978-1-59473-217-1 **$16.99**

Sacred Texts—continued

CHRISTIANITY—continued

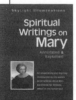

Spiritual Writings on Mary: Annotated & Explained
Annotation by Mary Ford-Grabowsky; Foreword by Andrew Harvey
Examines the role of Mary, the mother of Jesus, as a source of inspiration in
history and in life today. 5½ x 8½, 288 pp, Quality PB, 978-1-59473-001-6 **$16.99**

The Way of a Pilgrim: The Jesus Prayer Journey—Annotated & Explained
Translation & Annotation by Gleb Pokrovsky; Foreword by Andrew Harvey
A classic of Russian Orthodox spirituality.
5½ x 8½, 160 pp, Illus., Quality PB, 978-1-893361-31-7 **$14.95**

GNOSTICISM

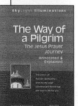

Gnostic Writings on the Soul: Annotated & Explained
Translation & Annotation by Andrew Phillip Smith; Foreword by Stephan A. Hoeller
Reveals the inspiring ways your soul can remember and return to its unique,
divine purpose. 5½ x 8½, 144 pp, Quality PB, 978-1-59473-220-1 **$16.99**

The Gospel of Philip: Annotated & Explained
Translation & Annotation by Andrew Phillip Smith; Foreword by Stevan Davies
Reveals otherwise unrecorded sayings of Jesus and fragments of Gnostic mythology.
5½ x 8½, 160 pp, Quality PB, 978-1-59473-111-2 **$16.99**

The Gospel of Thomas: Annotated & Explained
Translation & Annotation by Stevan Davies; Foreword by Andrew Harvey
Sheds new light on the origins of Christianity and portrays Jesus as a wisdom-loving sage.
5½ x 8½, 192 pp, Quality PB, 978-1-893361-45-4 **$16.99**

The Secret Book of John: The Gnostic Gospel—Annotated & Explained
Translation & Annotation by Stevan Davies The most significant and influential text of
the ancient Gnostic religion. 5½ x 8½, 208 pp, Quality PB, 978-1-59473-082-5 **$16.99**

JUDAISM

The Divine Feminine in Biblical Wisdom Literature
Selections Annotated & Explained
Translation & Annotation by Rabbi Rami Shapiro; Foreword by Rev. Cynthia Bourgeault, PhD
Uses the Hebrew Bible and Wisdom literature to explain Sophia's way of wisdom
and illustrate Her creative energy. 5½ x 8½, 240 pp, Quality PB, 978-1-59473-109-9 **$16.99**

Ecclesiastes: Annotated & Explained
Translation & Annotation by Rabbi Rami Shapiro; Foreword by Rev. Barbara Cawthorne Crafton
A timeless teaching on living well amid uncertainty and insecurity.
5½ x 8½, 160 pp, Quality PB, 978-1-59473-287-4 **$16.99**

Ethics of the Sages: Pirke Avot—Annotated & Explained
Translation & Annotation by Rabbi Rami Shapiro Clarifies the ethical teachings of the
early Rabbis. 5½ x 8½, 192 pp, Quality PB, 978-1-59473-207-2 **$16.99**

Hasidic Tales: Annotated & Explained
Translation & Annotation by Rabbi Rami Shapiro; Foreword by Andrew Harvey
Introduces the legendary tales of the impassioned Hasidic rabbis, presenting them as
stories rather than as parables. 5½ x 8½, 240 pp, Quality PB, 978-1-893361-86-7 **$16.95**

The Hebrew Prophets: Selections Annotated & Explained
Translation & Annotation by Rabbi Rami Shapiro; Foreword by Rabbi Zalman M. Schachter-Shalomi
5½ x 8½, 224 pp, Quality PB, 978-1-59473-037-5 **$16.99**

Tanya, the Masterpiece of Hasidic Wisdom: Selections Annotated &
Explained *Translation & Annotation by Rabbi Rami Shapiro; Foreword by Rabbi Zalman M.
Schachter-Shalomi* Clarifies one of the most powerful and potentially transforma-
tive books of Jewish wisdom. 5½ x 8½, 240 pp, Quality PB, 978-1-59473-275-1 **$16.99**

Zohar: Annotated & Explained *Translation & Annotation by Daniel C. Matt;
Foreword by Andrew Harvey* The canonical text of Jewish mystical tradition.
5½ x 8½, 176 pp, Quality PB, 978-1-893361-51-5 **$15.99**

Sacred Texts—continued

ISLAM

Ghazali on the Principles of Islamic Spirituality
Selections from *Forty Foundations of Religion*—Annotated & Explained
Translation & Annotation by Aaron Spevack, PhD
Makes the core message of this influential spiritual master relevant to anyone seeking a balanced understanding of Islam.
5½ x 8½, 208 pp (est), Quality PB, 978-1-59473-284-3 **$16.99**

The Qur'an and Sayings of Prophet Muhammad
Selections Annotated & Explained
Annotation by Sohaib N. Sultan; Translation by Yusuf Ali, Revised by Sohaib N. Sultan; Foreword by Jane I. Smith
Presents the foundational wisdom of Islam in an easy-to-use format.
5½ x 8½, 256 pp, Quality PB, 978-1-59473-222-5 **$16.99**

Rumi and Islam: Selections from His Stories, Poems, and Discourses—
Annotated & Explained *Translation & Annotation by Ibrahim Gamard*
Focuses on Rumi's place within the Sufi tradition of Islam, providing insight into the mystical side of the religion.
5½ x 8½, 240 pp, Quality PB, 978-1-59473-002-3 **$15.99**

EASTERN RELIGIONS

The Art of War—Spirituality for Conflict: Annotated & Explained
by Sun Tzu; Annotation by Thomas Huynh; Translation by Thomas Huynh and the Editors at Sonshi.com; Foreword by Marc Benioff; Preface by Thomas Cleary
Highlights principles that encourage a perceptive and spiritual approach to conflict.
5½ x 8½, 256 pp, Quality PB, 978-1-59473-244-7 **$16.99**

Bhagavad Gita: Annotated & Explained
Translation by Shri Purohit Swami; Annotation by Kendra Crossen Burroughs; Foreword by Andrew Harvey
Presents the classic text's teachings—with no previous knowledge of Hinduism required.
5½ x 8½, 192 pp, Quality PB, 978-1-893361-28-7 **$16.95**

Chuang-tzu: The Tao of Perfect Happiness—Selections Annotated & Explained
Translation & Annotation by Livia Kohn, PhD
Presents Taoism's central message of reverence for the "Way" of the natural world.
5½ x 8½, 240 pp, Quality PB, 978-1-59473-296-6 **$16.99**

Confucius, the *Analects:* The Path of the Sage—Selections Annotated &
Explained *Annotation by Rodney L. Taylor, PhD; Translation by James Legge, Revised by Rodney L. Taylor, PhD* Explores the ethical and spiritual meaning behind the Confucian way of learning and self-cultivation.
5½ x 8½, 176 pp (est), Quality PB, 978-1-59473-306-2 **$16.99**

Dhammapada: Annotated & Explained
Translation by Max Müller, revised by Jack Maguire; Annotation by Jack Maguire; Foreword by Andrew Harvey Contains all of Buddhism's key teachings, plus commentary that explains all the names, terms and references.
5½ x 8½, 160 pp, b/w photos, Quality PB, 978-1-893361-42-3 **$14.95**

Selections from the Gospel of Sri Ramakrishna: Annotated & Explained
Translation by Swami Nikhilananda; Annotation by Kendra Crossen Burroughs; Foreword by Andrew Harvey Introduces the fascinating world of the Indian mystic and the universal appeal of his message.
5½ x 8½, 240 pp, b/w photos, Quality PB, 978-1-893361-46-1 **$16.95**

Tao Te Ching: Annotated & Explained
Translation & Annotation by Derek Lin; Foreword by Lama Surya Das
Introduces an Eastern classic in an accessible, poetic and completely original way.
5½ x 8½, 208 pp, Quality PB, 978-1-59473-204-1 **$16.99**

Spiritual Poetry—The Mystic Poets

Experience these mystic poets as you never have before. Each beautiful, compact book includes a brief introduction to the poet's time and place, a summary of the major themes of the poet's mysticism and religious tradition, essential selections from the poet's most important works, and an appreciative preface by a contemporary spiritual writer.

Hafiz
The Mystic Poets
Translated and with Notes by Gertrude Bell
Preface by Ibrahim Gamard
Hafiz is known throughout the world as Persia's greatest poet, with sales of his poems in Iran today only surpassed by those of the Qur'an itself. His probing and joyful verse speaks to people from all backgrounds who long to taste and feel divine love and experience harmony with all living things.
5 x 7¼, 144 pp, HC, 978-1-59473-009-2 **$16.99**

Hopkins
The Mystic Poets
Preface by Rev. Thomas Ryan, CSP
Gerard Manley Hopkins, Christian mystical poet, is beloved for his use of fresh language and startling metaphors to describe the world around him. Although his verse is lovely, beneath the surface lies a searching soul, wrestling with and yearning for God.
5 x 7¼, 112 pp, HC, 978-1-59473-010-8 **$16.99**

Tagore
The Mystic Poets
Preface by Swami Adiswarananda
Rabindranath Tagore is often considered the Shakespeare of modern India. A great mystic, Tagore was the teacher of W. B. Yeats and Robert Frost, the close friend of Albert Einstein and Mahatma Gandhi, and the winner of the Nobel Prize for Literature. This beautiful sampling of Tagore's two most important works, *The Gardener* and *Gitanjali*, offers a glimpse into his spiritual vision that has inspired people around the world.
5 x 7¼, 144 pp, HC, 978-1-59473-008-5 **$16.99**

Whitman
The Mystic Poets
Preface by Gary David Comstock
Walt Whitman was the most innovative and influential poet of the nineteenth century. This beautiful sampling of Whitman's most important poetry from *Leaves of Grass*, and selections from his prose writings, offers a glimpse into the spiritual side of his most radical themes—love for country, love for others and love of self.
5 x 7¼, 192 pp, HC, 978-1-59473-041-2 **$16.99**

Children's Spirituality

Adam & Eve's First Sunset: God's New Day
by Sandy Eisenberg Sasso; Full-color illus. by Joani Keller Rothenberg 9 x 12, 32 pp, Full-color illus., HC,
978-1-58023-177-0 **$17.95*** *For ages 4 & up*

Because Nothing Looks Like God
by Lawrence Kushner and Karen Kushner; Full-color illus. by Dawn W. Majewski
Invites parents and children to explore the questions we all have about God.
11 x 8½, 32 pp, Full-color illus., HC, 978-1-58023-092-6 **$17.99*** *For ages 4 & up*

Also available: **Teacher's Guide** 8½ x 11, 22 pp, PB, 978-1-58023-140-4 **$6.95**

But God Remembered: Stories of Women from Creation to the
Promised Land   *by Sandy Eisenberg Sasso; Full-color illus. by Bethanne Andersen*
A fascinating collection of four different stories of women only briefly mentioned in biblical tradition and religious texts.
9 x 12, 32 pp, Full-color illus., Quality PB, 978-1-58023-372-9 **$8.99*** *For ages 8 & up*

Cain & Abel: Finding the Fruits of Peace
by Sandy Eisenberg Sasso; Full-color illus. by Joani Keller Rothenberg
A sensitive recasting of the ancient tale shows we have the power to deal with anger
in positive ways. "Editor's Choice." —American Library Association's *Booklist*
9 x 12, 32 pp, Full-color illus., HC, 978-1-58023-123-7 **$16.95*** *For ages 5 & up*

Does God Hear My Prayer?
by August Gold; Full-color photos by Diane Hardy Waller
Introduces preschoolers and young readers to prayer and how it helps them
express their own emotions.
10 x 8½, 32 pp, Full-color photo illus., Quality PB, 978-1-59473-102-0 **$8.99** *For ages 3–6*

The 11th Commandment: Wisdom from Our Children *by The Children of America*
"If there were an Eleventh Commandment, what would it be?" Children of many
religious denominations across America answer this question—in their own drawings and words. "A rare book of spiritual celebration for all people, of all ages,
for all time." —*Bookviews*   8 x 10, 48 pp, Full-color illus., HC, 978-1-879045-46-0 **$16.95***
For all ages

For Heaven's Sake *by Sandy Eisenberg Sasso; Full-color illus. by Kathryn Kunz Finney*
Heaven is often found where you least expect it.
9 x 12, 32 pp, Full-color illus., HC, 978-1-58023-054-4 **$16.95*** *For ages 4 & up*

God In Between *by Sandy Eisenberg Sasso; Full-color illus. by Sally Sweetland*
A magical, mythical tale that teaches that God can be found where we are.
9 x 12, 32 pp, Full-color illus., HC, 978-1-879045-86-6 **$16.95*** *For ages 4 & up*

God's Paintbrush: Special 10th Anniversary Edition
by Sandy Eisenberg Sasso; Full-color illus. by Annette Compton
Invites children of all faiths and backgrounds to encounter God through moments
in their own lives. 11 x 8½, 32 pp, Full-color illus., HC, 978-1-58023-195-4 **$17.95*** *For ages 4 & up*

Also available: **God's Paintbrush Teacher's Guide**
8½ x 11, 32 pp, PB, 978-1-879045-57-6 **$8.95**

God's Paintbrush Celebration Kit: A Spiritual Activity Kit for Teachers and
Students of All Faiths, All Backgrounds 9½ x 12, 40 Full-color Activity Sheets & Teacher Folder
w/ complete instructions, HC, 978-1-58023-050-6 **$21.95**
Additional activity sheets available:
8-Student Activity Sheet Pack (40 sheets/5 sessions), 978-1-58023-058-2 **$19.95**
Single-Student Activity Sheet Pack (5 sessions), 978-1-58023-059-9 **$3.95**

I Am God's Paintbrush (A Board Book)
by Sandy Eisenberg Sasso; Full-color illus. by Annette Compton
5 x 5, 24 pp, Full-color illus., Board Book, 978-1-59473-265-2 **$7.99** *For ages 0–4*

* A book from Jewish Lights, SkyLight Paths' sister imprint

Spirituality

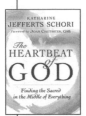

The Heartbeat of God: Finding the Sacred in the Middle of Everything
by Katharine Jefferts Schori; Foreword by Joan Chittister, OSB
Explores our connections to other people, to other nations and with the environment through the lens of faith.   6 x 9, 240 pp, HC, 978-1-59473-292-8 **$21.99**

A Dangerous Dozen: Twelve Christians Who Threatened the Status Quo but Taught Us to Live Like Jesus
by the Rev. Canon C. K. Robertson, PhD; Foreword by Archbishop Desmond Tutu
Profiles twelve visionary men and women who challenged society and showed the world a different way of living.   6 x 9, 208 pp, Quality PB, 978-1-59473-298-0 **$16.99**

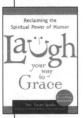

Decision Making & Spiritual Discernment: The Sacred Art of Finding Your Way   by Nancy L. Bieber
Presents three essential aspects of Spirit-led decision making: willingness, attentiveness and responsiveness.   5½ x 8½, 208 pp, Quality PB, 978-1-59473-289-8 **$16.99**

Laugh Your Way to Grace: Reclaiming the Spiritual Power of Humor
by Rev. Susan Sparks   A powerful, humorous case for laughter as a spiritual, healing path.   6 x 9, 176 pp, Quality PB, 978-1-59473-280-5 **$16.99**

Living into Hope: A Call to Spiritual Action for Such a Time as This
by Rev. Dr. Joan Brown Campbell; Foreword by Karen Armstrong
A visionary minister speaks out on the pressing issues that face us today, offering inspiration and challenge.   6 x 9, 208 pp, HC, 978-1-59473-283-6 **$21.99**

Claiming Earth as Common Ground: The Ecological Crisis through the Lens of Faith
by Andrea Cohen-Kiener; Foreword by Rev. Sally Bingham
6 x 9, 192 pp, Quality PB, 978-1-59473-261-4 **$16.99**

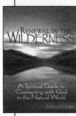

Bread, Body, Spirit: Finding the Sacred in Food
Edited and with Introductions by Alice Peck   6 x 9, 224 pp, Quality PB, 978-1-59473-242-3 **$19.99**

Creating a Spiritual Retirement: A Guide to the Unseen Possibilities in Our Lives
by Molly Srode   6 x 9, 208 pp, b/w photos, Quality PB, 978-1-59473-050-4 **$14.99**

Creative Aging: Rethinking Retirement and Non-Retirement in a Changing World
by Marjory Zoet Bankson   6 x 9, 160 pp, Quality PB, 978-1-59473-281-2 **$16.99**

Keeping Spiritual Balance as We Grow Older: More than 65 Creative Ways to Use Purpose, Prayer, and the Power of Spirit to Build a Meaningful Retirement
by Molly and Bernie Srode   8 x 8, 224 pp, Quality PB, 978-1-59473-042-9 **$16.99**

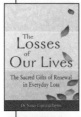

Hearing the Call across Traditions: Readings on Faith and Service
Edited by Adam Davis; Foreword by Eboo Patel
6 x 9, 352 pp, Quality PB, 978-1-59473-303-1 **$18.99**; HC, 978-1-59473-264-5 **$29.99**

Honoring Motherhood: Prayers, Ceremonies & Blessings
Edited and with Introductions by Lynn L. Caruso   5 x 7¼, 272 pp, HC, 978-1-59473-239-3 **$19.99**

Journeys of Simplicity: Traveling Light with Thomas Merton, Bashō, Edward Abbey, Annie Dillard & Others   by Philip Harnden
5 x 7¼, 144 pp, Quality PB, 978-1-59473-181-5 **$12.99**; 128 pp, HC, 978-1-893361-76-8 **$16.95**

The Losses of Our Lives: The Sacred Gifts of Renewal in Everyday Loss
by Dr. Nancy Copeland-Payton   6 x 9, 192 pp, HC, 978-1-59473-271-3 **$19.99**

Renewal in the Wilderness: A Spiritual Guide to Connecting with God in the Natural World   by John Lionberger
6 x 9, 176 pp, b/w photos, Quality PB, 978-1-59473-219-5 **$16.99**

Soul Fire: Accessing Your Creativity
by Thomas Ryan, CSP   6 x 9, 160 pp, Quality PB, 978-1-59473-243-0 **$16.99**

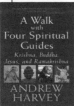

A Spirituality for Brokenness: Discovering Your Deepest Self in Difficult Times
by Terry Taylor   6 x 9, 176 pp, Quality PB, 978-1-59473-229-4 **$16.99**

A Walk with Four Spiritual Guides: Krishna, Buddha, Jesus, and Ramakrishna
by Andrew Harvey   5½ x 8½, 192 pp, b/w photos & illus., Quality PB, 978-1-59473-138-9 **$15.99**

The Workplace and Spirituality: New Perspectives on Research and Practice
Edited by Dr. Joan Marques, Dr. Satinder Dhiman and Dr. Richard King
6 x 9, 256 pp, HC, 978-1-59473-260-7 **$29.99**

Prayer / Meditation

Sacred Attention: A Spiritual Practice for Finding God in the Moment
by Margaret D. McGee
Framed on the Christian liturgical year, this inspiring guide explores ways to develop a practice of attention as a means of talking—and listening—to God.
6 x 9, 144 pp, Quality PB, 978-1-59473-291-1 **$16.99**

Women of Color Pray: Voices of Strength, Faith, Healing, Hope and Courage
Edited and with Introductions by Christal M. Jackson
Through these prayers, poetry, lyrics, meditations and affirmations, you will share in the strong and undeniable connection women of color share with God.
5 x 7¼, 208 pp, Quality PB, 978-1-59473-077-1 **$15.99**

Secrets of Prayer: A Multifaith Guide to Creating Personal Prayer in
Your Life *by Nancy Corcoran, CSJ*
This compelling, multifaith guidebook offers you companionship and encouragement on the journey to a healthy prayer life. 6 x 9, 160 pp, Quality PB, 978-1-59473-215-7 **$16.99**

Prayers to an Evolutionary God
by William Cleary; Afterword by Diarmuid O'Murchu
Inspired by the spiritual and scientific teachings of Diarmuid O'Murchu and Teilhard de Chardin, reveals that religion and science can be combined to create an expanding view of the universe—an evolutionary faith.
6 x 9, 208 pp, HC, 978-1-59473-006-1 **$21.99**

The Art of Public Prayer, 2nd Edition: Not for Clergy Only
by Lawrence A. Hoffman, PhD 6 x 9, 288 pp, Quality PB, 978-1-893361-06-5 **$19.99**

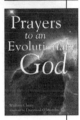

A Heart of Stillness: A Complete Guide to Learning the Art of Meditation
by David A. Cooper 5½ x 8½, 272 pp, Quality PB, 978-1-893361-03-4 **$18.99**

Meditation without Gurus: A Guide to the Heart of Practice
by Clark Strand 5½ x 8½, 192 pp, Quality PB, 978-1-893361-93-5 **$16.95**

Praying with Our Hands: 21 Practices of Embodied Prayer from the World's
Spiritual Traditions *by Jon M. Sweeney; Photos by Jennifer J. Wilson; Foreword by Mother Tessa Bielecki; Afterword by Taitetsu Unno, PhD*
8 x 8, 96 pp, 22 duotone photos, Quality PB, 978-1-893361-16-4 **$16.95**

Three Gates to Meditation Practice: A Personal Journey into Sufism, Buddhism, and Judaism *by David A. Cooper* 5½ x 8½, 240 pp, Quality PB, 978-1-893361-22-5 **$16.95**

Prayer / M. Basil Pennington, OCSO

Finding Grace at the Center, 3rd Edition: The Beginning of
Centering Prayer *with Thomas Keating, OCSO, and Thomas E. Clarke, SJ; Foreword by Rev. Cynthia Bourgeault, PhD* A practical guide to a simple and beautiful form of meditative prayer. 5 x 7¼, 128 pp, Quality PB, 978-1-59473-182-2 **$12.99**

The Monks of Mount Athos: A Western Monk's Extraordinary
Spiritual Journey on Eastern Holy Ground *Foreword by Archimandrite Dionysios*
Explores the landscape, monastic communities and food of Athos.
6 x 9, 352 pp, Quality PB, 978-1-893361-78-2 **$18.95**

Psalms: A Spiritual Commentary *Illus. by Phillip Ratner*
Reflections on some of the most beloved passages from the Bible's most widely read book. 6 x 9, 176 pp, 24 full-page b/w illus., Quality PB, 978-1-59473-234-8 **$16.99**

The Song of Songs: A Spiritual Commentary *Illus. by Phillip Ratner*
Explore the Bible's most challenging mystical text.
6 x 9, 160 pp, 14 full-page b/w illus., Quality PB, 978-1-59473-235-5 **$16.99**
HC, 978-1-59473-004-7 **$19.99**

Spirituality & Crafts

Beading—The Creative Spirit: Finding Your Sacred Center through the Art of Beadwork *by Rev. Wendy Ellsworth*
Invites you on a spiritual pilgrimage into the kaleidoscope world of glass and color. 7 x 9, 240 pp, 8-page color insert, 40+ b/w photos and 40 diagrams, Quality PB, 978-1-59473-267-6 **$18.99**

Contemplative Crochet: A Hands-On Guide for Interlocking Faith and Craft *by Cindy Crandall-Frazier; Foreword by Linda Skolnik*
Illuminates the spiritual lessons you can learn through crocheting.
7 x 9, 208 pp, b/w photos, Quality PB, 978-1-59473-238-6 **$16.99**

The Knitting Way: A Guide to Spiritual Self-Discovery
by Linda Skolnik and Janice MacDaniels Examines how you can explore and strengthen your spiritual life through knitting.
7 x 9, 240 pp, b/w photos, Quality PB, 978-1-59473-079-5 **$16.99**

The Painting Path: Embodying Spiritual Discovery through Yoga, Brush and Color *by Linda Novick; Foreword by Richard Segalman*
Explores the divine connection you can experience through art.
7 x 9, 208 pp, 8-page color insert, plus b/w photos, Quality PB, 978-1-59473-226-3 **$18.99**

The Quilting Path: A Guide to Spiritual Discovery through Fabric, Thread and Kabbalah *by Louise Silk*
Explores how to cultivate personal growth through quilt making.
7 x 9, 192 pp, b/w photos and illus., Quality PB, 978-1-59473-206-5 **$16.99**

The Scrapbooking Journey: A Hands-On Guide to Spiritual Discovery
by Cory Richardson-Lauve; Foreword by Stacy Julian   Reveals how this craft can become a practice used to deepen and shape your life.
7 x 9, 176 pp, 8-page color insert, plus b/w photos, Quality PB, 978-1-59473-216-4 **$18.99**

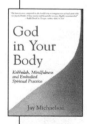

The Soulwork of Clay: A Hands-On Approach to Spirituality
by Marjory Zoet Bankson; Photos by Peter Bankson
Takes you through the seven-step process of making clay into a pot, drawing parallels at each stage to the process of spiritual growth.
7 x 9, 192 pp, b/w photos, Quality PB, 978-1-59473-249-2 **$16.99**

Kabbalah / Enneagram
(Books from Jewish Lights Publishing, SkyLight Paths' sister imprint)

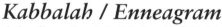

Cast in God's Image: Discover Your Personality Type Using the Enneagram and Kabbalah
by Rabbi Howard A. Addison, PhD 7 x 9, 176 pp, Quality PB, 978-1-58023-124-4 **$16.95**

Ehyeh: A Kabbalah for Tomorrow *by Rabbi Arthur Green, PhD*
6 x 9, 224 pp, Quality PB, 978-1-58023-213-5 **$18.99**

The Enneagram and Kabbalah, 2nd Edition: Reading Your Soul
by Rabbi Howard A. Addison, PhD 6 x 9, 192 pp, Quality PB, 978-1-58023-229-6 **$16.99**

The Gift of Kabbalah: Discovering the Secrets of Heaven, Renewing Your Life on Earth
by Tamar Frankiel, PhD 6 x 9, 256 pp, Quality PB, 978-1-58023-141-1 **$16.95**

God in Your Body: Kabbalah, Mindfulness and Embodied Spiritual Practice
by Jay Michaelson 6 x 9, 272 pp, Quality PB, 978-1-58023-304-0 **$18.99**

Jewish Mysticism and the Spiritual Life: Classical Texts, Contemporary Reflections
Edited by Dr. Lawrence Fine, Dr. Eitan Fishbane and Rabbi Or N. Rose
6 x 9, 256 pp, HC, 978-1-58023-434-4 **$24.99**

Kabbalah: A Brief Introduction for Christians
by Tamar Frankiel, PhD 5½ x 8½, 208 pp, Quality PB, 978-1-58023-303-3 **$16.99**

Zohar: Annotated & Explained *Translation & Annotation by Daniel C. Matt;*
Foreword by Andrew Harvey 5½ x 8½, 176 pp, Quality PB, 978-1-893361-51-5 **$15.99**

Spiritual Practice

Fly Fishing—The Sacred Art: Casting a Fly as a Spiritual Practice
by Rabbi Eric Eisenkramer and Rev. Michael Attas, MD
Illuminates what fly fishing can teach you about reflection, awe and wonder; the
benefits of solitude; the blessing of community and the search for the Divine.
5½ x 8½, 192 pp (est), Quality PB, 978-1-59473-299-7 **$16.99**

Lectio Divina—The Sacred Art: Transforming Words & Images into
Heart-Centered Prayer *by Christine Valters Paintner, PhD*
Expands the practice of sacred reading beyond scriptural texts and makes it acces-
sible in contemporary life. 5½ x 8½, 192 pp (est), Quality PB, 978-1-59473-300-0 **$16.99**

Haiku—The Sacred Art: A Spiritual Practice in Three Lines
by Margaret D. McGee 5½ x 8½, 192 pp, Quality PB, 978-1-59473-269-0 **$16.99**

Dance—The Sacred Art: The Joy of Movement as a Spiritual Practice
by Cynthia Winton-Henry 5½ x 8½, 224 pp, Quality PB, 978-1-59473-268-3 **$16.99**

Spiritual Adventures in the Snow: Skiing & Snowboarding as Renewal for Your
Soul *by Dr. Marcia McFee and Rev. Karen Foster; Foreword by Paul Arthur*
5½ x 8½, 208 pp, Quality PB, 978-1-59473-270-6 **$16.99**

Divining the Body: Reclaim the Holiness of Your Physical Self *by Jan Phillips*
8 x 8, 256 pp, Quality PB, 978-1-59473-080-1 **$16.99**

Everyday Herbs in Spiritual Life: A Guide to Many Practices
by Michael J. Caduto; Foreword by Rosemary Gladstar
7 x 9, 208 pp, 20+ b/w illus., Quality PB, 978-1-59473-174-7 **$16.99**

Giving—The Sacred Art: Creating a Lifestyle of Generosity
by Lauren Tyler Wright 5½ x 8½, 208 pp, Quality PB, 978-1-59473-224-9 **$16.99**

Hospitality—The Sacred Art: Discovering the Hidden Spiritual Power of Invitation
and Welcome *by Rev. Nanette Sawyer; Foreword by Rev. Dirk Ficca*
5½ x 8½, 208 pp, Quality PB, 978-1-59473-228-7 **$16.99**

Labyrinths from the Outside In: Walking to Spiritual Insight—A Beginner's Guide
by Donna Schaper and Carole Ann Camp
6 x 9, 208 pp, b/w illus. and photos, Quality PB, 978-1-893361-18-8 **$16.95**

Practicing the Sacred Art of Listening: A Guide to Enrich Your Relationships and
Kindle Your Spiritual Life *by Kay Lindahl* 8 x 8, 176 pp, Quality PB, 978-1-893361-85-0 **$16.95**

Recovery—The Sacred Art: The Twelve Steps as Spiritual Practice *by Rami Shapiro;
Foreword by Joan Borysenko, PhD* 5½ x 8½, 240 pp, Quality PB, 978-1-59473-259-1 **$16.99**

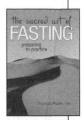

Running—The Sacred Art: Preparing to Practice *by Dr. Warren A. Kay; Foreword by
Kristin Armstrong* 5½ x 8½, 160 pp, Quality PB, 978-1-59473-227-0 **$16.99**

The Sacred Art of Chant: Preparing to Practice
by Ana Hernández 5½ x 8½, 192 pp, Quality PB, 978-1-59473-036-8 **$15.99**

The Sacred Art of Fasting: Preparing to Practice
by Thomas Ryan, CSP 5½ x 8½, 192 pp, Quality PB, 978-1-59473-078-8 **$15.99**

The Sacred Art of Forgiveness: Forgiving Ourselves and Others through God's Grace
by Marcia Ford 8 x 8, 176 pp, Quality PB, 978-1-59473-175-4 **$18.99**

The Sacred Art of Listening: Forty Reflections for Cultivating a Spiritual Practice
by Kay Lindahl; Illus. by Amy Schnapper 8 x 8, 160 pp, b/w illus., Quality PB, 978-1-893361-44-7 **$16.99**

The Sacred Art of Lovingkindness: Preparing to Practice
by Rabbi Rami Shapiro; Foreword by Marcia Ford 5½ x 8½, 176 pp, Quality PB, 978-1-59473-151-8 **$16.99**

Sacred Attention: A Spiritual Practice for Finding God in the Moment
by Margaret D. McGee 6 x 9, 144 pp, Quality PB, 978-1-59473-291-1 **$16.99**

Soul Fire: Accessing Your Creativity
by Thomas Ryan, CSP 6 x 9, 160 pp, Quality PB, 978-1-59473-243-0 **$16.99**

Thanking & Blessing—The Sacred Art: Spiritual Vitality through Gratefulness
by Jay Marshall, PhD; Foreword by Philip Gulley 5½ x 8½, 176 pp, Quality PB, 978-1-59473-231-7 **$16.99**

About SKYLIGHT PATHS Publishing

SkyLight Paths Publishing is creating a place where people of different spiritual traditions come together for challenge and inspiration, a place where we can help each other understand the mystery that lies at the heart of our existence.

Through spirituality, our religious beliefs are increasingly becoming a part of our lives—rather than *apart* from our lives. While many of us may be more interested than ever in spiritual growth, we may be less firmly planted in traditional religion. Yet, we do want to deepen our relationship to the sacred, to learn from our own as well as from other faith traditions, and to practice in new ways.

SkyLight Paths sees both believers and seekers as a community that increasingly transcends traditional boundaries of religion and denomination—people wanting to learn from each other, *walking together, finding the way.*

For your information and convenience, at the back of this book we have provided a list of other SkyLight Paths books you might find interesting and useful. They cover the following subjects:

Buddhism / Zen	Global Spiritual	Monasticism
Catholicism	Perspectives	Mysticism
Children's Books	Gnosticism	Poetry
Christianity	Hinduism /	Prayer
Comparative	Vedanta	Religious Etiquette
Religion	Inspiration	Retirement
Current Events	Islam / Sufism	Spiritual Biography
Earth-Based	Judaism	Spiritual Direction
Spirituality	Kabbalah	Spirituality
Enneagram	Meditation	Women's Interest
	Midrash Fiction	Worship

Or phone, fax, mail or e-mail to: SKYLIGHT PATHS Publishing
Sunset Farm Offices, Route 4 • P.O. Box 237 • Woodstock, Vermont 05091
Tel: (802) 457-4000 • Fax: (802) 457-4004 • www.skylightpaths.com
Credit card orders: (800) 962-4544 (8:30AM–5:30PM ET Monday–Friday)
Generous discounts on quantity orders. SATISFACTION GUARANTEED. Prices subject to change.

**For more information about each book,
visit our website at www.skylightpaths.com**